Going Down Slow

The Times of an Old Man Who Runs

Dallas Smith

Copyright 2011
Nightengale Press
A Nightengale Media LLC Company
All Rights Reserved

Going Down Slow

Copyright ©2011 by Dallas Smith
Cover Design ©2011 by Nightengale Press

All rights reserved. Printed in the United States of America. No part of this book may be reproduced or transmitted in any form or by any means, electronic or mechanical, including photocopying, recording, or by any information storage and retrieval system without written permission from the publisher, except for the inclusion of brief quotations in articles and reviews.

If you purchased this book without a cover, you should be aware that this book is stolen property. It was reported as "unsold and destroyed" to the publisher, and neither the author nor the publisher has received any payment for this "stripped book."

Disclaimer: This book relates the author's experiences traveling and training and competing in footraces and triathlons. It contains the author's opinions. Some names and identifying characteristics of individuals mentioned in the book have been changed to protect their privacy

For information about Nightengale Press please
visit our website at www.nightengalepress.com.
Email: publisher@nightengalepress.com
or send a letter to:
Nightengale Press
370 S. Lowe Avenue, Suite A-122
Cookeville, Tennessee

Library of Congress Cataloging-in-Publication Data

Smith, Dallas,

GOING DOWN SLOW/ Dallas Smith
ISBN 13: 978-1933449-95-1
Sports/Running/Memoir

Copyright Registered: 2011
First Published by Nightengale Press in the USA, the UK and Australia

October 2011

10 9 8 7 6 5 4 3 2 1

Printed in the USA, the UK and Australia

Contents

Prologue — Daddy's Blue Shoes	9
I. Turnaround	**13**
1. Turnaround	15
2. Punky Reggae Party	18
3. The Race No One Saw	56
4. On the Street Where You Live	61
5. Miracle on Fall Creek	71
6. The Best Marathon in the World	76
7. Twelve Gather for Supper	83
II. Spirits	**95**
8. Momma's Supper Table	97
9. Tip Your Hat to These Two Women	103
10. Katie's Angel	108
11. Prairie Chicken Capitol Redux	116
12. A Lonely Mesa, a Rude Visitor	136
13. What if a Neutrino Whacked Your Noggin?	142
14. Weather Report: Seville, Spain	148
15. The Editor Who Wanted Me to Write Stories	159
16. The Moment of Inertia	165
17. Iron Bill, Meet Queen Maeve	170
18. In My Father's Garden	179
III. Pathos	**185**
19. I Could See the Midnight Sun	187
20. Porch Is Gone	213
21. The Way Angela Runs	217
22. Ironma'am	224
23. The Hunter's Moon	233
24. Adventures in Paradise	241
25. Country Music Contrarian	256
26. Come Home, Hokie	269
27. I'll Take Manhattan	274
28. One Day in Funkytown	292
29. Summer Heat Reveals Artifact of Marathon Man	316
30. The Mystery of Water	321

IV. Pilgrimage — 323

31. She Threw Open Her Golden Gate — 325
32. The Old Slugger Remembered the Long Balls — 332
33. Nobody Wants to Crawl — 338
34. Dispatches from el Camino — 346
35. The Titan — 371
36. Four Who Ran Komen — 376
37. Wretched Undead Hound the Haunted Half — 389
38. A Special Guest at a Special Race — 393
39. Fourteen Elite Fools — 398
40. After the Flood — 405

Photos — 424

Appendix — My Winning Year — 431

Acknowledgments — 434

About the Author — 437

To Angela

My friend, I am going to tell you the story of my life, as you wish; and if it were only the story of my life I think I would not tell it; for what is one man that he should make much of his winters even when they bend him like a heavy snow? So many other men have lived and shall live that story, to be grass upon the hills.

— Black Elk to John Neihardt

Going Down Slow

PROLOGUE
Daddy's Blue Shoes

You won't catch me rhapsodizing about running. You may not even ever hear me say I like it. I'm not sure I do. It's severe and it trades in misery. It's the price I pay for living. It's just what I do. I reckon I'll keep it up until they scatter my ashes. My super-heated molecules will mix with the air, become part of it and circle the globe. You may run down the road and breathe a bit of me. It will give you strength.

Runners say the difference in a jogger and a runner is an entry form; a runner competes in races. By that definition, I became a runner in April of 1998 at the age of fifty-seven, after being a jogger for eighteen years, where I routinely logged six miles a day. I didn't know why I did that. I had the vague idea it was good for me somehow. After writing two books about running, I still don't know why I do it.

The first race I ran I wore my deceased father's shoes. I signed up secretly. The night before the race, a local 10K starting at Tennessee Tech, I told wife Jo Ann,

"I'm getting' up early in the morning and going to the campus to go running."

"Why?" She knew I hated getting up early.

"Cause I want to."

The shoes I wore I'd originally bought for my dad. He wore the same size I did. I'd bought myself a pair and got an extra pair for him. He wasn't a runner. He was an old man dying from lung disease. He'd spent a lifetime operating bulldozers in dust, welding dangerous metals, and smoking unfiltered Camel cigarettes. I used to smoke them too.

He wasn't able to do much except drive his pickup truck and sit around the house. The slightest exertion made him purse his lips and breathe hard. He took oxygen from a tank. So he didn't need the shoes for running. Soft and pliable as they were, I thought they'd be comfortable for him to loaf in. The shoes were eye-catching because they were navy blue, trimmed in white, unusual in those days; most running shoes were white then.

A thug soon stole my blue shoes. It was during one of the family's desperate attempts to get treatment for Daddy at Nashville's Baptist Hospital, seventy miles from his home, eighty from mine. Family members took turns staying in the hospital to help out and keep Momma company. I slept on the waiting room floor in my sleeping bag one night. We knew crooks roamed the halls. Some other visitors and I arranged the furniture into a fortress. I was exhausted from teaching at the university and spending nights at the hospital. I set my shoes under a coffee table at my head and went to sleep. Next morning the blue shoes were gone.

A few weeks after Daddy died, Momma gave his blue shoes to me. "I want you to have these back," she said. They were like new. But I had evil memories of those shoes. I put them out of sight on a closet shelf. They stayed there for nearly two years, until I signed up for the Golden Eagle 10K. I pulled them down and laced them on, already old by then, but hardly used.

I raced without anyone in the family knowing I was

going to. They accompanied me anyway. I wore something given me by each: Watch from Jo Ann; windbreaker from her parents; handkerchief from my youngest son; running socks from my daughter; hat from my oldest son; shirt from Jo Ann's oldest son; and shorts from her youngest son. And the blue shoes from Momma and Daddy.

Raced secretly, timid and afraid of failure, I guess. I needn't have been. Because I earned two trophies–first in my age group, and first master runner. That floored me. I had not figured on such a favorable outcome.

I had not figured on the next thing either: The man who presented the trophies, who twice shook my hand and handed me a tall mug, that man was my favorite student, a senior of civil engineering. He remains one of the most gifted students I ever advised or taught. As the cadet commander of the Army ROTC battalion, which organized the race, the job of race director fell to him.

All this happened. As cadet Philip Messer handed his professor one of the trophy mugs, the university photographer snapped a picture of us. Turning the tables, Jo Ann secretly purchased a print, framed it and gave it to me for a Christmas present. It's hanging on the wall yet. I just went and looked at it, student and professor smiling. Daddy's blue shoes stand out.

After the awards I got in my truck and headed home. When I pulled out on the main drag, I screamed so hard I hurt my throat.

Other races followed. In less than a year I moved to marathons, a couple years later to Ironman, and a year after that to 100-mile ultramarathons. For seven years I actually got faster, rising age notwithstanding. At age 65 I ran a certified 5K in 19:06, a 15K in 60:39. Then my speed leveled off. A gradual decline began.

Now I'm trying to stop the clock. At my age, if I run a

race this year I hope the clock won't show any more time than it did last year. If I run really well, I might even push the time back a bit. But, even if it's just the same, it's like improving–by, say, a minute on a half marathon, over two minutes on the full marathon.

You can learn that from studying the age-grading tables. Those numbers were gathered from decades of recording how aging runners decline. They bring a tale of woe: Your time is going to go up; your speed is going to go down. The columns of figures express biology. And it is destiny.

That's not a whine. I accept it. You're going to go down. I'm going to go down. But I don't claim there won't be a fight. Let's drag it out. I'm going down all right, but I'm going down slow – chasing every screaming second. That's the best hope now, going down slow.

TURNAROUND

1

TURNAROUND

The day I remember was a Wednesday. Overnight a front had swept through. The ides of March had come again. I went outside that morning, as I usually do.

The front's passing had left the air cold, the sky blue and not a cloud in sight. It was the kind of morning where if you ever liked the outside you'd want to be out.

I filled my tall water bottle, the one that holds enough for twelve miles, and headed north into a gentle wind, cold against my skin. The route meanders northwest six miles through countryside, makes a turnaround and snakes back along blacktops named for churches — Liberty Church, Shipley Church — familiar old roads that suit this morning's run.

It was still winter that March, although signs of spring were beginning to show. Daffodils marked a yellow border along a lawn's edge; crocuses thrust upward beneath a naked tree; a pastel blush tinged a maple's stark outline. The northern sky was blue as infinity, a color belonging to October, although it was March.

Four miles into the run a sharp crest offered a long view. To the right a fescue field cradled a small lake near the road, an occasional stopover place for waterfowl on their long

Going Down Slow

journeys north or south. On the left I saw scattered trees, a farm pond, a pasture; further south stood a wide stretch of gray woods. The road curved westward before me.

Ahead of me I saw something dark lying in the road near the lake. It was too far away to tell what it was. Maybe a skunk killed by a car—I had seen suchlike. But drawing closer, I could see feathers—a crow maybe.

But it was bigger than that, and, as I passed, I realized it was a duck. It lay in my lane only a few feet from the lake, likely hit by a car as someone rushed to work—destroyed by a device nature warned no duck about.

As I ran by, I glanced down briefly and kept on going.

It was just then that a white-winged duck passed low overhead, flying fast and straight, as in a missing-plane fly-over, honoring its fallen mate lying there in the road. Above me, his bright wings—for it was male—flashed in the harsh light, reminding me of a common merganser. It was the time of year when ducks migrate north, where they mate, build nests and raise their young. But this duck continued hard toward the south, showing not the slightest waver of direction or purpose, holding a precise course.

I watched him cross the pasture in a fury of speed you'd think he couldn't continue, staying level and straight. He passed the far end, where the woods start, and rushed on, skimming treetops as if ignoring in a blind rage their upstretched limbs.

Who can say how a duck might think? Perhaps in dim duck-thought he recalled the stopover they last made on the way north and was vainly returning to where he

Going Down Slow

thought his mate might once again be found. Maybe he was seeking a previous time, a previous place — one he can never find — a place in memory that remains how it was before. But who can say how a duck might think?

His image grew small, receding in the pale distance. We each traveled our own way, south for him, west for me.

But it looked like he must have had a change of heart. Before he vanished over the woods altogether he began to turn, swinging around to the left. He reversed direction, and headed back across the pasture in perfect retrograde to his previous course, aiming for another pass over the one that lay in the road. I turned to watch as he crossed.

This time he was climbing hard, setting a course north, into an infinite blue sky — a sky that belonged to October, although it was March.

2

PUNKY REGGAE PARTY

Whatever happened to Guadalupe Santos?

At the age of thirteen she was raped and then sent to prison for killing the creep who did it, a crime she did not commit—if, indeed, you could call it a crime; but then the episode happened in Latin America. In prison, Guadalupe Santos discovered she was pregnant, and gave birth to a daughter whom she had to surrender to the care of her older sister, a woman who later betrayed her.

After serving fifteen years and with credit for good behavior, her release date was drawing near. But calamity struck again. To save her life and the life of her best friend, she was forced to escape from prison. On the run, she worked her way north and crossed the border into the United States.

Rebuilding her life here, she met a man and fell in love. He didn't know her awful secret. Whether they had a future together seemed doubtful. She remained a prisoner of her past.

How things eventually worked out for Guadalupe will be forever lost from me. With remarkable bad timing the last three episodes of *Prisionera* air while I, myself, head toward Latin America.

Going Down Slow

On this December Thursday I ride an early morning flight from Nashville to Memphis, the first leg of a trip to Negril, Jamaica, where I plan to run the Reggae Marathon. I sit idly reflecting on the coincidence of my trip and the program's conclusion.

In an attempt to augment my Spanish lessons, I'd started watching *Prisionera*, a *telenovela* on Telemundo, only ten days earlier—I certainly needed the help. I'd never watched a soap opera before, and I thought they went on forever. I happened to pick one, however, that not only aimed to end two weeks after I started watching it but would manage to do so precisely while I make an unlikely December trip. Once again the ready occurrence of the highly improbable makes me wonder.

With several shows to choose from, why did I pick *Prisionera*? Simple—Guadalupe Santos. She grabbed my attention like a magnet grabs a compass. While maybe not the great beauty that some of the show's other women are, she is nevertheless *bonita* enough. But her attraction comes from something beyond mere physical perfection.

I decided to read about the character—another Spanish lesson. Telemundo's online literature described her as noble, strong and dreamy. I was surprised at how well those descriptions fit my impressions. The actor, Gabriela Spanic, who plays her, is able to convey those qualities without doing much of anything at all.

She can just stand there. When she cries, tears streak down her cheek and drip off her chin. Even her smile is tinged with sadness, and she seems to gaze into the distance. Her eyes are big, maybe too big, but all the

Going Down Slow

more poignantly expressive. Her lips pout and her profile suggests comic petulance.

Her beauty is flawed, and therefore the more exquisite.

This December morning I ride along, gazing out the Airbus window, my thoughts rambling in daydreams about beauty, about what it is—and why do I care? In an expansive mood, it seems I find it all around.

I pick up a book about Alaska I've brought to read during the warm days in the Caribbean. The book is called *Coming into the Country*, by John McPhee. It's a book full of rugged and beautiful images. McPhee's language has rare power. I read the book slowly, trying to make it last, scanning the words like a prospector looking for gold. I find a glittering nugget on every page.

He is describing a canoe trip on the Salmon River—one of thirteen Alaskan rivers so named—in the Brooks Range of northern Alaska. I want to be there with him. His party flew to the put-in with a helicopter pilot from the flat country of Louisiana who got them all lost. While they flew up and down river after river, the pilot handed the map to McPhee, a passenger and non-pilot, asking for his help in finding their position. Of the map, McPhee says, "…the mountains looked like calves' brains over bone china…" He describes the immensity of the wilderness: "…if anyone could figure out how to steal Italy, Alaska would be the place to hide it."

McPhee is skilled at evoking vivid images. He tells about a barber who was a lousy shot going on a bear hunting trip. He emptied his rifle and only hit the grizzly once, in the foot. "The damage the bear did to the barber

Going Down Slow

was enough to kill him several times."

A woman runs a small boarding house made of cottonwood logs at Talkeetna where mountain climbers stay. She works hard, enforces strict rules of behavior and prepares meals for which people make long drives. "She is dour, silent, stolid as a ceramic cat." Ceramic cat! No one can use that simile again. McPhee uses it up right here in this book.

Alaska is beautiful, but dangerous—beauty with a price, a price only a few are willing to pay. The flaw of danger is what protects Alaska's beauty. But is it enough?

I look up from the book and gaze out the window, savoring McPhee's thoughts. Thirty thousand feet below I see not Alaska, but west Tennessee. It is cold this morning, even on the ground—thick fog hindered my predawn drive to Nashville. The sun is up now, spilling a warm glow over the sleeping landscape.

I notice a scene unlike any I've spotted before. A river valley meanders endlessly through woodland. The valley is filled to the brim with fog, but not a droplet over. None spreads out over the surrounding countryside; it perfectly outlines the valley's imprint. From this height the fog looks solid. The slanting sun reveals its surface texture by shadowy shades of gray, like a glacier of dirty snow.

For some reason I suddenly remember John Dodson, conductor then of the Bryan Symphony, telling me why he likes the music of Gustav Mahler. It was like explaining Newtonian physics to our tan Shar-pei. I understood it poorly, and I can relate it only crudely.

He said Mahler's music unfolds with beautiful

Going Down Slow

promise but then somehow falls short—by design, I took it. It seems headed toward the perfect moment, like when you hit the ball *thock!* on the sweet spot and you know you've nailed it. Mahler instead pulls back, turns, preferring to introduce a deliberate shortfall, the perfect imperfection, a feature that makes his music intensely interesting. Some might consider that to be a flaw. If so, to John it was an exquisite one.

Then he said something surprising. "Amy is like that."

He was talking about Amy Dodson, my running colleague, who was then his wife. I hope he doesn't mind my mention of his comparison; I thought it was endearing. When he said it, we were standing on Laycock Bridge in Smith County, Tennessee while a movie crew of some fifty people filmed Amy running, beautiful and brave, across the shaky old bridge for a television commercial.

As she ran along the wooden floor, Amy's exquisite flaw was apparent to all—a graphite device that replaces her lower left leg. Perhaps John sensed that it is that very flaw that helps drive Amy to accomplish the feats she has, both as a runner and as a person. She had already become the first woman leg-amputee to compete in the Boston Marathon, a prestigious race with a 100-year-plus history. She has since gone on to set the woman's marathon *world* record for a one-leg amputee, and to finish Ironman races. Remembering her searing courage helps drive me through hard marathons such as Reggae, where the Caribbean heat raises the challenge.

This morning's flight to Memphis is brief. The pilot

Going Down Slow

must have gotten clearance for a straight-in approach. We've dropped steadily and I doubt any turns at this altitude. The morning sun is behind us. The angle is just right for me to watch our shadow sweeping the ground. It slides over the pastures, wafts through the bare woods, flicks across the freeway and swipes the roofs of warehouses, all the while growing larger and larger until finally—over grass now—it comes up and *thump* bumps into us.

We're down. First leg finished. I look around. The passengers are anxious to get off the plane. I don't know anybody. Next stop, Montego Bay.

Surviving the Road to Negril is my problem. The three old men are drunk, and getting drunker by the mile. It appears they had a few drinks on their plane, and now they've brought a few beers on the bus with them, in a cloth cooler managed by one of their wives. She occupies a jump seat in the aisle beside me, stowing the cooler underneath.

Eighteen of us are packed tight into a Toyota bus not much larger than a soccer mom's van. The last row of seats is piled high with luggage. We wind up a mountain overlooking Montego Bay heading toward Negril some fifty-six miles away.

The Caribbean is on our right, blue, sun-dappled and white-capped. The mountain, lush and green, is on our left; the road clings to the side of it. I have a window seat just behind the shotgun position, which is on the left in Jamaica, where cars travel the left side of the road. From

Going Down Slow

my angle, every truck coming down the mountain seems on a collision course with us.

The inebriated old men aren't worried; they raise a din of raucous banter, uproariously funny to them. They are from Michigan, something they remind us of frequently. They discuss people back home as if we on the bus want to hear about them. One complains about some woman there.

"Tell her to get a glass belly button so she can see where she's going when her head is up her ass," the head geezer says.

"Hee-hee-hee…." They have a laugh on the absent woman.

Head Geezer has a stiff white beard, and wears his baseball hat cocked high. He sits just behind the driver. The T-shirt stretched across his enormous belly asserts, "I survived the road to Negril!" That's the road we're on now.

I know next to nothing about Negril, except that the town advertises a beach and a marathon. Either one is a good enough excuse to come here on this December day. It is, however, the 26.2-mile race known as the Reggae Marathon that has drawn me to this tropical island.

Our driver wears a pinched look of perpetual worry. He shifts to third, and the Toyota crawls up the hill growling. While he loaded luggage prior to leaving the airport, Head Geezer was leaning across the seat, impatiently honking the bus horn, claiming it didn't work. He continues badgering the man for operating a bus equipped with a horn that won't blow. He won't let it go.

Going Down Slow

Finally the driver tries the horn button.

"It works," he says earnestly. Geezer can't hear it for the ringing in his own ears.

"Know what Davy Crockett said at the Alamo?" Geezer asks.

"Where'd all them damn roofers come from?"

"Hee-hee-hee."

Our driver is a patient man. Put dreadlocks on him and he would be the stereotype of Jamaican Man — slightly built, small bones, small head. His cap puckers in the back like a fifth-grade little leaguer. He looks hungry.

His lean frame is the same as that of the great African marathoners. I expect you'd find strong roadrunners in Jamaica, if young men — women, too — had the requisite opportunity. The driver's endurance today is of a different kind — abiding beer-drinking tourists from North America, geezers gone wild.

The young woman in front of me has fuzzy blond hair, bare shoulders and a diamond planted on the side of her nose. She seems to be helping our driver with his cell phone duties. One problem is to find it among the pile of litter on the console between them. I lean forward and ask her if she works for the bus company.

"No, I'm on holiday. I've been traveling around. This is the place I decided to hang out."

She's from Scotland, she says; her accent confirms it. I take it she is a part-time resident of Jamaica.

"It looks like *the* place if you like water and you like warm," I say. She does.

I drop it. I don't need to waste any energy socializing

Going Down Slow

before the race. I especially don't want to get caught up in the men's circus across the aisle. The silent matron sitting between them and me provides insulation. I keep my marathon plans and my easy-to-remember name to myself.

This marathon hangs over me like doom. This will be my twenty-fourth race this year — a few too many. My body is worn out, and I feel myself sinking. I need a break from it.

So I can't expect much in this race, especially in view of the heat here. My main hope is to get through it without a crippling overuse injury. Afterwards, if I can walk away, it will be like ducking a bullet.

This race has been on my calendar for months. There is nothing I can do now — except get the rest I know I must have. That means avoiding the orbit of the partying men. The emotional uproar sucks out energy worse than shoveling coal.

I want to look at the countryside. I gaze quietly out the window. The scene is a bit disheartening. The slopes are rocky and steep. Little frame houses propped on blocks tell a story of poverty. Most of the land is uncleared. There's an occasional pasture — I spot a few cattle and some goats. A dozen horses stand listless in a pasture grazed to the bare ground. Elsewhere, vegetation is rampant, lush.

At one lush place, a naked man stands in a pool of ankle-deep creek water taking a bath. Head bowed, arms upraised, he pours water over his dreadlocks. His virile black body glistens under a burning sun. He rises from the water like a primeval god reigning over Eden. The image

Going Down Slow

is at once innocent and sensual.

The striking scene slips past my window. I wonder if I am the only one who saw it. Bushes concealed the man until the bus was near him. You had to be paying attention at the right time. I listen, but no one says a thing about it. Certainly the Michigan beer drinkers didn't see him; it would have touched off a barrage of salacious one-liners.

I wonder if any woman on the bus saw it. Will she remember tonight? And tomorrow on the beach when the gentle waves whisper and a hot breeze lifts her hair, will she lay aside her book and gaze into the distance? Will she hold the secret in her heart, never telling anyone?

I don't know. I'm just a man, not qualified to speak for any woman. All I saw was a man taking a bath in a creek. When I was a small boy my maternal grandfather and I did the same thing.

The men from Michigan, apparently ignorant of the bathing man, carry on with the same kind of rowdy comments as before. Harmless fun mostly. They're just a little drunk, is all.

"How can you tell when David is lying?" Geezer wants to know.

"When his lips are moving," the friend answers.

Our road winds through three towns. The streets are narrow, sometimes lacking even a sidewalk. The buildings come right up to my window. I look through the open doors into the stores and bars.

At one place a round woman in a cotton print dress wobbles heavily along a walk. At the precise moment we pass she angrily slashes a shrub with her machete. What

Going Down Slow

does the gesture mean?

Geezer figures it out.

"Damn! You wouldn't want to jump her!" he observes, reasonably enough. That touches off a round of predictable comments.

"Hee-hee-hee."

The Michigan wife next to me endures her husband's road show without a word. Twice, in passing, I make a friendly comment to her. Each time she meets me with stony silence. She hardened like concrete years ago.

Negril turns out to be seven miles of two-lane blacktop next to a beach—further south is Towne Centre, I will learn. From the road you can't actually see the beach most of the time for the intervening trees, resorts, villas and restaurants. To the east is the Great Morass, a canopied swampland stretching to the horizon. The mountains have drifted away.

It has taken us two hours to cover the fifty-six miles. It seems longer. The driver makes the rounds of the resorts, dropping people off.

"Of all the things I've ever lost, my mind bothers me the most," Geezer says.

I have successfully kept quiet and not spoken with the Michigan men. Despite that, at least one has learned what I am up to. The bus pulls up to Negril Tree House, where I plan to stay. As I get out of my seat, the man's eyes meet mine.

"Good luck, Dallas," he says.

How I blew my cover, is another story.

✻ ✻ ✻

Going Down Slow

The last morning before the Reggae Marathon, I figured a walk along the beach would be relaxing. So I struck out down Negril's seven-mile beach, pride of western Jamaica, the brochure says. The sun was bright and warm, unlike the foggy December day I'd left behind in Tennessee.

Then a guy tried to sell me dope. Here he came, a stout young man wearing black droopy shorts, dreadlocks and a heavy ring on a gold chain around his neck, bling enough for the beach. He checked me out by offering a ride on the para-glider. But I wasn't interested in any excitement. From my white beard, he concluded he faced an unreformed hippie—leastwise, a safe bet.

"I know a guy. I can get you some good smokes," he said. I knew he could.

"No thanks, I wouldn't care for any," I said.

"It's good stuff."

"No, I don't want any. Thanks."

"You don't want that?" Puzzled, he turned and walked away.

His offer came on top of the female companionship a guy had tried to sell me the previous day, when I was in the airport restroom at Montego Bay.

The two incidents, maybe trifling and small, reflect a bigger problem for Jamaica: The economy is shattered. And where poverty goes, drugs, HIV, murder and other crimes follow.

A third of the population falls below the poverty line; the inflation rate hovers in double digits, and so does unemployment.

Going Down Slow

The Jamaican dollar is slipping. During the late nineties, thirty-five Jamaican dollars (J$35) bought one U.S. dollar (US$1.00). Then the slide quickened. As I planned my trip I saw an exchange rate of J$50. By the time I actually made the trip a few weeks later, it had reached J$60.

That may be good news for the traveler, but terrible news for Jamaicans. When their dollar falls from J$35 to J$60, their ability to buy groceries and other things likewise falls. Since this island country must import most of her staples, devaluation of its dollar hits doubly hard. Finally it takes a sack full of money to buy anything.

A gallon of gas costs J$140, a soda J$150, a beer J$200 and a speeding ticket J$10,000.

"They love the American dollar," a fellow traveler told me. Little wonder—the U.S. dollar represents lasting value, while the Jamaican dollar erodes away like sand under foot. Realizing that, I paid for most of my purchases with U.S. dollars.

Despite the hardship around me, my days passed pleasantly. I sat at a table on the veranda of my villa working and reading. A garden of shrubs and flowers comes up to the porch. Walks to other villas criss-cross the garden. Maids and maintenance men go about their work, singing as they pass—pop songs and reggae tunes mostly. But in the distance, briefly I heard a man's voice booming two lines:

When we all get to heaven,
We will meet on that beautiful shore.

Going Down Slow

Not waiting for the sweet by and by, I promptly went down and sat on that beautiful shore.

The singing and the friendly demeanor of the Jamaicans that I met seemed at odds with the difficult conditions they face. A wide smile and a, "Yah Mon," are what I saw.

But it was not always so peaceful. One day I sat working, reading and writing. An angry argument flared up between two men in the driveway near my porch. Although I couldn't see the two men for a picket fence, the sound was more than enough.

The volume hit a shrill pitch I thought only the hard shock of a 9-mm would end. Or maybe a scream gurgled by a sharp blade. It was like a taunt rubber band stretched to the limit. The invectives screamed out in Spanish came in waves, and the altercation gradually drifted down the drive to the road. I hoped they'd take it a mile on down the road. But it continued there.

A car passed and drowned the argument under the loud wailing of Bob Marley. But just for a few seconds. Then the argument resurfaced. It was more than wearisome — it was unnerving. In it all, I hear two reasonable words shouted out *en inglés*.

"Shut up! Shut up!"

After twenty minutes it finally played out, from sheer exhaustion I guess. While it lasted, the strident Spanish set my primordial reflexes a-twitch, and I couldn't concentrate on my work. I was studying my Spanish assignment.

Tourists are important to Jamaicans. They want you to come back. Tourism is one resource they do have. But,

Going Down Slow

of course, lots of other places have the stuff of tourism, the beaches and sunshine. But Jamaica has something more, something no one else has, and something no one can claim or take away: Bob Marley.

Or rather Bob Marley's legacy. His dreadlock image is everywhere—in photographs, on woodcarvings, on tee shirts. Though he died in 1981 his reggae music lives on, celebrated with fervor in Jamaica. His song, "One Love," has become a Jamaican anthem, if not a world one.

Besides running the marathon, my main goal was to search out a place where I could hear live reggae music played by a steel band. I need not have worried. Race organizers had arranged for the Caribbean Regal Steel Band to play in the park at the pre-race supper. The ten-member mixed-gender group filled that space with music. I pulled my folding chair up to the front and center, and let the music wash over me.

In one stretch they played—what else—"One Love," swung into—I swear!—Glen Miller's "In the Mood," sailed into "Rocking Robin," and chased that with "Tequila"—something for everyone. Their music was complex, melodic, joyous, clear as a bell. I believe they could have played Beethoven's Ninth.

Oil drum: The ordinary fifty-five-gallon steel barrel. Detritus of petroleum the world over: it took the descendants of slaves in nearby Trinidad to fashion it into a musical instrument. They cut the end off and hammered it into a concave surface, making a drum that sings. Strike it at different places and you make different notes. Shape another drumhead differently and you get a different tonal

Going Down Slow

range. Ten such drums make a band spanning several octaves, one that can emulate a grand piano.

From oil drums, music, from oppression, joy. The human spirit wrenches beauty from bleakness. Is there a better example than this? A steel band in flight is the human heart singing.

The night after the marathon, I sat at the resort beach bar ready for supper. The electricity went off. I read the menu with my key chain light and ordered curry goat, a treat. The food is cooked in a separate building, one that I hoped had some kind of power. The bar's concrete floor extends to the ocean; the waves washed gently against the edge where I sat. The restaurant has a roof but no walls. Beach walkers can drift through, and they do.

A young man suddenly sat down at my table and stuck out his hand. We shook. His approach was direct.

"I'm hungry," he said.

He'd been in jail. The police arrested him for selling peanuts and cigarettes, he said

"They did? Man tried to sell me peanuts today."

"They arrested me for selling without a license. You have to have a license."

"Have you talked to the folks at the restaurant about working for food?"

He wanted more than just food; his situation was critical, he said. He'd just gotten out that day. Unlikely, I thought, since it was Sunday. The earnest man wanted to raise enough money to get a bicycle and ride up and down the road to see if he could take tourists to the water park.

"You just got out today?"

Going Down Slow

"Yes."

I handed him J$500 and wished him luck. He headed on down the beach, but stopped under a beach light—the power was back on. He stood there, head down, counting his money. Suddenly he turned aside, and sat down with two tourists resting in the shadows.

I could've given his spiel.

On the day after the Reggae Marathon, I took a walk south to Negril's Towne Centre. It was about two miles from my room. The sun was bright and hot, and my legs were sore from the race.

A small bridge arches over the Negril River at its estuary, and then the road enters a roundabout. Yesterday's early-morning marathon had made a turnaround here before dawn and headed back north. I wanted to see the place in daylight.

Afterwards, walking back to my hotel, the sun got hotter. I waved at a cab. He pulled over.

"How much to the Tree House?"

He stretched across the seat, laboring to roll down the window. He started to say three but then changed it to five in mid-sentence when he looked up and saw an old gent. It came out like:

"Thre-uh-five."

"Five? You said three the first time."

"Three? No, I didn't say three! Hee-hee."

I pressed the point, derisively.

"Is that five Jamaican dollars?" (Roughly one US dime)

Going Down Slow

"Hee-hee-hee. No, not Jamaican."

He knew he'd messed up. He also knew that it was a buyer's market. If he left, there'd be another taxi along shortly, and he hated losing the fare. Finally, he said,

"How much you wanna pay?"

I'd won the argument. The ride was mine for three. So, I said:

"I'll give you five."

I sat down beside him. I wanted to be generous; it's hard in Jamaica.

"It's hard in Jamaica," he said. "I don't mean for *you* — for *us* living in Jamaica."

"Why is it hard?" I asked.

"There's too much unemployment and lots of poor people," he said.

He appreciates tourist coming down. He wanted me to know that. He made the point twice. He rarely gets to the states, to Miami occasionally.

My generosity turned out to be a good investment; the man opened up.

"Money won't buy anything," he said.

"I've heard about the Jamaican dollar falling."

"You go to the grocery store, a thousand dollars won't buy anything — three little sacks," he said. "I can remember when a thousand would actually buy something. A thousand dollars is small money now."

With the decline of Jamaica's economy has come an increase in drug trafficking, and other crimes, further sucking the lifeblood out of the country. A Kingston paper, *The Sunday Gleaner*, proudly shouted some news

Going Down Slow

in a tall red two-word headline: "KINGFISH JACKPOT." The story was about teaming up with Scotland Yard to catch some of Jamaica's "Kingfish" drug lords. Upon careful reading, the front-page story details more the *hope* of catching Kingfish than the actual catching of them. It reports only one caught so far, and he was caught, charged and tried in Great Britain, not Jamaica.

But officials are optimistic and upbeat. I don't know. My thought is that for every Kingfish caught, likely two more will be waiting to take his place. Crime pays. And for drug trafficking, Jamaica lies conveniently placed, just ninety miles south of Cuba, a perfect transshipment point for cocaine traveling north from South America to North America and Europe.

A separate problem originates within the country — the illicit cultivation of cannabis, one confirmed by my earlier encounter on the beach with a man selling "smokes." The government has a cannabis eradication program, but, as usual, corruption is a problem.

And what accompanies the drugs? *The Gleaner* reflects that, too: HIV, murder, social upheaval, and so on. I only have to scan the story titles: "AIDS, Disability and Insensitivity," "A Crisis in Human Sexuality." Numerous columns, stories and letters pursue this particular theme.

Kevin O'Brien Chang's column on murder is eye popping. He said the murder rate was poised to top 1,500 for the year. He contrasted that with only 423 back in 1989. He went on to note that "...Kingston is quite possibly the murder capital of the world...."

That is not the title Kingston needs when Jamaica uses

Going Down Slow

the "One Love" theme to promote tourism, and it is not a title befitting the home place of its late author, Jamaican hero and musician, Bob Marley.

Caught in the swirl of all this ugliness are the children, the beautiful little children, standing roadside in clusters waiting for the bus, smiling in their school uniforms — khaki shirt and trousers for the boys, khaki skirt and maroon blouse for the girls. In the education of the children lies Jamaica's hope for the future. But fear rests there, too — the fear that those same children may not escape the grip of drugs, HIV and shootings already raging across the country. They seem caught in a downward spiral.

On my last afternoon in Negril I sat in the beach bar nursing a Red Stripe beer and looking north along the shore. A few feet away a little Jamaican girl, about seven years old, worked hard in the sand, digging with a green plastic shovel. She eventually built herself a sandcastle and then excavated a moat around it. She knew a moat should be filled with water, and she tried to coax the waves into doing the job. She lay beside the moat. Each time a wave ran up the beach toward the castle, she attempted to swipe some of its water into the trench. Her little hand didn't catch enough to fill it.

Her little sister, maybe four years old, had an idea. She waded into the surf and filled a black plastic shopping bag. Then she ran up the slope with the bulging bag, jets squirting from holes in it, and dumped the contents into the moat. The older girl caught the idea and likewise filled a cardboard carton. They both ran back and forth, working hard and seriously, ferrying water to the moat. Finally the

Going Down Slow

box softened and the bottom fell out.

They gave up then. All was lost. All the water they'd managed to pour into the moat seeped into the sand and drained away.

First, I couldn't find any bananas, and then the man latched onto me like a hungry tick.

I was at the pre-race pasta supper the night before the race. A long line of open tents covering tables of food had been set up in a sports park. Serving would start soon. At a separate tent I'd just registered and picked up a plastic goodie bag containing my race bib, timing chip, tee shirt and other complimentary items.

The one item of food I was looking for on this tropical island and could not find was the same one every other runner wanted but could not find: a banana. At the registration tent I learned the problem. A handwritten sign stated, "Yes we have no bananas, courtesy of Hurricane Ivan." Ivan had barged into town a few weeks earlier. He stayed for a couple of days and blew the bananas slam off the plants.

Runners milled around, waiting for the food lines to open. I wanted to talk with some of them, but a man from New York had taken over my party. He was friendly enough — *too* friendly enough. I thought he was going to talk my leg off. His life history was mine for the taking — or listening. Philip was red-bearded, maybe fifty years old, and he was wearing a bicycling hat like riders in Europe use.

He'd gotten lucky and won the lottery at his

Going Down Slow

running club back home. The prize was a trip to Jamaica for the Reggae Marathon. He was observing the race, not actually planning to run it. The club paid his way just to promote the race. He'd already decided to come back and run the race next year.

Philip's wife had come too. But that was not lucky. Their plane had been scheduled to leave New York at seven in the morning. Everything unraveled; it was a long story. There were mechanical problems, plane substitutions, rescheduling and so on. They flew errant flights around the eastern United States for a while before actually heading toward Jamaica. Instead of arriving in Negril later that afternoon as planned, they didn't arrive until three in the morning the next day.

His wife was mad as a wet hen.

"She had to go five hours without a cigarette," he shouted. "Even after we got on the ground, she couldn't smoke until we cleared immigration. She's still back at the hotel," he told me. "We're on a section of the beach where clothes are optional. She can smoke there. That's a good place for her."

"Next year I'm bringing my girlfriend instead of my wife," he said with conviction. "That'll work out a lot better. She likes to swim and bike and run. Yeah, that'll be a lot better. Oh, I still live with his wife, you know—that's not a big problem—but it's just that my girlfriend likes to do the same things I do."

Of course, he hadn't been looking for a girlfriend—she just came along. "We went running together a few times," he explained. "She was just a running partner. But

Going Down Slow

one thing, you know, led to another. We got to be friends. Then we went bicycling together. And so on. It was just natural. She likes the same stuff I do."

He'd made up his mind about the matter. I was clear on that—next year he was bringing his girlfriend. Even his wife might like that better.

He was friendly, but I needed to scrub him off before he started talking about real estate and brothers-in-laws. I couldn't even catch a chance to look through my goodie bag. A woman from California saved me. She sat down behind me and started talking about San Diego's Rock and Roll Marathon, of which the back of my tee shirt reminded her. She was as big a talker as Philip, and for a minute I thought I'd made a mistake taking her on. I was caught in crossfire, yammering coming from two directions instead of one.

Then I had an inspiration. I gently deflected her comments to Philip, nurturing a tentative dialog between them. It blossomed into a full-blown storm, an even match. I took the opportunity to duck out. I wanted to find Burt Carlson.

I found Burt sitting on the curb at the head of the line of food tents, waiting for the food bars to open. He's a story. When he finishes this Reggae Marathon it will bring his total to 268 marathons. He's seventy-nine-years old (this was in 2004) and he's here to run in this humidity and heat. A doctor wouldn't recommend it.

But I wasn't surprised; I'd seen his picture in the online race literature, where he'd run the race the previous year. I figured he'd show up. Burt is a runner who's going

Going Down Slow

down slow, the way a runner should. Still, how old do you get before you learn you won't be back? Older than seventy-nine, if you're Burt.

It was Burt who blew my cover on the bus ride from Montego Bay where a bunch of beer-drinking senior citizens had been throwing a loud party. A situation I don't recall confronting before that day—*rowdy senior citizens!* I'd hoped to keep my mind quiet by avoiding marathon questions from people who I figured didn't know a marathon from a motorcycle.

The driver had made a restroom stop for his revelers—smart driver. As passengers climbed back on, someone tapped me on the shoulder and I looked up.

"Have you run this one before?" Burt Carlson asked.

I hadn't seen him on the bus—he'd been seated behind me somewhere. He looked surprised when I called his name.

Actually, I'd run a race with him, the forty-one-mile Strolling Jim ultramarathon in Wartrace, Tennessee, on an unseasonably warm day in May four years earlier. A man from St. Louis had introduced us. The man from St. Louis quit the race, got in his truck and split for home. Burt kept going, even past the hilly section they refer to in the plural as "the walls." He kept going—on through that day's heat—until he got to the finish line where the race's namesake, Strolling Jim, the first world champion walking horse, is buried. The race director was drinking beer and grilling barbecue chicken, a victorious woman runner was throwing up while her mate tenderly held her hand, and I was sitting very still in a folding chair concentrating hard

Going Down Slow

on staying conscious.

Images of a race, I remember Burt.

The food line opened, and Burt and I started through. I believe it was the most elaborately abundant collection of food I've ever seen. It was not a fiesta; it was several; each tent was a fiesta unto itself. Here were local delicacies — curry goat, jerk chicken, whitefish — and a variety of cooked vegetables. Food of every description was kept warm over open flames, attended by chefs in white hats. One tent featured a table piled high with baked bread shaped like animals — squid, fish, snake, alligator....

From the total available, only a tiny sample was possible. I had primavera, seafood pasta, boiled dumplings, sliced tomatoes and fried eggplant. Sadly, that was all I could allow myself the night before a marathon.

Burt and I sat in folding chairs eating. A man with a gray goatee walked up and asked me if I was Burt Carlson — I'm pretty old, too. "No, but he's right there," I said pointing. He handed Burt a laminated copy of a page from the local paper, and walked away. Burt sat looking at it bemused — he hadn't seen it until that moment. It was a story dated November — after Burt had registered for this year's race. Twin headlines told the news — "Burt's Coming Back" — and announced a profundity I wish I'd written: "The Human Body Was Made to Run."

Next morning, the stroke of five-fifteen would prove it.

Soon enough it comes time to run the race. You stand and wait. And you know you are forever doomed to

Going Down Slow

be a wretched runner. The pre-race fiesta, a night of fitful sleep and the dark-shrouded ride to Long Bay State Park, where the race starts, are all past. Finally, you stand at the starting line, as we do now. It is a moment that hums with primordial emotion.

We're all here: Two young black women each weighing maybe eighty-five pounds stand next to me, looking like they could run down a cheetah. Young black men in dreadlocks are here, as are housewives from North America. Old white guys like Burt Carlson and me, we're here too.

Somewhere up front, Pamenos Ballantyne, the soft-spoken thirty-year old Olympic marathoner from St. Vincent and the Grenadines, prepares to win this edition of the Reggae Marathon.

Temporary floodlights cast light on the immediate area around us. Except for that, we stand on the highway in the dark and face south, the direction we will start running. A giant wall of speakers sits in the grass pumping out reggae music.

They have lighted torches. The wavering flames along the side of the road will help guide us until daylight comes.

It can't be long now. The crowd shifts forward gently and tightens up. Bodies are close, and you can look square into the wide wild eyes of the young woman standing nearby.

Despite closeness, each runner is alone. The road ahead opens on twenty-six miles of mystery — but reveals no mile, betrays no suspense. It opens instead on your

Going Down Slow

soul. What do you see, marathoner?

Answers vary. Some are stricken by dread, fear. I recall a man from Maryland, at an Iowa marathon, telling me that as soon as the race starts, he immediately has to go to the restroom. Just nerves. He always runs quickly to the bushes, wherever he can, he said.

I recall a young woman standing next to me just before the start of the Boston Marathon. Her eyes darted about like a trapped animal.

"Nervous?" I said.

"Yeah! Aren't you?"

The truth is I wasn't—and never have been at the start of a marathon. That seems strange to say. I am by nature shy and timid, usually overcoming those tendencies with some effort. But a marathon does not intimidate me, despite all that might happen in it. Perhaps my running habit has changed me. Certainly it has.

As for now, while runners press in, I stand casually scanning the night sky. Overhead the moon is at third quarter, half full. Despite its glare and that of the floodlights, I can see stars with a sparkling brilliance I haven't witnessed in years. The glorious view comes as a surprise. It is due to the relative darkness surrounding Negril. On the western tip of Jamaica, Negril is surrounded by a dark ocean. And inland, the swampland known as the Great Morass is dark too.

The town itself has little wasted light flooding empty parking lots. Neon lights advertising stores to a sleeping town scarcely exist. Nor do security lights, so helpful to the crooks. At night, it is dark. As it should be. Light pollution

Going Down Slow

so common in the States—even in the countryside now—is largely absent here. And in the absence of this photonic indulgence, what do you get? The greatest view in the universe—the very universe itself.

We've nearly managed to blot it out in Tennessee, where I live. The dusty glow we radiate into space blanks the dim stars and dims the bright ones, leaving little to see. Take a survey: How many people under thirty have ever seen the Milky Way? We've pulled the curtain on a panorama that guided and awed humankind for millennia in everything from religion to agriculture.

Here I've found a new way to wait for the race to start—study the heavens. There in the east is the red giant, Arcturus, burning bright. Arching to the north my eye skips along the handle of the Big Dipper, a big bopper of a constellation everyone ought to know. It's upside down now, spilling a cosmic drink, the front edge shooting straight toward Polaris, the North Star. Always at true north, the star is lower than I've ever seen it. At Negril's latitude of eighteen degrees, Polaris appears just eighteen degrees above the horizon, geometry tells us.

A bright light is just south of Arcturus, where no bright star should be; it must be one of the wanderers. Not red enough for Mars, too high for Venus and too bright for all the other planets save one, I reason, by Jupiter, it must be Jupiter.

To the west, Orion the hunter marches off this night's stage followed by Canis Major the big dog. Sirius, the dog's nose, is the brightest star in the sky—except for the one we circle, the sun.

Going Down Slow

The race starts and jolts me out of my astronomical idyll. I run south with the pack, trying not to step on people. At three miles we cross the Negril River, make a turnaround at a traffic roundabout in Towne Centre, and head north.

Approaching the turnaround, I realize that I must have already met Pamenos, the race leader. But it is still so dark I never knew when.

On we go, heading north now. The course goes past where we started and continues on north, following the meandering coastline past Bloody Bay and Orange Bay, to finally arrive at Green Island Harbor, where it makes a second turnaround at the sixteen-mile marker. From there the ten-mile return to Long Bay State Park brings the total distance to precisely 26.2 miles.

At the aid stations they hand out water packaged like I've never seen before—sealed in a clear plastic bag, hand-sized, a little water pillow. It can't splash out like a cup. You can bite the corner and conveniently squirt it in your mouth without stopping.

Somewhere around mile nine the sun rises. We can't see it for clouds. What we see are the green-shrouded trees of the Great Morass in stark relief against gray-streaked salmon stratus.

Soon afterwards my run wilts in the heat. I expected it—just not so soon. At mile eleven, my pace creeps over eight minutes per mile. By comparison, my average pace at the last Country Music Marathon had been seven twenty-five. Here I can't even hang onto eight—and I know it will get worse.

Going Down Slow

Part of the problem is that this is my twenty-fourth race this year, way too many. I'm declaring a rest the moment I finish. If I do—because you don't know. Just past mile thirteen, I am running alone, when here comes Pamenous going the other way. The man is miles ahead of me. He has already made the turnaround at mile sixteen and is headed back, well clear of challengers, who aren't even in sight.

Two lone marathoners meet on the road. Separate in culture and speed and over a generation apart in age, we spare a common experience here today—and run exactly the same distance. He looks relaxed, comfortable, just running fast enough to win. We pass.

"Go, Pamenous," I yell.

"Yeah." A little smile.

By the time I make the turnaround and reach eighteen-and-a-half miles, near where he is now, he will be breaking the tape at Long Bay, winning this marathon for the third time in four years.

Actually by the time I reach mile eighteen, something else happens—my watch shows me nine twelve, a number greater than nine minutes for the first time. In the eight miles remaining, I will manage to push the pace below nine in only three of them. Eight minutes, slow early on, has now become a wistful dream.

The mercury pushes into the eighties, and the sun bears down.

At the little town of Orange Bay a scattering of people stand on the roadside gossiping, watching, applauding. Little kids play and ride bikes.

Going Down Slow

My slog continues. A sardonic fathom narrates:

"Stand aside, ladies and gentlemen! Pay attention. Here comes one. Look! Witness his heroic effort! Note how ponderous it is — how puny the effect. See, his energy is gone. See how his knees barely bend, how his feet nearly scrape the ground."

"And see how, even knowing that, he keeps going, trying harder and harder — and gets slower and slower. Check his loss of muscle strength, too! — see that, the slumping body, the loss of posture. Pathetic, I tell you."

"I got to say 'desperation.' That's the word. Look at that face, folks. A grimace frozen, a death mask, if you ever saw one. He's not alone either. Here come some more. Applaud if you will. Shed a tear, sentimental fans. These wretched souls, can't stop. They are forever doomed to run, run, run."

"And here's the damnedest thing: I swear — can you believe it? — by tomorrow they'll be describing this as 'fun,' and using expressions like 'words can't explain…' and so and so on. Yes, they will!"

"Stand back, folks. Make room. Don't get too close!"

My feeble trudge ends after three hours, thirty-seven minutes and twenty-five seconds, my slowest time in years. For the sixty and over age group, I've finished first — not because I ran fast, but for the good and usual reason that no one else ran faster.

It seemed likely I'd never find Jason. Following the race, I sent an e-mail to the race director. After a couple of months I quit thinking about it. Then a message suddenly arrived from Gail Jackson. "I know that kid," the message said.

Going Down Slow

Gail owned the hotel in Negril where I'd stayed and she'd worked on the marathon's registration committee.

"I was at his school yesterday...and asked if after the race did he go for a swim and talk to a white man?" she wrote. The boy's answer had been yes. He was the one. His real name was Oraine.

I promptly mailed one of my hundred-lap Ironman watches to Gail to give to the boy. It was a watch I'd actually used in an Ironman triathlon. Sending him a watch I'd used seemed more personal than buying a new one. I put it in the original box with it's instructions along with a note of good wishes from me.

A month later, Oraine sent a letter thanking me. He liked to draw, and he included a pencil-drawn portrait on green paper. In his letter he said, "If there is anything you want me to do for you in drawing don't be afraid to ask."

But... at the race that day:

After I crossed the finish line I quit running and starting staggering, stumbling like a backward-walking drunk. I was okay. But my legs were confused — by fatigue and the sudden non-running. The music was pouring down, and the heat was humming.

I'd just crossed the finish line at Long Bay State Park. A young man sharply dressed in a white polo shirt and dark slacks handed me a cell phone.

"Want to call home?" he asked.

"Good idea. Thanks."

The free call was a promotion of the carrier for which he worked. I dialed my home number but couldn't get an answer — or rather I couldn't tell if I got an answer, the

Going Down Slow

music was so loud. So I walked a hundred yards away from the stack of speakers pumping out reggae, across a field of grass toward the ocean, and tried again.

And there was Jo Ann's comfortable voice from far-away Tennessee, bouncing off a satellite, sounding next door. She'd answered the first time, she said, but couldn't hear anything except noise. I told her I was okay, that I'd had a poor run, but that I wasn't surprised by that. The usual stuff.

After returning the phone, I went to check on partial results posted on a board past the booming speakers, and discovered that for the male age-group 60-99 I'd finished first with a time of three thirty-seven twenty-five. At most places where I run that wouldn't win a cakewalk. The competitive field was not very deep, and the heat was a factor.

Under the female 20-29 age group, I saw that a young woman named Shannon from West Virginia had finished third. With about a mile to go, I'd pulled even with her. We were both just trying to survive, and we chatted a bit. But she was running a little slower than I was. Finally I went on. I knew she was feeling terrible.

"I'll see you at the finish line—if I get there," I said.

"Oh, you'll make it; you look strong," she said.

Runners! Bless their happy little hearts—always upbeat and encouraging. They'll say you're looking good and running smooth, even when you're dying—even when *they're* dying. They can't help it; it's how they are. Running makes them crazy.

I meant to keep my promise to Shannon, so now I

Going Down Slow

went back toward the finish line looking for her. I found her glued to a chair under a beach tent. She hadn't gotten very far. When I told her she'd taken third she was so pleased she began warming to the idea of going to the Country Music Marathon that I'd told her about.

"That's not very far..." she said, and trailed off, visualizing another marathon—even while the pain of this one was still in her legs. Here you see another trait of runners: terrible memory.

When I was a kid my dad liked to drink coconut water—he called it coconut milk. He'd drive a nail into the eyes to make holes and pour the water into a glass. I learned to like that, too.

At this race, that was a piece of good luck. A man was trimming the shucks off coconuts with a machete, deftly whacking away over a plywood board that served as a chopping block. With the last whack he sliced the top off one and held it out to me. I dropped in a drinking straw and walked away sucking on the coconut, a new kind of post-race hydration—one lacking carbonation, artificial coloring, preservative or sweetener.

Race management had set up a medical center in the beach house, an open-air, wooden structure the size of a five-car garage. Dehydrated runners lying on cots and tables were getting IVs and massages. I didn't need either one. I asked the woman doctor if I could leave my shoes in the corner.

"That's an unusual request! But I guess it's all right," she said.

"I don't want to lose my shoes—it's a mile walk back

Going Down Slow

to the hotel. I'm going for a swim," I told her.

"Go north. We're only ninety miles from Cuba," she said.

"I need to practice."

I walked straight into the Caribbean wearing my sunglasses, cap, running shorts and singlet, race number still pinned to it, marathon medal dangling around my neck. The water was exactly the right temperature.

Nearby a half-dozen Jamaican men and women of mixed age tossed a soccer ball around. One woman's enormous breasts swung heavily and stretched her transparent tee. A young boy dived in my direction. I watched as he swam the whole distance under water. He came up facing me wearing a friendly smile, a handsome lad with short dense hair.

"Did you run the marathon?" he asked.

I told him I had. He said he had run the half-marathon distance as a member of a three-man relay team, a special competition organizers had provided for the school children, one I didn't know about until that moment.

It's a wonderfully idea to involve the children in something as positive as a race; they face an uncertain future in a country wracked by so many problems.

Here we were, an old white man standing in the ocean with an eighth-grade Jamaican boy talking about running. We shook hands. I told him my name, and he said he was Jason.

"My relay team won second place!" he said.

"That's great, congratulations."

Jamaica's children left a poignant impression on me,

Going Down Slow

none more so than Jason. His easy, endearing smile was as natural as sunshine. He admired my sports watch, an eye-catching black and yellow number Jo Ann had given me.

"I want to get a watch like that," he said.

"You can get one about like it at Wal-Mart for thirty or forty dollars."

I actually said that! And with that utterance I proved I could be as arrogantly stupid as any North American tourist who ever landed on Jamaican soil.

Exactly which Wal-Mart should he go to, one in Miami or Key West? Well, he'll just have to check the airline schedules. And what about the forty bucks? — just a bit over 2,000 Jamaican dollars. He'll just have to save his lunch money.

The hard truth is a watch is not likely for him any time soon. I wanted Jason to have a watch. To develop his running skills, he needs basic training tools. Who knows what he might accomplish? My impulse was to strip my watch off and hand it to him on the spot — I had two others at home. But Jo Ann had given it to me; and, too, it held my mile splits stored in the memory, not yet transferred to my file.

A few weeks after the race, I mounted an e-mail campaign to find Jason. Weeks went by with no luck, until one day the e-mail suddenly arrived from Gail Jackson. Through her, I finally sent Jason a watch.

What *could* Jason accomplish? Most Jamaicans are of African or mixed African-European descent, and, hence likely share the genes of the Kenyans who currently dominate marathon competition.

Going Down Slow

The success of Pomenos Ballantyne suggests the potential. The King of Caribbean marathons — so-called by the *Sunday Gleaner*, a Kingston paper — is from neighboring St. Vincent, and he'd easily won the marathon.

At the Negril Tree House on my first night in Jamaica, I had gone to the lobby, an open-air room. A leanly chiseled black man came up to me.

"Did you run the Stockholm Marathon?" he asked.

My tee shirt proclaimed it; I admitted it. At first I was wary and not very warm, thinking he might be a crook. After we chatted a bit I realized that the man was indeed a marathoner. He wrote his name for me — Pomenos Ballantyne. And when he told me that his time in the Trinidad Marathon was something like two seventeen — the number I recall — I realized more.

"Oh...you're an elite marathoner."

"Yeah, elite," he said.

Over the next few days I talked with him several times. I asked him how fast he thought he could run a marathon in cool weather away from the Caribbean heat.

"Two eleven," he said.

"That would win the Country Music Marathon! They give big prize money and a new car," I said.

In fact, that time would win most marathons.

On the Sunday morning after the marathon, I went up to the roof terrace of the Tree House for the breakfast buffet there. In the corner a jazz trio — bass, keyboards, drums — was playing the barn-burner "Mercy, Mercy." People were celebrating the marathon. Hotel owner Gail Jackson herself was there, wearing a flowing chartreuse

Going Down Slow

dress, marathon metal around her neck, smiling at everyone. She had run the race, too. Not only that, but the race winner, Pomenos Ballantyne, had stayed at her hotel.

Pomenos was there too, busy talking with people. A tall picture had appeared in the *Sunday Gleaner*, showing his calm intensity during the race. He was a hero. Not wanting to intrude on his party, I sat down at another table.

The band went through Roberta Flack's "Killing Me Softly" and then took off on "Wind Beneath My Wings." Pomenos showed why men run races. Women crowded around, waiting to have their picture made with him.

Bette Midler's familiar melody about soaring higher than an eagle wafted across the terrace and drifted out over a calm blue ocean. Her voice wafted through my head.

Pomenos stood with his arms wrapped around two smiling young women — and soared higher than the song's eagle.

As he left the terrace, he angled by my table to say goodbye. He was heading back home to St. Vincent. I urged him to come to Nashville for the Country Music Marathon.

"I'd very much like to do that," he said.

But I didn't expect it. Travel money was a problem.

3

THE RACE NO ONE SAW

To start at the end, this is the moral: Sometimes a door stands open, unseen until it closes. That's the way of life. An opportunity sometimes passes before it's even known to be one.

Megan Prandtl could have been a scholarship runner. I ought to know; I saw what she did.

You step through the revolving gate in the chain link fence that surrounds Tennessee Tech's Tucker Stadium in Cookeville, Tennessee and you find yourself standing on a nine-lane track encircling Overall Field. It's the place I go to run intervals. A standard track, one lap is 400 meters long, a quarter mile.

It was 400-meter intervals I'd been practicing on that June morning, pressing hard for a full lap, followed by a one-lap recovery of easy jogging, doing the hard laps in a time of one-thirty. That's not too fast, but, then, I'm old and I have to take that.

The morning was warm and calm, and I had the track, the football field, the stadium—the whole shebang—to myself. I'd finished the required eight repeats and was jogging through a two-mile cool down when two college-aged men entered the area. They slouched around on the

Going Down Slow

infield near the 400-meter start/finish line, doing nothing much, putting in time, maybe considering some exercise. One was lean and wiry, the other pudgy. The wiry one was wearing baggy black shorts; he peeled his shirt off. As I approached the finish line they seemed to be waiting for something.

Then I saw a young woman gliding across the parking lot south of the stadium, running tall, head and shoulders visible above the parked cars. She wore earphones and a sandy ponytail that swished about. In her hand she held a water bottle. Her stride was easy and fluid—a Tech varsity runner, I figured. She soon joined the two guys in the infield.

I watched as I jogged, wondering what the three were up to. They milled around, kicking the turf, making plans it seemed, mulling things over. Something was going to happen.

I soon decided I knew what it was. The wiry boy had a problem. He'd maybe shot his mouth off and talked himself into a corner. It had gone too far, and now there was no backing out. Only his legs could save him. And those legs looked too short, their appearance made the more so by his droopy pants. His cocky quick movements failed to betray that knowledge, I thought. The pudgy one was going to be the timekeeper.

The short legs, the baggy shorts—they were clues. And I'd seen the woman float across the parking lot—another clue. I knew where I was putting my money.

The wiry boy and the smooth girl lined up, leaning forward, tensed, waiting while I approached the start line

Going Down Slow

from behind them. Allowing me to close meant I'd be past the line and out of their way when they came back around. So it was going to be 400 meters then, a 400-meter battle between Man and Woman.

I drew near, the timekeeper signaled, the racers bolted. An audience of precisely two caught its collective breath, captivated by the sight.

I didn't know Megan then, but on a later jog she told me how that race had come about. The wiry man with baggy shorts was a co-worker of hers. At work they'd been talking about running, something he knew Megan enjoyed. I guess he liked to tease her. He'd bragged that he could beat her.

"Was he a runner?" I asked.

"No. Thing was—what got me—he just thought he could beat me, uh, you know, without even knowing, uh…"

She was having a hard time saying it to another man. I helped her.

"You mean, because you're a woman?"

"Yeah, yeah, exactly."

Five seconds after the race started he was a wiser man. Megan snatched the lead at once. Going around the first turn she stretched the gap, piling yards on him like cordwood. Down the backstretch she opened the space to maybe twenty-five yards by the time she hit the 200-meter mark where the second turn begins.

She was sailing like a lark swooping. The man's legs whipped the baggy shorts into a flapping fury. He was running hard and ugly, elbows and knees pumping herky-

Going Down Slow

jerky with no regard for form. He hoped Megan would fade in the second half, I guess. It seemed to work—at least enough to stop the piling on. Around the first part of the second turn he managed to halt the deficit. Then he began to take back yards. He was game, but it was getting late,

The danger was that Megan had initially run too fast. Perhaps she was beginning to slow. If so, really, it was quite slight, I think. When she came out of the turn and entered the final straight, her posture was tall, gallant, her stride still fluid. I realized she wasn't spent at all. The man gained very little after that point. Finally, he couldn't gain a whisker. His fate was sealed.

I watched them from across the field, as they sailed down the home stretch. The moving space between them froze, passed before the empty stands like a discreet entity, tangible and inviolate, attached at each end to a runner.

Megan beat him by twenty yards.

After the racers recovered their breath, the three walked around the track, laughing and talking, still friends. Continuing my jog, I pulled alongside them.

"That was pretty fast. What did you run that in?" I asked.

"One-ten," she said; her eyes said it too.

"That's pretty fast."

That's pretty fast—a varsity runner all right.

Three months later, she won a local 5K. I'd jogged the race's companion10K as part of a thirty-mile training run for an ultramarathon. After finishing the 10K, I continued on my jog without meeting her. Later that day, my route,

Going Down Slow

by unlikely coincidence, took me down the street where she happened to live.

She and her mother were out for a stroll. I stopped to meet them. Megan has large striking eyes. I asked her if she'd won the 5K that morning. She had, of course.

"Are you a Tech runner?" I asked.

"No, I've already finished college. Idaho State. Out west."

"Did you run in college?"

"No."

No! I was astonished at that answer.

"I just like to run," she said.

"But you could've had a scholarship! Saved Mom some money!"

She could have won a college scholarship, something she never realized or considered. That door is closed now. Anyway, as she says, "I just like to run." In the end, maybe that's the bigger prize.

Despite her potential for speed, she told me she doesn't like speed training, preferring long slow runs instead. A few months later, I saw her taking those long runs more often than usual. Her easy stride and swinging ponytail graced the streets of Cookeville as she trained for the Boston Marathon—a dream for any runner.

4

ON THE STREET WHERE YOU LIVE

My eleventh-floor balcony door looks west over San Diego Bay. The sunset spreads a warm glow over the expansive scene. But my view in the near foreground is more arresting, one fecund with the drama of elemental life. I watch a daily struggle.

The scene beneath me includes an improvised parking lot, one made from the concrete floor slab of a demolished building. On the east side, the side near me, the wall has been razed to the ground so that cars can drive in. Along the north and west sides, remnants of the demolished walls stand waist-high like jagged parapets. A derelict building with a sound wall but a collapsed roof sprawls along the south side. These are the borders of the temple. Life, primal and raw, plays out on this shabby slab.

Cars fill the lot during working hours, but leave at quitting time. Homeless people take the lot then. They make their homes against the wall, spreading blankets beside it, setting their belongings around them. Being tallest, the south wall is popular, but the west wall is a favorite too. No one wants to be in the middle of the slab, vulnerable on all sides. No one makes his bed on the north wall, running along Ash Street; that wall is the toilet. When

Going Down Slow

I walked by it once the soured stench of human excrement filled my sinsuses, and altered a hamburger's taste thirty minutes later. Thereafter, I detoured north a block to avoid the latrene's smell. Each morning the homeless fade into the city and the cars come back to the slab. Another workday begins.

Scattered just east of this scene, new office towers sprout tall—high finance and big money abundantly evident. The money pours into rampant construction while the city ignores a greater, but less-appealing, problem—the very people on the street.

I had come to San Diego to run the Rock and Roll Marathon—a grandiose urban race famous for media attention, glamour, glitz and noise. Runners encounter loud bands playing in each mile along the course. Because it spawned other similar races, including the Country Music Marathon, all managed by the same San Diego company, it's sometimes called the mother of musical marathons.

By most measures, my race went well, but the street life was more interesting than the race. I stayed a couple of extra days.

San Diego seems an apt place for the first musical marathon; a center for endurance sports, the world's first triathlon was held here. Ironman legends, Mark Allen and Scott Tinely, live here, among others. San Diego: city of Sea World and sunshine; beaches, surf, golden girls and golden boys running in the sand. The men who sleep on the slab at Ash Street know nothing of this.

The homeless have a home in San Diego. The

Going Down Slow

weather is a help. It rains only fifteen inches per year, and temperatures are pleasant. It's a good place to be homeless.

Their presence sears the cityscape. Iron gates and chain link fences guard entrances to alleys, to any alcove that offers shelter. Chain link fences, sometimes topped by razor wire, run around parking lots. That leaves parks, public squares, unfenced parking lots, and the street itself, for the homeless. Otherwise, the city is barred and fenced. Closed. Don't even think about it — even the restrooms in fast food restaurants are locked; you need a quarter.

Most of the homeless are men, of course. But not all. One day on Broadway, close to the fast food places, a college-aged woman wearing a backpack approached me. Her face was drawn in a pathetic scowl like a stray dog expecting to be kicked. She hated asking me:

"Sir, can you spare some money for food?"

"Sorry."

During the week I spent some time riding the buses and trolleys. The city's public transportation system is an asset that works well. A special wide area is provided at the front of the buses for senior citizens and those with disabilities. Being a senior citizen I was not only qualified but sometimes even compelled to sit there, especially if the bus was crowded. I loved the secret irony of a marathoner riding in such gentle style.

One day a homeless man rode standing over me, bracing his cart of stuff in the wheelchair space. He wore a heavy coat despite the warm temperature; a coarse mane of dirty hair swept back above his collar. We rode along. He decided to give the citizens on the bus a lecture. I was

Going Down Slow

closest and could hear him best. I glanced up occasionally; the rest ignored him.

He rambled a bit, and I had trouble following—something about medical care. His concluding words were delivered with conviction and passion: "...and that's why we need Medicare!"

A ringing conclusion. Except that it didn't turn out to be the conlusion after all. Just as the bus braked for his stop, he decided to announce one more thing: "I wouldn't recommend my dentist to anyone!"

I looked into his face. A chicken has more teeth.

San Diego's destiny is shaped by an infinite supply of poverty just fifteen miles south, at Tijuana, across the Mexican border. Earlier I had ridden the trolley to its southern terminal and walked over the border to the town, as tourists do. One-and-a-quarter million souls live there in apparent chaos and deprivation. The city spreads across the scrubland like dried scum. Maybe that's too harsh. Some progress is evident—street construction was underway. But a good deal of the town seems a collection of shoddy open-air stores unevenly cobbled together and thrown down. Merchants chase after you flashing cheap jewelry.

Visitors encounter panhandlers. A young woman with wild frightened eyes approached me, four small kids trailing behind her.

"Sir, can you spare some money in our need?" she begged.

I kept walking like a Philistine. But I remember her eyes.

After I'd crossed the border back stateside, I sat at the Tijuana Stop waiting for the train to San Diego. I struck

Going Down Slow

up a conversation with an old white-haired man from San Diego. Retired now, he had worked at a clerical job in Tijuana, and he occasionally goes back for visits. I said it appeared San Diego has a problem with the homeless. He agreed; it was a subject he'd thought about a lot. I offered the opinion that many were mentally handicapped.

"They are!" he exclaimed. "It started with Reagan. "Anybody capable of living on their own had to be released from the hospital." He went on complaining about how many patients had been turned out to fend for themselves.

Apparently he was referring to a policy implemented when Ronald Reagan was governor of California, a controversial one I vaguely recall from the news. That was a long time ago. The policy seems callous and wrong; you'd think it would've been amended by now.

The homeless problem is not unique to San Diego, of course. It's here close to home too—in Nashville and even Cookeville, my home town. On my daily runs through Dogwood Park one summer I often talked to a man who took shelter in the gazebo there.

San Diego's problem is acute. The city willfully turns a blind eye to it. At quitting time, downtown workers drive away in cars with air-conditioning, stereos and tinted glass. They don't see the homeless. The downtown dwellers live in high rise apartments behind iron gates. The city compensates with fences and gates for a public policy lacking in compassion and pity. For that, the city suffers. But the ones who suffer the most are those without a car to drive or a gate to bar—like the men on the slab at Ash Street.

Going Down Slow

* * *

It was on my last night in town when I saw the man in motion. I was walking to supper east along Ash Street, a downtown street mostly empty after quitting time; the people who work in the office towers had already merged their cars with the traffic streams draining downtown.

I glanced down a side street and saw the man a baseball pitch away. He shuffled and waved his arms around, talking with someone only he could see. His body jerked with sudden movements. A bony wrist shot out of his cuff when he gestured; he wouldn't have weighed 120 pounds.

He was a black man of vague age dressed in black shirt, black pants and a black baseball cap turned backwards. His clothes were dark like those of the other homeless men I'd seen. Dark eats light and theirs were usually dark, whether by choice or from dirt of the street—maybe both. You see them in the distance—dark figures drifting languidly across the scene like barely visible spirits that people pretend not to see.

But the man in motion was anything but languid; he buzzed with misdirected energy. His clothes, though dark and a bit shabby, appeared recently laundered. Breaking the black theme, his sneakers shined brightly white. I couldn't help but notice that. The white shoes described his foot trajectories like reflectors on bicycle spokes.

He glanced in my direction. I turned my gaze frontward and hurried on, not wanting an encounter with a panhandler.

I had come to San Diego for the Rock and Roll

Going Down Slow

Marathon, of course, a race so famous for its Hollywood-like atmosphere that you feel like you ought to make a pilgrimage to it. By most measures I ran well, clocking three hours and fifteen minutes to earn second place in my age division. A highlight came in mile twenty-five when I was locked in a struggle. I passed Frank Shorter going the opposite way! Amid all the hoopla, the only American man to ever win an Olympic gold medal in the marathon was out for a casual morning jog.

My race was successful and memorable, but so was the street life.

Now on my way to get supper, I hurried down Ash Street, leaving the man in motion behind, shuffling, flapping and jerking, talking to spirits. I had walked along this same street two hours before daylight on race morning, dressed in my running clothes then. The distance to Balboa Park, where the race started, was two miles. The street was dark and lonely at that time of morning. I saw only one person then. At a parking lot where homeless men sleep, a man stood on the curb urinating in the street.

On this last evening, I went into Caparelli's, a neighborhood bar and restaurant on the fringe of downtown. It faces First Avenue, just off Ash Street. It was my customary place to eat. The salads and spaghetti were good, and those had been what I needed before the race. I needed the same food still, to recover from the race. The patrons were all local—and not many of them, at that. No tourists at all—save for one: me. My waitress was a high-school-aged girl in a tight sweater top.

I sat in a booth and looked through a wide window at

Going Down Slow

the traffic on the street outside. The cars headed north, out of town on the one-way street. But the rush was over now; traffic was light. Directly across First Avenue set Mixon Deli and Market, a convenience store. Customers came and went at the store. I watched as I ate.

A car stopped on the curb in front of the restaurant. I was vaguely aware that someone got out of the car. A two-and-a-half-foot-tall man entered the restaurant. He walked to a table where two men sat — he was barely as tall as the table. After a loud conversation making arrangements of some sort, he left, and the car pulled away. I wanted to see how he could operate the car, but my view was obstructed. Maybe the car has hand controls like a motorcycle, and he drives standing in the seat. I don't know.

After the two-and-a-half-foot man left, the man in motion appeared. He stood on the walk in front of Mixon Market across the street, still jerking, flapping and talking to the wind. The white shoes flashed; he had energy, lots of energy. But he didn't have anything else, any visible possessions. Most homeless men carried some belongings, if nothing more than a dirty blanket across their shoulder.

I finished my supper and watched a vignette unfold in front of the market. The man in motion yacked, and shuffled, bony hands flapping. My waitress came. She seemed to know people in the neighborhood.

"What about the man in black, do you know him?" I asked. She studied him through the window a second.

"No."

"I thought maybe he was a local character," I said.

"Nope. Never saw him before."

Going Down Slow

She wasn't interested.

A sedan stopped on the curb in front of the market. A tall black man with a shaved head got out. His clothes looked expensive, professional at the least. He was big enough to play linebacker for the Chargers. He talked across the car to the man in motion a bit. Then he walked around the car and stood towering over the little man, who talked and gestured fast, only now it was to a physical presence. Whatever he was saying, he pled the case with ernest emotion.

"Parole officer," I was thinking. The man in motion is going to get busted for violating parole. The tall man pulled out a cell phone, turned away from the man in motion and made a call, while the little man talked to his triceps. A squad car will be here soon, I thought.

Error is the risk of guessing. I was wrong. Soon, without ever entering the store, the tall man got into his car and pulled away, leaving the man in motion on the walk by himself, still talking and flapping.

The man in motion went into the store. He returned to the walk with a bag of chips. He waved each chip like a baton while he talked and chomped. The store clerk, a tall skinny white man, came out and told him something. The man in motion moved to the side of the store, an empty parking lot. He leaned back against a metal post, the kind that stops cars from hitting the building, and ate the chips. Chips dropped to the ground without his notice.

Suddenly he wheeled around and looked intently at the post he'd been leaning on. It seemed a new discovery. The incessant motion ceased. He bent forward and tenderly caressed the post, a new thing he'd found. A few seconds passed while he gazed at it lovingly, like a mother watching her baby sleep.

The moment passed; he dismissed the post and turned his back to it. It was just a post. He casually propped on it again and resumed waving, chomping and yacking. Finally he drifted from the store to the center of the empty parking lot, where he stood talking and flapping his hands.

I paid for my supper and crossed the street to the market. I wanted to buy a snack for later on in the evening. I laid my snack items and money on the counter in front of the tall clerk.

"What's the story on that man in black waving his arms all around?" I asked.

"What?"

"He was in here a few minutes ago—he waved his arms around..." I said.

"There was a black woman in here."

"...had on black clothes and his cap turned backwards," I continued.

"It was a woman freaked out on drugs...or something."

"I thought it was a man," I said.

"She's freaked out on drugs, or something."

I thanked him, took my snack sack and headed back down Ash toward the hotel. The man in motion stood in the middle of the parking lot waving and talking just as before, white shoes flashing. Only he wasn't a man.

The man in motion was a freaking-out woman.

It was the last lesson San Diego taught me. I left town the next morning.

5

MIRACLE ON FALL CREEK

March comes around, too, just like October, the two months linked like a bridge in my runner's mind—one edging into the gloom of winter, the other heralding the bright breakout from it. Today it is March I'm thinking about.

It's hard to get it right when you tell a story like this one. You end up looking like a puffed-up fool if you aren't careful how you say it. Despite that danger, this story needs telling. It comes from astonishment, wild, exuberant amazement, not puffery.

There are times I've been broken by races. I've told those stories just the same. Maybe I've earned the right to tell one about success. Ironically, it's easier to write about failure—little chance for conceit there. Runners are generous people; if old devil pride rears his ugly head, forgive me.

I ran a miracle race.

It happened in the Fall Creek Thaw 15K at Fall Creek State Park one Saturday morning in March. That race is the last of the Tennessee State Park Running Tour, a grand prix of then-fifteen races. On that 9.32-mile course I ran a time of sixty-two twenty-nine, finishing eighth overall. And I want to tell it to somebody who knows something

Going Down Slow

about running. Or anybody who'll listen.

That finishing time, alone and of itself, is of little interest. Until you learn that Porch Patrol, the tan Shar-Pei that lived with us then had recently celebrated his sixty-fourth birthday — in equivalent human years — and mine would follow just three months later. Marching into codgerhood, going down slow, Porch and I were.

So I was already old, and I ran a pretty good 15K. But that's not the miracle.

The course was kissed by nature, especially so on that morning. Hard rains overnight had downed the trail along the last mile and a half. Flowing runoff and stretches of standing water covered portions, sometimes two or three inches deep. I splashed through like a kid in a puddle. My shoes grew leaden, taking on all the water they could hold.

Nature carved a pretty rough course to begin with. Miles 2 through 5 snake across steep rollers clinging to the rim of the gorges carved by Piney Creek and Cane Creek. Mile 6 spans a steady one-mile-long climb that adds forty extra seconds. Then you enter a twisting trail that winds through the woods.

So the course is hard, and I ran a pretty good race. But that's not the miracle.

I was just putting in time that morning. The race meant nothing. It came at the end of a week of high-mileage marathon training. I knew the race wouldn't change my grand prix points total, since only the best eight races are counted and I'd already won eight: I'd already clinched the Senior Division and couldn't be upset. Going in, I was four pounds too heavy. I didn't need anything, didn't

Going Down Slow

expect much, didn't care much.

The miracle fully emerged later when I examined the race details embedded in my split times. At the 3-mile mark came a personal record. I was six seconds ahead of my pace in a 5K I'd run just the previous Saturday, where I had set a single-age state record of 19:45. At four miles came another personal record, thirty-eight seconds better than my last four-mile race, also a state record. At five miles another personal record, an eight-second improvement over a record I'd recently set. That trend continued. At the 10K point — interpolating — I was nearly a minute ahead of my 10K best.

Finally, when I splashed to the finish line I was six seconds ahead of my last 15K, a state record I'd set on the supremely flat Shelby Bottom Boogie course in Nashville. Since the Fall Creek course was certified, I would eventually get official credit, thus breaking my own 15K record.

All those personal records mentioned refer to official state records for a certain old male runner: me. Dismissing, now, all the annoying — but necessary — numbers, in their aggregate the miracle emerges:

I outran five state records in one race. And those five records were mine to begin with.

I had set each one within the last seven months, running the best I could at that time. In one pyrotechnic blast I shattered them all.

How could such a run happen? You don't run a 5K pace in a 15K race. It violates a principle of running that racers know down to their toes — the longer the race, the slower the pace.

Going Down Slow

If gravity suddenly reverses, the furniture falls against the ceiling, the house rips out its foundation and tumbles into infinite space—a startling violation of our expectations. Of course, a principle of running doesn't hold the same gravitas as a law of nature.

Still...the run astonishes. I can't explain it, and I didn't expect it. Was it the shredded wheat I had for breakfast? The coffee?—maybe I need more next time. I don't know....

Was the race a breakthrough or just a fluke? What did it portend for the Tom King Half Marathon, which was coming up the very next Saturday? For the races following that? Had I used up all my luck in one explosive blast, I wondered?

There was this I *did* know about the miracle 15K. It wasn't hard. I blew around the course, silently singing Liz Johnson's "Blue Prelude," without myself being the least bit blue. At the one-mile mark I saw my split, 6:13, and I thought: *I got the juice! Set the throttle, hang on.*

It was about that easy. And after it was over, I wasn't tired. My marathon training demanded a twenty-mile total that day. To get that mileage I ran around the course again.

The second time I looked at the scenery.

March rolled on, as it always does, as the year always does. I duly ran the Tom King Half Marathon I'd worried about and posted a time of 1:29:21, which was also a state record. And I celebrated the birthday I couldn't evade. By the end of the year, I'd run twenty-four races and officially set twelve single-age state records, three times breaking my own record.

Going Down Slow

If my saying that appears immodest, forgive me. I felt like it ought to be mentioned.

6

THE BEST MARATHON IN THE WORLD

Marathoners were streaming into the west side of the stadium. They would run a partial lap around the track before ending their 26.2-mile journey at the finish line I'd just crossed.

I wanted to have one last look. I glanced back down the track at the finish line fifty yards behind me, up at the expectant faces looking down from the stands. The people in those stands in 1912 had watched Jim Thorpe win two Olympic gold medals—later stripped from him for having played two seasons of semi-professional baseball. The decision was controversial and the medals were restored after his death.

I turned to walk through the archway. On the wall high above, a staff held out the Swedish colors, a yellow cross on a sky-blue background. The flag whipped and snapped in the wind.

I ambled through the archway, clutching my plastic blanket and finisher's medal. On this June day the Stockholm Marathon had for me already become history, my 3:26:44 finish converted to mere blips on a computer disk. I was dismayed at what had happened. Once again the awful distance had declared its mystery, sprung its trap.

Going Down Slow

My legs hurt.

I walked a short ways to a soccer field and stopped in front of a blue-eyed blond girl, exemplar of Scandinavian beauty. She looked up and, noticing the tiny American flag printed on the corner of my bib, spoke in perfect idiom:

"Did you run good?"

"I did the best I could."

"That's the best!"

Then she went to work with her knife, reclaiming the timing chip.

Legs aching, I walked on to a table stacked with T-shirts marked "L." They might be *too* big, I thought. Standing there was a square-jawed blond boy—another stereotype.

"How large are they?"

"They're large. Americans are so very large."

"Not this one."

He had noticed my nationality too. We were a tiny minority. Among 16,000 runners from fifty-four countries, only 180 were Americans. I slung the shirt over my shoulder. Too big or not, it didn't much matter.

Among thousands of recovering finishers I found a vacant spot of grass, spread my plastic blanket, and stretched out, although I knew what would happen: I wouldn't be able to get back up. My legs were twitching and jerking, electricity darting like Saint Elmo's fire. I lay very still, hoping against a cramp. I'd done the best I could. Sometimes it just doesn't work out.

With a good run I had a chance for a trophy, I'd thought. But today there'd be no trophy. The *Ultimate*

Going Down Slow

Guide to International Marathons picked this marathon as the best marathon in the world — in arguably the most beautiful city in the world. That brings out world-class runners.

Now as I lay in the grass, a rock band behind me was in full flight, playing a Bob Seger tune. When the singer came across the words "running against the wind," I suddenly started sobbing. I stopped quickly, ashamed.

Why did my run go so badly here on this beautiful, flat course? I wondered. I didn't want to wreck again. My plan had been to run each 5K segment at 22:30. That would bring me to the finish in 3:09:53 — not over-reaching, within my capability, I thought. At the first 5K marker I pushed the button on my Timex and saw frozen there precisely the numbers I wanted — 22:30. I had nailed it.

Despite that, news was not good. Instead of the expected pulse rate — 141 beats — my heart monitor had been pushing 150, foretelling trouble. My system was under stress, probably from all the sleep lost in the four days prior to the race. Over three of those days I'd had a total of six hours of sleep. A night of sleep lost on the overnight flight, and subsequent jet lag had blasted my body rhythm.

The next 5K took forty-six seconds too long, the next one eighty-five seconds, and so on. My time goal slipped away, and there was nothing I could do about it. It became a matter of playing out my string. At the halfway point the darts of electricity started in my feet and legs — hard cramps were coming soon, I knew.

They started around 30K. Crippling cramps seized

Going Down Slow

my feet, calves and hamstrings in mid-stride so suddenly and so hard I'd nearly smack the pavement. "Relax, take it easy!" I whispered to those muscles. I slowed to a jog.

I felt lucky to make it to the finish line. Races that go bust are the ones taking the greatest courage. I did the best I could. Marathons are unpredictable.

My time ranked me twelfth among the 446 finishers in my division, I would learn. I needed my best game, but brought my worst one.

Now I lay trying to recover, looking up at a Stockholm sky of the purest blue—I understund why the Swedish flag is sky blue. Fleecy clouds were running fast from the south. A nearby oak tree stretched its leaves out. An occasional gull sailed over, eyeing this festival of pain.

My T-shirt lay wadded on my chest, weighted by the medal. A marathoner walked by, looked down and smiled. He said something but not in English. I just smiled. The kindness of strangers!—it stabs me with sudden joy. I started sobbing again.

Is it that simple?—a stranger's smile, a sudden joy. Why do people run marathons?

That night after the marathon, French writer Antoine de Saint-Exupery offered an answer. Despite exhaustion, I still couldn't sleep. My legs were twitching and jerking. At 3:00 a.m., daylight peeped through the drapes. I gave up on sleep and pulled out *Wind, Sand and Stars*, a beautiful book I'd been rereading. On the second page I read I found: "Everything about mankind is paradox." Then Saint-Exupery linked joy to misery: "...a sudden joy that came when nothing in the world had forewarned us...a joy

Going Down Slow

so thrilling that if it was born of misery we remember even the misery with tenderness."

There is ample misery in a marathon. Runners remember it with tenderness, tell stories about it. They treasure that intense moment; it's part of their truth, like soil is part of a farmer's truth. But there is also the simple smile of a stranger. They remember that, too, and treasure that, too. I do.

But lying in the grass now after the race I wasn't wondering why; I was wondering how to get up. I watched as the fleecy clouds thickened and finally blotted out the blue sky. Day turned gray. The temperature fell; I got cold.

I managed to gain a sitting position. But when I bent my knee to gather my feet, the calf muscle jerked into a hard knot. I slammed the leg straight and lay back grimacing. Finally it eased. I tried again. And again. Each time cramps shot an arrow through my calf. Getting up took several minutes. But I finally found myself standing again.

Since I was cold, I put on the T-shirt. Then I wrapped the plastic sheet around my legs and tied it, forming a sarong. That screened the wind.

After a hot dog and beer I headed toward the hotel, walking down a street called Sturegatan. A surging river of runners still flowed the other way, heading toward the stadium. They'd been running an hour longer than I ran. After such a long time, they had the finish line near now, and nothing could stop them. They would cross the line. Each one knew that, each face told you. What could they gain there? And why were they so willing to suffer so

Going Down Slow

much to reach it? I couldn't answer. Their long-suffering seemed to embody the whole world's suffering, and I could only watch in unknowing pity and wonder.

A strange thing had happened on this street. I walked along it to the pasta supper the night before the race, gazing at the buildings. A gray flag hung from a pole mounted on the wall between two windows on the second story. The flag contained in big letters a single word: "Dallas." My name, my name waving bravely in the wind! The name of a Swedish company maybe. I didn't know, but it was the last thing I expected to see. A good omen, I thought.

The next day on my way to the race I walked along Sturegatan again, watching for the flag, my race talisman. But what I saw was bleak. The wind had snarled the flag in a wad around the pole; my name lay trapped in a crumpled heap. Overnight the lucky omen had turned to a gloomy one. My spirit sank.

Now, my race over, I walked along that street again. The flag had been right. I watched for it one last time. But I knew what I'd see. The flag was still tangled just like before. It had kept its promise.

From the mass of passing runners someone suddenly yelled, "Dallas!" I looked over to see Keith Lewis, a Californian I'd met three days earlier. He swerved to the curb to slap hands. "Go man!" I yelled.

He was about to finish his 100th marathon. No stranger to this city; he had visited here in 1995 when his father won the Nobel Prize for his research in genetics. Keith carries on that work. Their research shows how, at the genetic level, humans are very similar to all other life,

Going Down Slow

even plants, he'd told me.

The unity of life is perhaps a hopeful notion, if frightening.

Keith melted back into the stream. Against all conceivable odds, my name had been heralded twice on this singular street in this foreign place — once from a desultory flag, once more from the scientist son of a Nobel Laureate.

My head was awhirl. I'd seen majesty: Today's run had taken me through the hunting garden of ancient kings, across the Baltic Sea, by the walls of medieval buildings and across lake water pure enough to drink. And I'd seen mystery: A marathoner running nude but for a bra, jock strap and head band, a blood-like smear on his right thigh. And so on.

These events swirl around the marathon like so much turbulent fog. Despite all the tumult, at its canonical heart the story remains the same: a primal struggle against 26.2 implacable miles. It will always be so.

I drifted on down Sturegatan, a shabby spectacle in a plastic skirt, amazed at it all.

7

TWELVE GATHER FOR SUPPER

The party wasn't scheduled to start until 7:30; I was a full forty-five minutes early. The trouble I'd allowed for on the drive to Nashville didn't happen; I'd made better time than I expected. I found the address on Nineteenth Avenue and parked on the curb nearby. The street was quiet on this Saturday afternoon.

Overnight a sudden change in the weather had brought a cool October-like respite to the August swelter. It had brought a sky of exquisite blue, too, a color that makes me restless. I had time to kill before the party. There was only one sensible thing to do—take a walk.

I knew where I was going too. To the south I could see a tall bell tower hovering above the trees. That needed checking out.

A short walk down a shaded street brought me to the Scarritt-Bennet Center, a building of collegiate gothic architecture constructed from sandstone blocks quarried on the nearby Cumberland Plateau. I'd recognize that sandstone anywhere. The building formerly belonged to Scarritt College, which became Scarritt Graduate School in 1980, and finally closed in 1988, I would later learn. On this end stood the bell tower, poking high into the day's

Going Down Slow

incredible blue sky. Near the tower's top, arched openings on each side allowed the now silent pealing out—or the intruding pigeons in. A chapel anchored the south end of the building.

The use of native sandstone together with the classic architecture produced a charming building of unexpected elegance and dignity. The pink, buff and charcoal hues of the sandstone had dimmed and softened a bit over the years. A wide concrete walk led through an archway. Beside the walk stood the largest magnolia tree I've ever seen; the trunk looked to be two-and-a-half feet thick.

I drifted through the archway into an open courtyard, stopping to feel the rough hard surface of a sandstone block—good honest material carved directly from the earth. It promises not to fail its purpose—and keeps its promise. The building seemed timeless, solid and as lasting as the earth itself.

Walks crisscrossed the courtyard, and a bench sat in the middle—a good place to sit and read, I reflected. The courtyard opened to the east, on the far side. I walked along the near edge and returned to the front through a second archway, emerging next to the chapel.

I noticed young women in long dresses standing on the walk at the front of the chapel. Others from the chapel soon joined them. Six wore identical long blue dresses, the same wonderful blue as the day's sky. *Bridesmaids, they're having a wedding*, I thought. The ceremony had just ended. A white limousine idled on the curb, guarded by a big man wearing a black suit, a Fu Manchu and black wrap arounds. He stood at alert, arms crossed, facing the

Going Down Slow

chapel, waiting.

The crowd grew. There were young men in black tuxedos with shiny stripes down the legs. They held bottles of soap and waved wands around making soap bubbles. There was scarcely a breath of wind — clusters of bubbles hung in the air, refracting bright colors, barely drifting, slowly settling.

A photographer took a position near the limousine; his two assistants scurried about. The crowd milled around and watched the chapel door, waiting for the bride and groom to appear. I wondered idly who the couple was and thought about asking the chauffeur, but his forbidding visage dissuaded me. Instead I joined the back of the crowd and waited too. A low parapet wall ran along the sidewalk. I stepped up on it to get a better view.

Soon enough the young couple appeared. There was a stir — I couldn't see why. I suppose the bride tossed her bouquet. The two came side by side down the walk toward the limousine; the crowd parted. The couple stopped; the groom lifted his bride in his arms. He toted her toward the waiting car; his lips stretched thin in a brittle smile, his face red with embarrassment and muscle strain.

At the car he started to let her down. With a rustle of gown material, her legs slipped from his arms. Her high heels — *clonk!* – hit the concrete hard. She managed to stay upright, no damage. The big chauffeur held the door open; they got in.

The show was over; it was only a wedding. I ambled away from the crowd, back down the sidewalk, by chance walking apace with the photographer. After a few yards

Going Down Slow

we stopped and looked back as the white limousine pulled away from the curb and approached us.

The car stopped beside the photographer and the window went down for one last picture. As he aimed the camera, the bride smiled and waved at the photographer. Since I stood just behind him, she was waving at me too — or well might have been. In any case, I smiled and waved my good wishes back, the last person at the wedding to do so.

Who knows what the future holds for them, for their children…?

I don't know. I have read that by the time their children are middle aged, they may face a dying world. Pondering the future of his soon-to-be-born granddaughter, one writer referred to a possible, "…global catastrophe unprecedented in human history." These gloomy warnings, I must recognize, are based on actual measurements: of glaciers melting, of oceans rising, of species vanishing, of the earth warming.

Of an earth dying. All in a swooping geological blink. All on our watch.

I believe that. And yet…

Standing there, I could see the day's incredible sky, that special heartbreaking shade of blue, one untainted by clouds, haze or pollution, the very color for which the Spanish word *celeste* must be meant, a color imbuing a celestial quality indeed, a pure hue of restless and expansive hope. Standing there, it seemed possible to believe that God didn't blunder after all, that humans might yet somehow fail to wreck the garden.

Going Down Slow

There the blue sky was. There the hope was.

I don't know. I think I may have been wrong. But I chose hope.

So I waved hopeful good wishes to the happy couple. The photographer finished, and the window swished up. The limousine rolled down the shaded street, bearing the couple away.

They were headed toward the new life they'd just started; I was headed to a party I had doubts about. Being such an old man, I wasn't sure I should attend a party of runners, most of them much younger. But I had to keep my word. I turned and walked toward Music Row to look for a party.

We sit around a long table in the Mellow Mushroom on Nashville's Music Row, five women and seven men, eating, drinking and talking. A meeting is in progress. But this meeting is not one called by any of the usual functionaries; it's more important than that. It is a meeting of friends sharing the simple joy of companionship, the comfort that in its better moments, human society sometimes provides. This meeting is a party.

Susan, in fact, called this meeting. We gathered thirty minutes ago this Saturday night at her boyfriend's apartment, a short block from here; then we walked to this restaurant for supper. After supper, the plan is to walk back and sample some of Susan's homemade dessert.

Susan and her boyfriend, Hal, a music publisher, are bothered by over-use injuries which curtail their running. But they miss seeing their little training group. Susan

Going Down Slow

decided why not get together anyway. So she sent out invitations to their running buddies and to some of their friends.

And here we are.

Being friends of friends, some here didn't know the others until thirty minutes ago. But no onlooker would guess that; there is an instant friendly connection between runners. I'm here because Albino, a member of their little group, is also a friend of mine. He visited me earlier today at my Cookeville home for a morning run.

Originally from Seville, Spain, Albino now temporarily lives in Hopkinsville, Kentucky, where as an accountant he monitors the financial matters of a Spanish-owned company there. Three years will not pass before his work calls him back to Spain. But on the summer night of this supper, he doesn't yet know that. At thirty-three he is perhaps the youngest at the table; at sixty-four, I am easily the oldest.

Hal, the publisher, originally from Oklahoma, sits at the center with his back to the wall. He is tall and slender and his graying hair sweeps back stylishly; his kindly manner and soft voice exudes serenity. By his side sits Susan, a Connecticut Yankee, educated in Florida, an intense young woman whose wavy auburn hair frames a finely featured face you'd likely call beautiful. Hal tells about how she became his girlfriend.

"We went running four or five times. She kept talking about how her love life was all screwed up," he says.

Susan jumps in quickly: "I'd gotten so used to talking about it on runs with Stan that I didn't realize I was still

Going Down Slow

doing it!" she explains.

After a few runs spent listening to her lovelorn tales, the Oklahoma boy began to get ideas. As a result, Susan's troubles flew away like gray birds.

By "Stan," I reckon Susan is talking about the man sitting on Hal's left, one of her running buddies. Stan, in his fifties, is a songwriter from Massachusetts; he's accompanied by his cheerful wife, Joy. Stan is a strong man with close-cut hair and a neat mustache. He seems perfectly comfortable, always at ease. The surface calm masks the fire in his poet's heart. He brought his guitar to Hopkinsville for Albino's thirty-third birthday party a couple of months past and sang some of his songs. A favorite of this Massachusetts man is Flatt and Scruggs' *Jimmy Brown, the Newsboy* (written by A. P. Carter) a song about a poor boy who sells the morning paper to help his mother. Though not his, Stan sang that song at Albino's party, too.

I admire Stan for his songwriting. Songwriters have precious ability to wring emotion from just a few words. Henry Mancini's *A Slow Hot Wind* says more in the title alone than 200 pages of some books I've read.

Jimmy Brown connects with me, too. I used to hear Flatt and Scruggs sing their songs every morning on the AM radio that sat on top of the refrigerator. Momma listened to their program while she cooked breakfast. The Hot Rize theme sang me out of bed before daylight. It was like my alarm clock. Into the dark and cold I went to feed the livestock and milk the cows. Shoot a monkey! I remember those mornings.

Going Down Slow

That was long ago. Here at the table tonight, a dozen people are having a roaring good time. Teasing questions and snappy answers fly back and forth; stories spin out.

"What time you running tomorrow, Dallas?" Lu asks me.

His crooked grin tells me he's teasing. Lu is from Vietnam; he smiles easily. In his mid thirties, he would have been around seven years old when Saigon fell. If growing up in that ravaged country left a scar, you won't see it in his smile. He seems genuinely content.

"The war scattered everyone," he says pleasantly.

"The war scattered everyone," I reflect. "And now it's a tourist destination. I have a friend who just left to go there."

"Really?" he says, smiling, pleased to hear someone say something good about his homeland.

Lu goes back to Vietnam frequently, even though the trip is expensive. Later he will tell me about his best friend. On his last visit home, he and his friend made a 1,000-mile trip together on their motorcycles. "He's sixty-three years old, but he's still my best friend," Lu tells me.

That comment touches me. His friendship with the old man is like Albino's friendship with me, somehow bridging a gulf of nearly two generations.

Lu has come to the party with Luz Maria, a thirty-three-year-old engineer from Mexico—she has a beautiful name that I love. Sitting between Lu and Albino now, she exudes charm and strength equally. The strength is real too; she runs a blazing marathon.

Sitting next to me is Tammy, an engaging woman with bright eyes and short blond hair, originally from Smithville, Tennessee. She's telling Susan and me a lively

Going Down Slow

story about how she met her Tunisian boyfriend. At first sight she had been smitten by the man. But because of timidity, she had missed her chance to get acquainted. She was crushed by the loss, angry with herself.

But providence intervened for her, and she found her nerve — both later that very same night. She was a passenger in a friend's car. As they backed out of their parking spot beside a convertible she suddenly saw the Tunisian man getting into that convertible. Defying improbable odds, their car had been parked beside his.

"Wait, wait! Pull back in!" she yelled to her friend.

She wasn't going to miss another chance. She jumped out of the car, ran up to the man and pressed her phone number into his hand.

"Call me sometime!" she told him, and quickly ran back to her friend's car, leaving a very surprised man sitting in a convertible.

"By the time I got home, I had a message from him," she says.

She finishes the story. Her eyes sparkle as she laughs at how wickedly bold she had been, surprised at herself still.

The man from Tunisia sits beside Tammy now. As she finishes the story, he strokes his chin and smiles shyly. Tall and handsome, with wavy black hair, he works in telecommunications and speaks a number of languages fluently. But he had never had a chance. The woman from Tennessee reeled him in like a largemouth bass.

Sitting at our table is only one person who admits to being a homegrown Nashville native — Nick, who looks strong enough to drive fence posts. His supportive wife,

Going Down Slow

Carla, loves going to Bell Buckle when Nick runs that annual race.

Suddenly I'm startled by a remarkable thought: These twelve humans come from places flung down across the globe. They represent five countries. And that's not counting Massachusetts. Four continents! Grounded in academia, I'm accustomed to a cosmopolitan crowd. But this is not an academic setting; it's a casual gathering of friends, here by choice rather than institutional imperative.

The unexpected wedding I witnessed earlier had brought together a collection of family and friends in a joyful affirmation of life. To equal degree, so does this simple gathering of runners—but in a unique and surprising way.

This group shatters every boundary of culture, religion, politics, geography and rearing. Backgrounds vary from urban to rural, from aristocratic to red-dirt poor. Some are Roman Catholics; I can estimate a Muslim, a Buddhist, maybe a backsliding Baptist, and a heathen or two. And who knows what else?

And who cares? That's precisely the point. Because, the most amazing thing about it all is this: *no one here seems to notice*. Despite all the walls erected by politics, religion, and even tectonic plates, we have happily gathered here tonight. No one thinks it's unusual that we have. In microcosm this group represents the world John Lennon naively dreamed of in *Imagine*.

These friends have been convened here by a thing as innocent as running, by Susan and Hal reaching out to their training buddies. In this, I find reason for hope.

Going Down Slow

Running, the most elemental of all human athletic skills, has trumped all the hate-engendering bugaboos contrived through millenia of humankind invention and generalized bungling.

It seems child-like to notice.

Running can't stop war. It can't reverse melting of the Arctic ice shelf or stop the dogwoods from dying. It can't prevent world hunger or cure HIV.

Running can't save the world.

But on this Saturday night it has brought together a dozen souls in a harmony of goodwill, friendship, joy, and even love.

And that's a lot.

SPIRITS

8

MOMMA'S SUPPER TABLE

On the Sunday supper table at Momma's: chicken and dressing, giblets gravy, cranberry sauce, fried rattlesnake, boiled potatoes, fried corn, pinto beans, black-eyed peas, poke sallet, sliced tomatoes, green peppers, fruit salad, homemade relish, cornbread, biscuits, pecan pie and coconut pie.

That supper was on September 23, 1984 in the Smith Bend community of Jackson County, Tennessee. Just an ordinary Sunday feast—except for the rattlesnake whose head I had chopped off after he failed to bite my brother and me. We dressed the snake, Momma cooked the meat. It would have been a feast even without it. Poke sallet? Momma served that delicious weed even in wintertime; she canned it.

I know what was on the table that long ago day because as the women cleaned the dishes, I asked Momma for a pencil and piece of paper. She tore a sheet from a spiral binder and handed me a ballpoint pen, and I wrote down the list.

Just before Christmas fourteen years later, we held Momma's funeral. I gave the list to preacher Draper Murphy, a family friend. He read it at the service. When he

Going Down Slow

came to the rattlesnake, he said, "She'd fix about anything those boys brought in." Hearing him read out the items on that list, the people in the little chapel smiled knowingly. They didn't doubt the lavish menu; they'd sat at Margaret Smith's table. That list told more about Momma than a room full of sermonizing.

Momma shouldn't have died. At the age of seventy-eight she was in surpassingly good health. She stood five-four and weighed 105 pounds. She could outwork two good men—and often did. Her teeth, all still where God installed them, were porcelain white and contained not a single filling. Before I knew what toothpaste was, she'd taught us to brush our teeth with a mixture of salt and baking soda. No surgeon's knife had gashed her skin.

She died because of how she lived—allowing no concessions, yielding not an inch. Following Daddy's death two years earlier, she had continued living on the farm, pasturing twenty head of cattle and a herd of goats. Neighbors unable to contact her on the phone would be shocked when they learned she had been back in the hills checking on her cattle. "Something could happen to you back there and nobody would know about it for days," they'd say.

When we were kids—my sister, my two brothers and I—she used to take us to those hills in the fall to collect hickory nuts and walnuts. She used the hickory nuts in pies, doing the painstaking work to crack the hard shells and pick out enough kernels. No pecan pie could compete with her hickory nut pie.

On Friday nights I'd drive to her house, some thirty

Going Down Slow

miles in the country, and take her to supper, and then go back to her house on Sunday for the big lunch and supper she'd cook up. One Friday I suggested eating at Pizza Hut, where I knew I could get pasta. She didn't know why I wanted to eat there, since I had not before. The pasta was for my very first race, a 10K, on the next morning. I kept the race a secret until the following Sunday. Then I showed her my tee shirt and the two trophies, heavy mugs, I'd earned for winning both my age group and the master category.

She was proud. With that race, she saw the very beginning of my running. A few months later, it was too late. She never got to see my later success. I know she would have been surprised and pleased.

We didn't take her high blood pressure seriously. She wouldn't have listened if we had. Her abiding fatalism trumped any worry. "If it happens, it's supposed to," she had always said. Throughout her life, that sense of resignation gave her the endurance to work in the field all day, and to then come home and cook supper while the men rested. I think the running events I seek out express that ability she had to work, uncomplaining, at a steady pace for a long time. Any stoic endurance I have I got from her.

Best we can figure she had the stroke on a Thursday. She had been out cutting weeds with a swing blade in the heat of a June day. That's the way she was. It must have been a small stroke. People who talked to her Thursday and Friday noticed that she wasn't quite herself. I, myself, took her to supper Friday night, and noticed she seemed a

Going Down Slow

bit unsteady. But I didn't suspect the awful truth.

Afterwards, I dropped her off at her house. "Wait a minute," she said. She went into the house and came out with a present, a polo shirt for my birthday, which fell later in the week.

"My birthday's not until Thursday."

"I might not see you then."

She wanted me to stay the night. I had to go. I backed the truck out. I remember her standing there looking into the glare of my truck lights. Her oldest son was leaving; she stood helpless and utterly alone. I missed the best chance anyone had to get her prompt medical help, essential in the case of stroke. The next day, still ignorant, I remarked to a friend, "Last night Momma seemed old for the first time."

My sister found her that day when she went for a visit. Momma was confused, and Sis checked her into a hospital.

At first, we were sure she would recover. But then she had another stoke, in the hospital, and was taken from Carthage to a big hospital in Nashville. A vigil began. We took turns staying with her night and day. My turn came on my fifty-eight birthday. Momma and I faced the struggle in the hospital room just as precisely fifty-eight years earlier we had faced a similar struggle in a two-room log house in Jackson County. Just the two of us again — except now it was my turn to help her live.

But I was inadequate. After six months Momma died in a Donelson Rest Home. We had chosen that particular home for its location, just a few blocks from my Sister's

Going Down Slow

house. Sis had visited her daily, bringing treats, staying to comb and plait her hair.

The night she died I drove to Donelson. My daughter Jill rode with me. In her room, Momma lay peacefully in the bed, her hands crossed. The nurses discretely withdrew. Sis, Jill and I stood there looking down.

After a few minutes, I left the room and walked outside. Jill followed. I walked along the path where I used to push Momma in her wheel chair—she always liked to be outside. The path led to a gap in a fencerow where we had always stopped. Looking west across a parking lot, we would watch the traffic on Donelson Pike.

It was a fencerow like the ones in Smith Bend where Momma had always lived, thick with tall Sassafras bushes, honeysuckle and briars. Jill and I stood there in the dark now, not speaking. I saw a wild grape vine hanging from the bushes. I slashed it off with my knife and yanked the severed vine with the sudden fury of a savage. Dead leaves and twigs rained down, branches snapped, bowing to the violence. I ripped the whole vine from the tree down to its last clinging tendril.

I rolled the fallen vine into a hoop, twisting the bushy branches around the main limb, and tucking the curlicues. When I finished, I had a platter-sized wreath.

I took it inside to Momma's room and handed it to Sis. She turned it in her hands, admiring the curly twigs. "It needs a bow," I said. Sis had an idea. A vase of flowers sat on the table, a small card attached by a pink ribbon. She untied the ribbon, and looped it into a graceful bow. Then she fastened the bow to the wreath and held it up. It was

Going Down Slow

an elegant little wreath. She stepped forward and gently laid it on Momma's folded hands. "It's the last thing we can give you, Momma," she said.

Two days later they closed the casket. It was twelve days before Christmas 1998.

My oldest son flew in from his Texas home. The night before the funeral, he and I spent the night in Momma's house. Everything was just as she had left it six months earlier.

A rose bush Momma had recently planted stood at the corner of the front porch. It was thin and scrawny and hadn't had much chance to grow. Though it was December, the sad little bush reached up a single red rose.

We gathered at Momma and Daddy's house for Christmas that December as we always had. My sister, my two brothers and I, our families, kids and grandkids were all there. Gene, my youngest brother, had put up a cedar tree and decorated it just like Momma used to do. Gerald, my other brother, brought his shotguns for skeet shooting. We gathered around the tree and opened presents. Kids with new toys romped through the house squealing, raising a happy din.

The women brought a feast like Momma always fixed. Once again we sat around the big long table in front of the picture window that looks out over Cordell Hull Lake and the hills beyond.

It was a joyous Christmas obeying the spirit of past ones. But Momma now rested beside Daddy in the family graveyard a few paces from the back porch. A glance in that direction reminded us — it would never be the same.

9

TIP YOUR HAT TO THESE TWO WOMEN

You should have seen Margie and Marie.

They had not met each other before Saturday morning that September. They were acquainted only by reputation.

Margie Stoll, then sixty-three, was the fastest senior runner in Tennessee, dominant at all distances from one mile to the half-marathon, having recently run a 5K in a time of 21:54. She sets an age-group state record every time she runs. She will go on to set over four dozen new marks. A few years later she will gain a national ranking of third in *Running Times* magazine, and go on to earn two gold medals and two silver medals at the National Senior Games.

She doesn't just win. She destroys. She destroys records, and leaves her competition far behind her, out of sight over the hill somewhere. I see her frequently around Nashville, where she runs most of her races.

Marie Threadgill, also then sixty-three, was more of an occasional racer. She hails from West Tennessee, runs races in that area, and runs a few of the Tennessee State Park Tour races. She is fast too; when she runs, she wins. I had gotten to know her a bit at the Tour races.

So Margie and Marie usually run different races.

Going Down Slow

Their paths had never crossed—not until that Saturday morning.

A story about two women old enough to be your mom, you say? Bite your tongue, sonny. Yes, if you insist. They would not deny it. They are age-group athletes after all. Old enough to be your mom maybe. But, on the racecourse, fast enough to run your legs off. Walk a little slower when you walk by them. And tip your hat, or, by grab, there might be trouble.

There is a mark painted on the road in front of the River View picnic shelter in Nashville's Shelby Park. The Nashville Striders running club put it there. It marks the beginning of 15,000 meters, or 9.32 miles. At 7:30 on that Saturday morning, Margie and Marie stood with several hundred other runners behind that mark when a man fired a starter pistol.

Then they met. Somewhere along nine miles of exquisite agony they became acquainted; they both suddenly *knew*.

A race sorts things out. Soon the crowd around you thins out; the pack gets strung out along the course. You look around and find out who's with you, find out who your competition is. There comes a moment—as I think it did with Marie—when you suddenly realize, *there she is!*

And the next phase of your life changes. You pour every desperate last atom of energy into getting to the finish line first. In that moment, nothing else in the world matters at all.

Of course Marie's chances were poor against Margie, a runner who had probably never been beaten in her age

Going Down Slow

group. If you saw her you would understand why. She is tall and slender, and her long legs make each stride count, lapping up the miles. Marie is smaller, maybe standing five feet three, but with the quickness of a point guard. Quickness aside, nobody beats Margie.

That day Marie did.

Afterwards, she was as giddy as a schoolgirl. Her bright eyes flashed.

"I won!" she said.

"What? You beat Margie?" I barely believed it. I'd missed their finish myself, recovering.

Margie, in defeat, was gracious. Her eyes twinkled; she seemed as happy as Marie was.

"Did you know Margie before today?" I asked Marie.

"No, but someone pointed her out to me before the race." Marie had known whom she faced. I asked Margie if she had ever seen Marie before.

"No, we met on the course," she said.

So they did.

Marie covered the 9.32 miles in one hour, twelve minutes and two seconds, Margie just seven seconds slower. These two smart, funny, friendly, generous, gracious ladies competed as fiercely as fighting bantams.

You should have seen them.

How good was their run? Well, in endurance sports, men hit their peak around the age of thirty. So I looked at the performance of the men in the 30-34 year-old age group, thirty runners that day. Margie and Marie would've placed in the top half of that group. In other words, these senior women beat the majority of the men who were in

Going Down Slow

their prime. Overall, they easily placed in the top third of the whole pack of 375 racers.

Do I have to say it again? Tip your hat.

Look what these women have done! Can't somebody learn from that? Isn't the lesson plain? Get moving. Do something—anything!—the opposite of nothing. In motion is life, in stasis, death. Soon enough it's over and done. Don't mess around.

We stood around that Saturday waiting for the awards ceremony like a few hundred sweaty people at a cocktail party of Gatorade, bagels and bananas. Margie and Marie had become inseparable, although they'd never met until that morning. Every time I looked around they were huddled, talking and laughing, sometimes with others, sometimes alone.

They reminded me of sorority sisters reunited after a long time. Perhaps they had played intramural football. Given her height advantage, Margie played quarterback and Marie, with her quick feet, played wide receiver. They formed a spiritual bond in that game long ago, a bond flicking from Margie's throwing arm along the ball's delicate arc to Marie's outstretched hands, a bond undiminished by time. And now they were together again, a team again, like time hadn't passed.

Of course that never happened; they'd just met. Had it happened, I doubt they would have been better friends than they seemed to be. Their meeting two hours earlier had been a galvanizing one.

Margie and Marie went to school long before Title IX, before women had many opportunities in sports, before

Going Down Slow

people knew what women could do.

Driving home that day, I wished I'd told Marie more about how impressive her performance was. Before daylight that morning when her alarm rang, she must have had second thoughts about throwing off the covers only to drive to Nashville and face a runner everyone knew was invincible. That takes courage. She has plenty of grit in her craw.

And Margie—I wished I'd told her something, too. Her loss didn't diminish her one sliver. Instead, it made her stronger. It may have been the luckiest run she ever made. It will certainly be one of the most memorable. I've been on the losing end of a duel or two, and the memories of those are the most vivid of all. Margie will always remember the race fondly.

As the awards ceremony started that Saturday, Margie and Marie stood there side by side, sweaty like we all were, their hair hanging limp in wet strings, soppy as rags. They were a mess.

They were beautiful.

They were magnificent.

You should have seen them.

10

KATIE'S ANGEL

The young woman was having trouble finding my race packet. It contained my race number, tee shirt and race instructions, all inside a big manila envelope. I needed it if I was going to run the Wichita Marathon the next morning. It was among a few hundred others alphabetically arranged in boxes sitting on the floor of the hotel lobby.

She sifted through them and turned to me puzzled. "What did you say your name was?" she asked.

"Dallas—as in Texas—Smith. I have a Texas name, but I'm from Tennessee." That, just in case they were arranged by state.

She hunkered down and searched some more. Soon she rose, reaching the envelope out. "Someone put it in the Rs," she said smiling.

Except for that filings blunder, I would never have met Katie or heard her remarkable story.

"You had me worried there for a minute," I said. A bit of chitchat naturally followed. "You know my name; now what's yours?"

And so she told me. She looked to be in her mid twenties, had sun streaked blond hair, gray azure eyes

Going Down Slow

and dark symmetric eyebrows — the outdoorsy good looks of a model in a truck commercial. She wore no makeup, and needed none.

She had moved to Wichita after finishing college at Pittsburg State in eastern Kansas; and she worked as a commercial artist for a Wichita developer. She spoke with a smile, delighted to talk.

"Wichita is full of surprises," I said. "Like this hotel. I've stayed in hotels from Honolulu to Boston, but I think this is the best room I've ever had." (The ceilings were twelve feet high.)

Which Boston hotel, she wanted to know. I named one of the three I'd stayed in there. From that, I learned that she had run the Boston Marathon the past April. She further told me that she had qualified for Boston at the Dallas White Rocks Marathon. She was young and had scant experience but had already qualified for the Boston Marathon.

She introduced me to her coach, Leon, a kindly senior runner. He was helping out at the registration desk, too. He had more than a little to do with Katie's success at Dallas, I figured. I eventually found out that I hadn't the foggiest notion what had really happened.

I thanked Katie and headed to the pasta supper at a restaurant across the street. I wanted to have an early dinner, get some rest and save my energy for the next day.

After supper I drifted back through the hotel lobby. It was mostly empty. No one was around the registration table; marathoners had already picked up their packets or were waiting until the morning. Katie and another

Going Down Slow

woman sat nearby, keeping a watch on things. I picked up a brochure.

"How was your meal?" Katie asked. It was good, I told her—pasta and salad, standard stuff, but good.

"I love food; I love to eat!" she said. Her enthusiasm surprised me.

"And being a runner, you can eat."

"I can eat," she said.

She told me about a festival a few weeks earlier that featured all kinds of food and alcohol. "I get cut off—not from alcohol, but from food," she said. She wasn't interested in alcohol. "I just eat and eat. My husband cut me off," she said. "He said, 'you gotta quit eating; you're embarrassing me.'"

"He's just jealous," I said. 'Envious' would have been a better word, but she knew what I meant.

"He's just jealous," she echoed.

The other woman got up to attend to a chore, and didn't come back. After a while, I took her seat. Katie and I sat in posh armchairs talking, mostly alone in the huge space.

The lobby around us was decorated with flowers and tall-standing plants. A fountain nearby burbled and cascaded into a pool below. The atrium rose to the roof trusses that supported the skylights and cupola high above us. Room balconies projected from the wall opposite us. Mirrors on the wall behind us reached to the roof, reflecting the balconies. It was a grand, luxurious space. For the time being, Katie and I owned it.

Her warm smile was unconscious. Talking with her

Going Down Slow

was easy. I told her about my harsh experiences in the Heartland 100-mile race, an ultramarathon held each October just fifty miles north of where we sat. She had an uncle who ran it the same time I did, two years ago.

It's not a story I usually tell a stranger. But Katie didn't seem like a stranger. She listened carefully and then grew quiet and pensive.

Then she leaned forward and spoke softly, "I want to tell you mine. I don't know if I can without tears."

The story was about her first marathon, the Dallas White Rocks Marathon.

Leon, her coach, whom I'd met, had volunteered to help her train. For four long months she trained hard, working toward a tough goal.

"I meant to run a pace of 8:23," she explained.

"You had it down to the second…"

"I wanted to qualify for Boston. I had to run it in 3:40."

"You qualified for Boston in your first marathon!" I already knew she had run the Boston Marathon; now I suddenly realized she'd qualified for it in her first marathon, the one she was telling me about. To qualify in your first marathon is unusual.

She told me about her regimen, that she had done three twenty-mile runs and that Leon was with her every step of the way. And when it came time for the race, he ran the marathon with her too, providing pacing.

But during the race, disaster struck. In the confusion at a water station, around Mile 17, Katie lost contact with Leon. Among the thong of runners, she couldn't find him. She didn't even know if he was behind her or ahead. He

Going Down Slow

had run on. They were unable to find each other again until after the race.

She was lost without Leon. His presence had been constant, guiding her for months. Now when she needed him most, he was lost from her.

"You were going solo...."

"I was solo," she answered.

She could only go on. But the hardest miles were ahead. What would she do? Around mile 20 she felt it all coming undone.

"I felt like I couldn't go on," she said.

Her family, there to watch, had noticed too. They had started traveling ahead along the route to meet her at every mile, trying to cheer her on. A man behind her noticed her cheering family and moved up to run with her.

"He said, 'I'm running with you. I'm feeding off that.'" The man wanted to get some of that cheering too.

"It was kinda like tough love," she said. "Around Mile 23, I said I just I can't go on. He said, 'Yes you can! Get your butt moving! You gonna cross that line.'"

The stranger wouldn't let her quit. He had taken the place of Leon, her lost coach.

Katie's eyes watered as she recalled the moment. It seemed a miracle to her — this man arriving just when she needed help the most.

"I finished, and it was because of him," she said softly.

"Did you talk to him then?" I asked.

"No. When we got close [to the finish], he took off."

"Did you ever talk to him, find him in the crowd later?"

Going Down Slow

She shook her head no.

"So you'll never see him again?" I asked, knowing the answer.

"Un-uh."

But I knew.

I said, "You know, I wrote in my book that some of the best friends I ever had, I had just for a day — and never saw again."

"Un-huh, that's how it was."

Only I didn't know it all.

Katie wasn't through with her story. The rest became a bit disjointed, and, at times, I had to infer things between sentences. She went on.

"But here's the thing — I didn't find this out until the next day… My grandmother still lives in Kansas, and she's hard of hearing."

Katie had to wait until she returned to Kansas and talked with her grandmother in person to learn the next. Before the marathon Katie had asked her parents to tell her grandmother to pray for her success in that race. What Katie later learned was this:

As her grandmother went into the little Kansas church on the Sunday morning of the race, she had told her companions: "We've got to remember to pray for Katie."

They did remember, too.

"I realized that just about the time I was having a hard time was the same time they were praying for me," Katie said.

She paused.

"Their prayers sent the man?" I half asked, half stated.

Going Down Slow

"I just believe I couldn't have made it without that," she said.

It was an intensely personal story, told to a stranger. I glanced at Katie, her eyes dewy, and, sitting there in the hotel lobby, I didn't know what to say.

"That's a great story," I finally mumbled.

But I still didn't know it all.

I'd interrupted her again; she wasn't through.

"Here's the thing...the pictures—my family was making pictures, they were meeting me every mile—in all the pictures...the man was right beside me."

"He took Leon's place," I said.

"In the pictures...uh, he was forty. Leon's sixty-one. But in the pictures he looked just like Leon."

Her eyes were wet. She said it again, absently, softly.

"In every picture he looked just like Leon."

In Katie's darkest hour, the timely prayers of her grandmother had sent an angel to replace her lost coach. He pulled her through the race—and vanished. And it's no accident that the recorded images of the angel are the same as the coach he replaced.

Katie doesn't doubt this. Nor should she. The episode affirmed her deepest beliefs and seared her like a hot iron. It gave her a standard by which she will measure all of life's events. Already a part of her lore and her family's lore, she will tell it to her children, and to their children. It will not die. It is her truth.

Nearly half a million people run a marathon in this country each year. Every last one of them has a story. You don't need to be a runner to understand the story. You

Going Down Slow

only need to know something about aspiration, hope, striving, pain, failure and success, victory and defeat. You only need to know something about life.

The next day I saw Katie twice. During the race, at mile 10, I was turning to enter McConnell Air Force Base, where fans weren't allowed. A group stood at the entrance. I heard my name.

"Go Dallas! Let's go, Dallas." When you are where no one knows you, it is heartening to hear your name called out. I glanced up. Katie was jumping up and down and yelling like a varsity cheerleader.

I saw her a second time, at the awards ceremony that afternoon. As I sat in the crowd, she rushed about doing chores. Afterwards, when the crowd was breaking up, I went up to her. She was pouring ice from a cooler into a tub.

I thanked her for cheering for me.

"And you won some money!" she said, beaming. It was true; I'd won fifty dollars for placing third among master runners, those over forty.

I thanked her for telling me her marathon story. "That was the sweetest story I ever heard," I said.

When I said that, she suddenly hugged me, as runners will do. I wished her good luck and told her to take care. Then turned and walked to the hotel.

11

PRAIRIE CHICKEN CAPITOL REDUX

A man I knew flew C-47 cargo planes from Burma into China, over a chunk of the Himalayas they called "the Hump." That was a long time ago, during World War II. But he told me his story.

It was dangerous work, and many of the planes and crews didn't make it back; navigation, communications and meteorology were primitive then, at least by today's standards. The clouds and mountains were quick to claim a plane in trouble. He'd lost a lot of his friends, he told me.

"You would be talking to them on the radio one minute—and then they'd be gone," he said. "Just not there." The mountains and jungle were unforgiving.

Against advice—and maybe orders, too—he had a habit of flying without wearing his parachute. The straps were uncomfortable, and, after all, the chute was always there handy, a part of his seat; he figured if he ever needed to, he could quickly slip it on.

Then the day came when one of the crew members yelled that a fire was in the back of the plane. Now he grabbed for the familiar old chute. He twisted and turned in his seat, pulling and jerking at the straps. But the chute had become foreign and complex, a strange puzzle he couldn't solve.

Going Down Slow

He couldn't get it on. He flailed around in desperation and failure. Finally the co-pilot piped up:

"What are you gonna do Cap'n?"

He quit wrestling the chute.

"I'm gonna go back and put the fire out," he said.

So leaving the chute, his last-ditch chance, his lifeline, he went back and fought the fire, eventually putting out the blaze. That act saved his plane and crew. And it made him a hero. But he didn't say it that way, and I don't believe he was even thinking it. Because in the retelling, after all those years, the one thing that still astonished him was that in the stress of the moment he was unable to do such an easy and simple thing as put on his chute.

The story would come to mind as I logged 140 miles per week training for the Heartland 100 ultramarathon. You have time to think then. I would recall the stress of that race and the stress of the Arkansas Traveler 100, which I'd done just one week before it. The stress in those races is slow-building, but eventually just as insidious in its effects as the sudden stress on the C-47 pilot. It eats away the ability to do even simple things and finally drowns the mind in confusion and fog.

Of course the heroics of running an ultramarathon pale to nothing compared with flying the Hump. Running a 100-mile race is at best a personal quest, maybe even a silly and selfish one at that, not at all comparable to wartime flying. Those airmen over the Hump were *real* heroes — facing death over and over in their daily missions.

Just the same, on the course I knew the stress would be there and that I needed to practice techniques until they

Going Down Slow

became instinct on race day, rather than trying to figure out things in the moment.

"All the front-runners have handlers or crews," an ultramarathoner told me once the night before a race. "Late in the race you can't think. You need someone to tell you what to do." That was his judgment.

The next day I was just behind him when he made a mistake. It was only a small mistake, but his angry expletive underscored what he had told me about the difficulty of thinking.

Most problems, I knew, would come at night; fatigue, sleep deprivation, exposure and loneliness add to the accumulating stress. At Heartland, the prairie is lonely, with scarcely ever a house or car, and not many runners scattered along the course.

On my first attempt there I ran through the cold, windy night without seeing another runner. My cold fingers suffered a mild case of frostbite. My vision faded. I didn't know then that the vision loss was temporary. Instead I had good reason to believe it was permanent and irreparable. Finding the course markers was a challenge; getting lost in that austere place was dangerous, and I'd been lost just the previous week at the Arkansas Traveler 100, when my vision was good.

There were gloves in my pack that might have helped my freezing fingers that night, but I didn't think so then. The waxing moon had set at midnight, and the prairie was dark. The glow of my flashlight became a smudge drifting like a specter through the windy night. Only the coyotes kept me company. Their pathetic squalls filled the prairie

Going Down Slow

with sadness and pierced my lonely heart.

Through ravaged eyes I saw my light hitting the back of a road sign ahead. It seemed to be maybe fifty yards ahead. The idea was ridiculous, of course; there generally were no signs — or anything else, for that matter — on that dirt road. The sign faced the wrong way, to boot — or was on the wrong side of the road; and my little light was too weak to reflect off of anything more than a few feet away. Didn't matter, it was a road sign to me, something familiar, something to hang onto, something forward, the direction a racer looks, a beacon to follow, to look toward.

And I did look at it, glowing in the darkness. The sign had a wonderful quality — no matter how long I ran toward it, it hovered just fifty yards ahead. I accepted that behavior completely and didn't worry myself about how it did that; I just kept running toward it.

But after a mile or two — how can I know which? — a disquieting notion began to gradually gnaw its way into my consciousness: *that sign's not acting right*. But so what? What could I do? The sign remained fifty yards ahead, the way it always had, out of my control, separate and distinct. That was an empirical fact. It obeyed its physics; I obeyed mine.

Eventually though the traveling sign began to pester me a bit, and finally to annoy by its unorthodox behavior.

In time, the mystery was solved, as most eventually are. It wasn't a sign at all. It was a distant security light at a house. A house meant I was getting close to Cassoday, the little town at the end of the run. My diminished vision had transformed the distant point of light into a nearby

Going Down Slow

diffused reflection, like the back of a sign.

That's the technical explanation.

The first Heartland 100 taught me that time becomes an obsession at night. So, for my second attempt there, I adopted a training technique, using two sports watches, one on each wrist. There were two reasons for two watches. Time is the only familiar reference at night. In a strange place at night there is no passing of landmarks, no stretch of visible land extending to the horizon, or the top of the hill. Progress is hard to realize. Time is the only gage. If a watch failed, I wanted a spare.

There's another reason. In its main register—the one large enough I can easily see it—one watch would show my total race time, the other watch would show the "lap" time, the time since my last drink. Every ten minutes I planned to walk for one minute while I took a drink.

With only one watch, measuring one minute was hard, I'd discovered. Soon, I didn't know if I'd walked one minute or two. I had to actually read the total time, say 41:38, remember that, add one minute, and start running again at 42:38. But sometimes I'd be occupied with other chores, digging something out of the pack, putting on gloves, looking for a course marker and so on. Because of that—and the stress of the race, too—soon I'd forgotten the time when I started walking, or confuse the one when I should start running again with when I started walking. Or confuse the seconds with the minutes—was that 41:38 or 38:41? Sometimes I'd even forget to note the start-walk time altogether. Once the race makes you stupid, there are more boring ways to mess up than I can list.

Going Down Slow

A lap timer would make it simpler, I thought. Start to walk, I push the button; the time resets to zero, and when fifty-nine seconds flashes to one minute, it's time to run again. The procedure is the same each time, over and over. But there were other complications with time management—I would also use a walk break at five-minute intervals, on the "fives," but no drink on the fives. Except that once I got confused and was swigging my standard drink on the fives, too. Eventually, I realized I was drinking just twice the fluid I needed. My fingers had swollen, puffy and pudgy from the extra fluid.

The man was right—you can't think.

So I practiced the technique of tiny details, hoping to reduce correct action to rote, one not requiring thought. I doubted it would work. I always figured something unexpected could come along and knock me out of the groove. And then I wouldn't be able to do something as simple as don a parachute. I just wondered what the hell it'd be. I hoped it wouldn't be incipient blindness again—that would be a bore.

You do the race and you find out. On my second attempt at Heartland 100, the one for which I'd practiced so carefully, a completely new experience reared up as I'd feared it might, one so blindingly unexpected it left me wondering, disoriented and uncertain about ultramarathoning. So uncertain was I that I returned to the scene a third year, not for the race, but for a visit only, for a chance to ponder and bring peace to my running soul.

Place of misery and pain, place of deliverance and

Going Down Slow

exultation—place of whimpering failure, too: I returned to Cassoday.

Cassoday, Kansas, Population 99, a cluster of white houses sitting on the tall-grass prairie in the Flint Hills. In the town you find a restaurant, a school, a post office, a market and the United Methodist Church, everything you need. You also find where the Heartland 100-mile foot race begins and ends—an extra thing you may not need. I'd run that race the last two years. Now I was here to think.

I drove into town on a pleasant October day. I'd been fifty miles south at Wichita that week anyway and decided to visit. As I drove in, a freshly painted sign erected by the Lion's Club welcomed me to "The Prairie Chicken Capitol of the World," as it had almost precisely two years earlier when I was here for my first attempt. Two hundred yards further and I was through town. An identical sign faced the other way.

At the second sign, I came to City Park, a low grassy field among a rare—for the prairie—grove of trees, mostly walnuts and hackberries. I parked beside the swing set. Nobody was around. From the distance across the street came the sound of children playing in the schoolyard.

I looked around for squirrels and saw none. The walnut crop had failed.

I had a seat in one of the swings and took a ride. The chains are strong and well supported; you can swing high with no fear—as I'd done before, two years earlier.

There's a frost-free faucet standing in front of the band shell. I remembered the water from that faucet. It has a stony taste that reminds me of the limestone well

Going Down Slow

water on the farm where I grew up. So once again, I filled my bottles at the faucet. I remembered taking hold of the handle two years before. A gray jumping spider lived in the mechanism then. He'd stalked out, annoyed. After holding his ground a few seconds, he jumped into the grass and hid. That's a strange thing to remember.

It was memories of the Heartland 100-mile race that drew me back to this park. I'd camped overnight here two years in a row for that race. I still wrestle with the outcomes of those races. Now I sat recalling what happened.

The first race stands as perhaps the bravest episode of my life—or maybe, the most foolish, maybe both. We had started running in pitch dark and light rain two hours before dawn. The course follows lonely dirt roads across the prairie. During the day, the rain gave way to hard gusty wind, and the temperature dropped.

We ran through the day, strung out and separate. Darkness came. Light left, the wind stayed, it got cold. My fingers nearly froze; they haven't fully recovered yet. All night long I ran without seeing another flashlight.

My eyesight began to fail around nightfall. As it grew dimmer, I worried about finding my way and about freezing if I got lost.

But there was an even greater worry. A dozen prior eye surgeries told me the vision loss might be permanent. The surgeries had stemmed from last-chance attempts by specialists to repair badly torn and detached retinas. Only one eye recovered. And now that eye was going dim. My luck had finally run out; all that surgery had weakened the structure of my eye too much for the stress of the race, I figured.

Going Down Slow

Here is a thing to wonder about: Alone in the dark in that vast prairie, freezing and going blind and already way beyond ordinary exhaustion from having run for twenty hours, would you believe what I was thinking? How could you? I barely do. Even believing I might be blinded for life, troubled I had ruined myself forever, or worried I might get lost and freeze to death anyway — even believing those things, what was I thinking about? One thing.

The race.

I wanted to finish the race in twenty-four hours, finish before 6 a.m., before our starting time the previous day — run a hundred miles in one day. That's what I was thinking about, that's what I wanted to do. The other things were distractions.

One wonders about that. To balance profound loss against an arbitrary goal, and still pick the race seems crazy. One could criticize my decision. But endurance athletes would not think it unusual. Endurance means enduring. Training instills the belief that you will keep going, and you must have that belief. Other runners would have done the same. Indeed, many stories of runners and triathletes going past the limits of health confirm the truth of it.

In any case, I failed my goal by six minutes, taking twenty-four hours and six minutes to cross a finish line I never saw. I remember it, all right.

My vision loss turned out to be temporary. Most of it returned the next day, and improved to normal over the next four or five days. The problem was due to corneal edema, swelling prompted by cold conditions, low blood

Going Down Slow

sugar, fatigue and exertion.

Then I returned to Cassoday the following year determined to rub out the extra six minutes. Experienced and thoroughly prepared this time, I expected to crush it. But again I failed to see the finish line—but for a completely different reason than before.

I failed to finish. Thoroughly prepared, I totally failed. The race crushed me. An utterly new race outcome. It was the first race I'd failed to finish, despite dozens of strenuous races. I simply quit the race, walked off the course and sat down. And I still don't understand why. Around midnight I simply quit—this time under pleasant weather conditions and a beautiful full moon.

After running seventy-five miles I somehow had a mental failure. My resolve tipped over. Polarity reversed. I decided not to just passively quit but to actively oppose finishing. I wanted to kill ultrarunning, shove a knife through its cruel heart. I had decided the race was an evil thing. Despite the urgings of fellow runners to keep going, my resolution held steady and strong. No temptation could dent it.

I had no injuries. The reversal signified a catastrophic failure of the will—an ignoble crash lacking either grace or endurance. I reckon you could say that. It was shameful and cowardly. I reckon you could say that, too. I'm still dismayed by it. But, of course, that experience has happened to other ultra endurance athletes.

Paula Newby-Frazer, holder of six Ironman world championships, is maybe the most successful athlete in the history of that sport. Yet in one championship race

Going Down Slow

she approached the finish line on Hawaii's Alii Drive and, though having completed nearly 140 miles, suddenly stopped and sat down on the curb. Despite attempts by fans to urge her on, she sat there while a woman in her wake ran by and took the crown.

Failure has happened to better athletes than I. I know that, but find little consolation in it.

Today's non-running visit to Cassoday comes just one week after this year's Heartland 100. I'd learned that twenty-four runners finished the race. I found myself wishing I'd been here for it, and I don't know why.

The course winds out across the prairie and back, all on dirt roads except for the first and last half-mile. It starts and ends at a derelict two-story school building. I'd attempted the race twice without ever seeing the finish line. Now on my visit I went looking for it. I stopped the truck and got out opposite an ornamental shrub in the old school's yard.

There painted across the road I saw a faded white line worn away except at each end. It bears faint testimony to the toil of all the runners who've crossed it.

A faded white line seems absurdly inadequate, less strength of evidence — even if it is physical — than my own memory. And so my thoughts fly back to that very first race; I drift away, recalling:

The lonely miles stretch through the long night. It is nearing midnight, and I've been running seventeen hours; I have seven more to go if I'm going to turn in a respectable time for a 100-mile distance. Around three dozen of us are

Going Down Slow

strung out along dirt roads.

So widely spaced are we, no runner's light is visible. No vehicles or houses are in sight. I run alone, as I like to do. No human turns me from what I want to see and hear, or alters the thoughts I think.

The running has blurred my sight. I can distinguish shapes but details are foggy—the Heartland 100-cum-American Impressionism.

I stop in the road and stand looking at the heavens—all blurry, the moon and stars. I turn out my light to sky-gaze better. The moon is a fat crescent and will set long before I finish this race. A few clouds to the south glow translucent around the edges, outlined by the moon's backlighting. There's nothing here but the wind, the prairie, and me. This road may not see a car all day long. The view is marred by blinking lights, beacons on the horizon, visible across impossible distance in this open space. They annoy me, and I'd like to snuff them out.

I turn eastward, gazing skyward. In the corner of my eye, suddenly I see a dark figure lunge at my back. It's too late! I spin around to face the assault, fumbling with the light switch. The beam flashes.

The light blasts the intruder into cosmic ether.

Gathering myself, I make a discovery that makes me feel like a fool. It's my shadow, my moon shadow, nothing else. I stand looking stupidly at the figure in the road, its menacing darkness unwelcome in my post fright. I aim my light at it, blasting the wicked thing in two; the bright spot vaporizes its heart. I kill it at will and just as easily resurrect it. Turn the light away; the shadow lives again,

Going Down Slow

none the worst for its recent death. It exists on my whim.

But it's only a shadow. I turn my back and trot on. My benevolence is large, my study of the heavens is finished. The run remains.

The synthetic world presses in, an unwelcome intrusion. Strobe lights and rotating beacons flash their warning, "tower here." Some blink in clusters, like a field of towers—somebody cultivating the ugly invaders like photonic corn. I see cities, too, sprawling light clumps on the distant horizon, spreading a glow into the prairie night. It's a panoramic surplus of light, an orgy of photons. Perspective lost to the dark makes the lights seem close. They are…just…right there. You aren't lost, they say to the runner. This is a cozy place, a small space, after all. Just pick a light and go to it. There's an easy way out.

But I'm not buying it. The reality is the prairie; the illusion is the lights. Those lights lie; they are a long way off, too far to see in daylight. How far away?—twenty, thirty, forty miles? Who knows; take your pick. It's all the same to one on foot—a long way to anywhere. It's an illusion, diminishment of the prairie by those lights. They don't diminish the prairie; they diminish me. And mock my efforts to cross it. The prairie is real, austere; it doesn't care. Let the lights blink. These prairie hills are made of flint, a hard rock that wears slowly, abides long. The wind blows across them, the coyotes howl, and prairie chickens cluck to their chicks each spring. The prairie is true; the lights are false. I chose the prairie and curse the lights. Damn the lights.

A pack of coyotes starts up on a hill to my left—yelping,

Going Down Slow

barking, howling, yodeling squalls, everyone singing his part. The outcry could be mourning at a funeral, or rather a celebration of the coming Hunter's Moon. I don't know; the language is primal, not understood by me. There is the sudden nearby sound of hoofs pounding. A couple of nervous horses running away, maybe spooked by my light, wary this Saturday night. The canine singing continues. Soon a lone coyote answers from the right. The loner and the pack conduct a call-and-answer serenata across the road. Coyotes are pack animals. The lone one can't be too happy about being alone. I leave them to their coyote concerns and run on, passing out of hearing.

But the coyote action is not yet finished. Soon another one starts up near me, just to the right. The sound is pathetic and lonely. No one answers; he is alone. He squalls out agonized cries, formless screams of misery and pain. No one helps him. He cries alone in the night.

On my visit, I sit recalling my running in this prairie. The Cassoday park playground is quiet this Monday morning. All the swings hang slack except for the one I sit in. The band shell, too, is lifeless.

I sit where I twice camped and ponder my two 100-mile races here. The first race I not only attempted but actually managed to finish, and in a pretty good time under difficult conditions. With eye injuries threatening permanent blindness, the curtain drew down. I raced toward the finish trying to beat it. That lonely night turned into a desperate race.

That first race remains the most heroic run I've made,

Going Down Slow

or likely will make. A year later, the second attempt turned pathetically shameful—after seventy-five miles I quit like a craven coward. It was the first race I'd failed to finish—failed for no apparent reason, excepting maybe cowardice, or failure of will, or…

Those two races set like opposing bookends, embracing all the other races I've run, a spectrum spanning from heroic to dismal. What do they mean? It troubles me, and that's part of my visit.

But I must now set those thoughts aside. It is not solely the memory of those races that drew me back. I have still another mission: I want to see a spot of land.

The little town calls itself the Prairie Chicken Capitol of the World. These hills cradle one of the last strongholds of a scarce bird called the greater prairie chicken. In running the two 100-mile races here I never saw one.

The Nature Conservancy owns 2,000 acres of land not far from Cassoday, called the Flint Hills Tallgrass Prairie Preserve. After paying dues to the Conservancy a few decades, I decided I wanted to come see my land.

The Nature Conservancy saves wilderness by an eminently simple and utterly effective method: they buy it. That takes money. They get some of it from me.

I like the Flint Hills. I might want to move here and be the Preserve's caretaker, I thought, a good way to keep out of trouble.

I contacted the Kansas Chapter for directions to the property. Ruth Palmer, the Philanthropy and Communications Coordinator wrote right back.

"The fall color in the prairie grasses is beautiful right

Going Down Slow

now," she said. "Our preserve is 6 miles straight east of Cassoday."

I had my directions. I took a road apparently headed east, and noted my odometer setting. The road ran straight. At the six-mile mark it made a hard left turn. Continuing straight ahead was the gravel driveway to a ranch house. I stopped and pondered—she'd not mentioned a house. While the drive ended at the house, a four-wheel drive path continued over a hill out of sight.

Could be it, I thought. I decided to follow the paved road a bit further first. After a few miles without seeing the land, I returned to the ranch house and headed down the gravel drive. Coming toward me was a four-wheel-drive truck pulling a goose-necked stock trailer loaded with cattle. I pulled over and stopped.

A black-spotted white fice played a daring game—darting in front of the trailer wheels and back out just before getting squashed, all the while yapping murderous threats. Not afraid to ask directions, I motioned the driver to stop.

He pulled up, a stern, raw-boned guy with big hands and a big hat. He sat without expression, maybe irked at having to stop his rig.

"That dog lives dangerously," I said.

Faint smile. "Yeah."

Black wrap-a-rounds hid his eyes, although the sky was overcast. The edge of a Band-Aid peeked from behind the left lens. A black eye behind those glasses maybe, maybe two. I asked him where the Conservancy land was. He told me to go to Cassoday and head east.

Going Down Slow

I thought I'd traveled east, but with the sun hidden it was hard to tell direction.

"Which road is that?" I asked.

"Do you know First Street?" he asked. Cassoday has numbered streets! I stifled a grin.

"Nah. I know where the school is—there's a road beside it."

Take that road he told me. I thanked him. As the rig pulled away the belligerent little dog resumed his chase, playing the dangerous game with the wheels, darting in and out, screaming invectives.

I turned my truck around. The fice returned unscathed. He ignored my trespass. It was the tandem-wheeled trailer he hated.

Back at Cassoday, I took the road beside the school; it soon turned to flinty dirt. At six miles I topped a hill. Suddenly I realized I was surrounded by grass three-feet tall. The previous pastures were grazed to the ground. I dropped into the hollow, where a tiny stream ran clear—head of the Cottonwood River—headed over the next hill and dropped into another swale, this one dry.

I parked on the gravely edge. The road climbed a hill ahead. On the right the tall grass continued. To the left the tall grass gave way to an over-grazed pasture. I'd found the Preserve.

To see land you need to walk on it. I headed up the road, leaving the truck in the hollow. After a quarter-mile I heard car wheels crunching gravel in the distance behind me. The car, a white SUV, stopped beside my truck while the driver inspected the unfamiliar vehicle parked there.

Going Down Slow

Then it came on and stopped beside me. I looked in to see a sturdy man around seventy with a dark tan and wavy gray hair.

"Are you okay?" he asked.

I told him I was fine and thanks for checking, that I was taking a walk to look at the land.

"Well, you see somebody walking out here and...." He trailed off. I knew what he meant. I asked him about the land with the tall grass, told him I thought it belonged to the Nature Conservancy.

"It does," he said.

"It looks ungrazed," I told him.

"They allow grazing but with lots of regulations," he said. Then he told me he owned 5,000 acres on its eastern border.

"That's a lot of land!" I said.

"Life has been good to me," he said, smiling kindly.

I have a hunch hard work had something to do with that. He got the brown tan working outdoors. I asked him if he grew up in the Flint Hills, and he said he had, that his daddy was an oil worker and that there had been an oil field nearby.

I reached in and shook his hand; it was thick and strong. His name was Frank Gaines. He spoke with a slight Johnny Cash tremor. On his print flannel shirt was the repeated scene of a fly fisherman landing a trout, his rod bent in a great arch, a sight foreign to this arid land.

I mentioned the beauty of the land.

"You should see it around the first of April to the fifteenth. They burn it all," he said.

Going Down Slow

"Uh—you mean to rejuvenate the pastures?"

"Yeah. It takes fire to get down to the woody plants," he said. Without fire woody plants diminish the grass.

"Does the Nature Conservancy burn theirs too?" I asked.

He answered with a wry smile. "If they don't set it, it gets set."

I guess so.

Truth is he liked the Conservancy. "We've worked with them a lot," he said. Their nearest representative is "an awful nice fellow."

He was in no hurry; we talked a good while. Finally we shook hands again, and he drove away.

In flagrant trespass, I slipped under the barbed wire fence into the Conservancy's tall grass. It came to my waist. I headed toward a half dozen cottonwood trees in the dry wash, where Frank had told me there was once a home place. I didn't need to find any artifacts. I just wanted to tread the soil, brush through the grass.

I worry about the Flint Hills. Commercial interests want to develop the land. That will destroy the austere beauty of the place. When that beauty goes, the greater prairie chicken goes, too. The ranchers could make a killing by leasing or selling out. Their love of the land is all that stops them. Through the years, they've been good stewards. Will future generations foster men like Frank Gaines? I don't know, but I worry.

I approached the bottom of the swale, where the big cottonwoods stand and the grass grows thickest. An old cow path revealed a big deer track. I stooped to look.

Going Down Slow

The startling roar of wings shattered the silence. The wary bird had flushed already beyond range of all but a good duck gun. He came around to the right for a passing shot, still out of range. A bit slower than an eastern grouse, I thought. His wing beat seemed syncopated, at intervals making a sort of stutter flap.

I stood fascinated, watching him recede in the distance. Short wings, chunky body, he walks on the ground and flies only when he needs to.

I'd finally seen a prairie chicken.

Come next spring I hope the hens walk this ground clucking to their chicks. I hope they don't vanish. I hope, but I worry.

12

A LONELY MESA, A RUDE VISITOR

Sometimes you walk. Sometimes you have to. Like deep in a 100-mile ultramarathon when running becomes too hard, walking is hard enough, and even mere standing seems hard, too. Other times you walk because you want to. You want extra time to look around, to pause when you need to in order to examine things more closely. That's what I'd been doing, walking because I wanted to look close at a terrifying place. But now I was leaving.

It was getting dark and I was driving the two-lane blacktop north along the Utah mesa known as Island in the Sky, a monolith a few miles wide and twenty miles long rising into the air on vertical cliffs 1,200 feet high. On my eastern flank jutted Dead Horse Point, a precipice named for the horses that once ran too close to the edge before they realized the awful truth.

Immediately around me the mesa looked like ordinary high plains. But I knew better; the abrupt cliffs are out there like the ultimate edge. A few miles north the cliffs play out enough that the road can wind its way down.

I was drifting through spring that year, on a solo trip around the Four Corners area. I'd been walking on the southern tip of Island in the Sky, a place known as

Going Down Slow

Grandview Point that overlooks the junction of the Green and Colorado Rivers. At the mesa's tip, the very last rock juts out into space like an anvil's point. I'd climbed out on that rock and gazed down into the terrible swooping distance below. The vista before me was as forbidding as it was immense, one scarred by deep canyons, standing rocks and mesas, raw naked rock, a case of geology gone mad. The Point earns its name.

The long walk over, I was leaving now, driving north. I needed a place to sleep. I spotted a Jeep path angling off to the west that looked like a good bet. I headed the truck down it, looking for a likely place to park. After a half mile, I came to a wide spot where it appeared campers had stayed before. I turned the truck around, ready for a quick get away, and parked it level beside the path.

The sky was clear and the moon was full, casting a yellow glow over the desert rocks. I looked forward to a peaceful, lonely night.

Stretching a hundred miles to the west lies some of the most barren land you can find — land so profoundly worthless as to be infinitely valuable. At least to the human soul. If a laser weapon high in space scorched the whole region, it would kill precious little; the sage bushes would turn black and the black bushes would just get blacker.

The next day I planned to venture into that space and find a canyon where the ancient ones, the Anasazi, left elaborate petroglyphs on the walls. Extended drought 700 years ago decimated the Anasazi and drove them from this region. But their stark art still decorates the canyon, ghostly images of spirits long departed.

Going Down Slow

It was too early to go to bed. I sat in the truck cab for a while and discovered an FM station in Salt Lake City playing mainstream jazz, a rare kind of program I was glad to find.

Suddenly headlights came bouncing along the truck path toward me. This was disappointing; I wasn't expecting company. A van rumbled by without stopping. I watched as it went on down the path. Probably just some camper looking for a place to sleep. Soon the taillights dipped out of sight over a rise. Good. Whatever they had in mind, it didn't look like they'd be doing it close to me.

It soon got too cold to sit in the truck without running the heater, and I wasn't going to do that. I stood around outside and sat on the tailgate. The moonlight was a pale liquid falling on an austere landscape of sand, rock and shrub. To the west the view faded to darkness, as if that harsh land swallowed light.

I had dismissed the van. It was time to go to bed. My truck had a camper shell and my sleeping bag was already stretched out in the back. I climbed in, closed the main tailgate, the camper gate, and slid into the warm bag, removing only my sneakers. Moon glow came through the windows, lighting the inside. I was tired and soon drifted off.

Crunching metal jarred me awake like a garbage truck. I sat bolt upright, grabbing my .38. Somebody's outside! What do they mean? You can't come raising hell in a stranger's camp! You'll get shot!

I sat there holding my breath, trying to get a fix on their direction, see if I could hear talking. It had sounded

Going Down Slow

like guys stomping beer cans just outside my truck. Anyone would have to know the hostility of that. Menace was their clear intent, and they probably weren't through, I thought.

My pulse was roaring. It seemed like all the blood in my body was trying to rush into my head.

I couldn't see anyone outside the windows. They could have crouched down beside the truck, I knew. As quietly as I could I leaned over to each side window and looked down, but saw nothing. The same for the back window. They may have retreated to the rocks a few yards away or be hidden toward the front of the truck.

One thing was obvious to everybody concerned — there was only one way out of the truck bed, and that was through the back. I had to get out. I was a sitting duck inside. I slipped on my sneakers as quietly as I could and got set to jump.

Here goes! I flipped up the camper door, slammed the main gate down and hit the ground facing the truck, pistol ready.

And saw nobody.

Not at the sides of the truck, not at the front. I fetched my flashlight and swept underneath the truck, but nobody was under there either. They had retreated to the rocks, I figured.

I checked the ground near the left rear wheel, where I thought the can crushing sounds had come from. There were no cans there. Neither was there any metal left over from a previous camper that could have caused the noise. From that, I assumed they had taken the cans with them

Going Down Slow

when they ran — all the better to annoy a lone camper.

Well, I wasn't leaving. I stood around, wondering. A hard moonlight fell on the desert rocks — which now took on a new evil dimension.

Oddly, I remember noticing the beauty of it all, too. The moon was so bright I could clearly see the snow on top of Tukuhnikivats, flagship peak of the La Sal Mountains, thirty miles to the east.

I went back to bed. I lay there not quite asleep.

The sound started again.

Again sitting up, I couldn't see a soul outside the truck. The sound had changed, I noticed, to a metallic crunching, something like a hack saw on sheet metal, a rhythmic sound akin to gnawing. Gnawing?

Ah, yes, there was my answer. It must be some kind of desert rodent gnawing on my truck. The metal bed of the truck had amplified the sound, making it louder, especially to my ears so close to the floor. I decided I'd get out and find the little varmint.

The commotion of my getting out made it stop the sound, of course. It'd be hiding. I scanned the underside of the truck with my light, expecting to see a furry scurrying. But it held tight.

I knew where it would be — the engine compartment. There's tasty stuff there. I raised the hood. It was cagey and probably small, but I figured I could find it or, at the least, make it run away. I inspected closely, looking inside the fan shroud, underneath the AC compressor and alternator, wherever it might be crouching.

I satisfied myself that it wasn't there, that it had

Going Down Slow

already bailed out. Everything was quiet. Good enough, I thought, a lesson learned for both of us, a happy outcome all around.

I returned to the back of the truck, prepared to go to bed once again. For some reason, before climbing in I decided to have one more look underneath the back of the truck. It wouldn't be there, of course. The commotion of slamming the hood and door would've already scared anything away.

I stooped down and shined my light on the rear axle and the spare tire area.

As if cued by the light, the metallic crunching suddenly started.

It was in front of my face, just past the tailgate, at precisely where I was pointing the light. As if mocking me, my light, my futile search, it scrunched and screeched, metallic and undaunted.

Crouched there on that harsh lonely mesa drowned by cold moonlight, I pointed my light at a grating sound made by something I could not see — and conveniently re-affirmed a long-held position, one unsupported by the immediate empirical data: I don't believe in ghosts.

With that, I climbed back into the truck and slipped into my bag. While it gnawed on the steel bowels of my truck I drifted gently into a sweet sleep.

13

WHAT IF A NEUTRINO WHACKED YOUR NOGGIN?

"Tell me the truth now—what happens if neutrinos have mass?" I heard Bob Seger ask the question in a song when I was running with my headphones on.

Don't usually run with headphones. But I was inside that day, six laps to the mile. Did thirty miles there one day, 180 laps. Which would have been a lot even without the broken ankle. Had a shoe that fit the air cast. I could do all right. I think I'll claim a distance record for that gym.

Anyway, I was running inside, headphones on, and there was Seger asking a deep question. Particle physics is not an issue normally considered by pop singers; but then Seger always did write evocative lyrics. The question is a dandy; I think I know what he's getting at.

Astronomers wonder what's going to happen to the universe. They peer into the night sky and see everything running away from us. The galaxies the furthest away are running away the fastest—a phenomenon first noticed by the American astronomer, Edwin Hubble. The discovery made him famous enough for the space telescope to carry his name.

The universe is expanding, and has been ever since the Big Bang started it. Is it going to just keep doing that—

Going Down Slow

exploding into an infinite void? If so, as density and energy diminish, then there finally comes the ultimate moment when all the stars have died and the very last photon blinks out. The universe falls cold and dark. The end of light; the end of time.

There's another possibility. If there's enough mass scattered around, gravity's pull will eventually put the brakes on run-away expansion, bringing everything to a terrible shuttering halt. Gravity doesn't sleep; it will keep pulling, gathering everything back in, all hurling inwards toward some center—and toward an incomprehensible cosmic collision, one without precedence. The Big Bang in reverse, the Big Crunch.

There's a problem in deciding which fate awaits. Is it the dark void or the Big Crunch? I'm not sure which one I favor. God planned it; I don't worry with it.

But astronomers do. They total up the mass of everything they can find, and they can't come up with enough to pull everything together again.

They don't like that answer. They think it ought to recycle. But without enough mass it won't. So they think there's dark matter out there that they can't "see." This has been referred to as the missing mass problem.

And this returns us to Seger's question. Maybe the missing mass is contained in all the neutrinos zipping around in the universe.

Trouble is, neutrinos are contrary sub-atomic particles, ill-behaved and hard to find. When I first read about them, I thought they had spilled out of a physicist's nightmare. They seemed too fantastic to be true.

Going Down Slow

For starters, they interact with matter so weakly that they can dash through, say, twelve feet of lead without hitting a single thing. Worse, the elusive particles can fly right through the very Earth itself, come out the other side and sail happily on, leaving not one scrap of evidence. You'd think they'd hit an atom somewhere along the way, but not so.

Practically nothing you put in front of them impedes their headlong flight the slightest, not even our world. But then a physicist will tell you that most things we think are solid — even a dense piece of lead — on the atomic scale, are mostly empty space. A neutrino can fly through them unscathed.

And how much do they weigh anyway?

I imagine Bob Seger running though the Hollywood Hills he sung about pondering that question, the very same way I mull over similar questions running the country roads around my little town. Maybe that's how he finds his lyrics and writes the hits. Running takes you far away sometimes, clear out of the galaxy this time. Running or not aside, what about the question? How would you measure the particle's mass?

For something as strange and evasive as a neutrino you'd need to design a strange detector. Physicists, I learned, were equal to the task. It was a matter of probability, they figured. If you place enough mass in their way and if there are enough neutrinos flying by, then you might net one — the more the mass, the more numerous the neutrinos, the better the odds.

Here's what they did: They filled an abandoned

Going Down Slow

underground mine in Michigan with a fluid. That was their mass. As I recall—and this seems too fantastic to say—the liquid they used was dry-cleaning fluid! Well, why not dry-cleaning fluid? That seems in perfect keeping with the whole bizarre scheme. Maybe Karo Syrup was too messy.

And they were optimistic. They placed photo detectors around the walls of this dark lake. If a neutrino ever did hit an atom, it would cause a photon—a little packet of light—to be ejected, like the 1-ball when a pool player makes his break shot. That 1-ball slams into the corner pocket.

So they worked with the angles. By knowing which photo detector caught the hypothetical light, they could even determine the direction from which the hypothetical neutrino came. If one ever hit.

They even built another detector, in Japan—similar, except it was filled with distilled water, if memory serves.

So there sat the two underground lakes of denatured fluid on opposite sides of the globe, in perfect darkness, and silence so profound it was disturbed by nothing but Earth's deep growling. They waited.

A subscriber at the time to *Sky and Telescope* magazine, I read about the neutrino detectors, and shook my head. Crazy beyond anything I'd encountered before, the best I could say about the whole scheme was that it at least seemed harmless, and it kept graduate students out of trouble.

Then came Supernova 1987A. A star exploded, the first such one of the year 1987, hence the "A" handle. It

Going Down Slow

was in the Large Magellanic Cloud, a companion galaxy in the Southern Hemisphere 170,000 light years away, not visible from either Michigan or my home in Cookeville. It was the first "nearby" supernova in three centuries.

A supernova blasts out a wave of neutrinos. A virtual storm came sailing toward Earth, like a cosmic swarm of starlings. At precisely the right moment the detectors in Michigan and Japan both registered hits, a total of nineteen. Both said the direction was toward 1987A. It was conclusive.

I was surprised, and shame-faced. The physicists had been right. I doubt they'd ever doubted it; they built the detectors, after all. A scientist in a different field, I shouldn't have doubted them in theirs. I will be slower to do so again.

So given enough mass and enough neutrinos a flash of light may be produced. What does that mean, I wondered? There are now seven billion people on Earth. That's quite a bit of mass right there. Has any person ever experienced a neutrino event? Did he or she thereby emit a flash of light? Or was it only a soft glow? Was it bright enough to see?

I was an engineering professor in those days; I wondered about these things aloud to my class one day. The students had just taken their seats in a large lecture room, one that sloped up high at the back. Before jumping into the technical lesson, I sometimes told a light-hearted story, something for their listening pleasure and enjoyment.

I told them about the neutrino detectors, about

Going Down Slow

Supernova 1987A, about how surprised I'd been. I wondered if a person would react to a neutrino by some kind of light display.

They listened quietly; I set the final scene: a woman and her boyfriend alone in the dark. At a tender moment suddenly a neutrino hit turns the woman's light on, perhaps a soft flash. That would be a miracle.

"If it's true that every couple has its moment then that would certainly be a very special one," I said.

The students smiled quietly, thinking secret thoughts. On the front row sat one of the brighter scholars. He'd leaned forward during my monologue, listening carefully. Finally he spoke up:

"You told that whole story just so you could use that line, didn't you?"

He was partly right. It was a good finish to the story. And every story needs a good finish.

14

WEATHER REPORT: SEVILLE, SPAIN

We went barreling into the roundabout too fast for the wet cobblestones. The car lurched into a sickening skid. Rafael jerked the wheel, and we swooped through the circle clean as a pin. The lucky fact that no other cars were about at that early hour helped.

My friend Albino was riding shotgun; his older brother, Rafael, was driving, and I was in the back. We burst out laughing. We didn't care. The danger seemed small compared to what we were rushing toward, the place where our minds already were.

Which was the XXI Maratón Ciudad de Sevilla. On a February day that had yet an hour to wait before dawning, we rushed along wet streets heading for a rendezvous with the brothers' running club. From there, according to plan, we would all drive to the marathon at Olympic Stadium.

The Peugeot's thermometer showed 4 degrees C and the wipers beat back the rain. A little colder and there wouldn't be rain — which would be an improvement. As it was, we'd be both cold and wet. Staying warm enough would be a problem.

"This is as bad as it gets, unless there's wind too," I said.

Going Down Slow

Then the wind started.

To this warm and dry city, an unusual weather system had sneaked overnight; the Seville Marathon was going to be a wet piece of business. Rafael had tuned in a station playing old pop hits from the United States. Dale Shannon was inconsolate: His little Run-Away had, sure enough, run away. "I'm walking in the rain...," sang he.

At the pre-race expo two days earlier, a sunny day, Albino had picked up a folded piece of plastic and extended it to me.

"We may need these," he'd said.

I doubted that but took it anyway. It was a plastic bag with a neck hole, the usual marathoner's raincoat. That bag saved my race.

After linking up with the running club—an indefatigable group as sunny as the dawning day was cloudy, everyone wearing matching warm-up suits—we arrived at the Stadium to find the parking lot layered with water. We posed for a foggy group picture there, one that turned out blurred because Albino's camera was inadvertently set for close-up photographs.

In cold conditions, what to wear is hard to decide. I don't want any extra clothes to slow me down. On the other hand, freezing doesn't help either. The plastic bag, I held in my hand. Sitting in the security of the Peugeot, I decided on shorts, tee shirt and glove liners, not gloves, for my hands—lightweight clothes for speed. I pulled the bag down over my head, and we walked through the rain to the start, a block from the Stadium.

I faced the gray day in just shorts and tee—and a

Going Down Slow

plastic bag, which I planned to throw away after a mile or two, when I got warm. My guess was that once the sun came up, the rain would stop and the sky clear. And that was not only optimistic but also wrong.

It turned out to be a day of unblemished gray. The rain never let up. We slopped along wet streets. Water pooled at intersections. We cut across curbs and corners, or went splashing through, high-stepping like a guy wading a tangle of snakes. The sun never showed, the air never warmed, the rain pattered, and the wind rattled our plastic coats.

Early on, I had punched two holes in the plastic bag so that I could stick my arms outside for a natural arm swing. That didn't work; my arms got too cold. I pulled them back inside. Thus cramped, I ran. Huddled, I ran. Nursing cold hands, I ran. Suffering wooden feet, I ran. Losing faith, I still ran.

It was easy. I couldn't do anything else.

A woman passed me. She had a crooked left leg. It bowed outward at her knee. I guess she knew it. To compensate, she ran leaning to the side. Her short hair ran in matted spikes down her neck. She had no coat to protect her from the wind, the cold, the rain. She faced it like the runner I am not. And she ran faster than I could.

But her race is not my race, and her truth is not my truth. Whatever happens to her is as singular and as lonely as whatever happens to me. We share the cold, and the hard miles. And, together, we are ever separate.

Marathon fans can be counted on. They came out to watch, huddling under umbrellas and storefront shelters.

Going Down Slow

"Animo, animo!" they shouted.

A man with slicked-back hair and horn-rimmed glasses stood puffing a cigarette under a kiosk. I hopped up on the curb and ran by him. He looked at an apparition in flapping plastic. Our eyes met.

"Vamos!" he said.

The encouragement helped fight back the cruel weather for a few strides. Which is the way one runs a marathon — one little piece at a time. An observer might imagine a smooth continuum of passion. It's not. Instead, one stitches together many patches and pieces along the way, finally unfolding a forty-two-kilometer pattern of random color previously hidden and hardly imaginable, like a Jackson Pollock painting.

Strange, what one remembers of the scenery. It is racing, after all, not sightseeing. The course crossed four bridges spanning Rio Guadalquivir. Two are modernistic and the most unusual I've seen. Having once designed bridges for a living, you'd think I would have noted each one.

But I can clearly remember crossing only one of those, the last one, Puente de la Barqueta. I remember it only because it was close to the finish line and because of a thought I had at the time: *I need to remember this.* From a high arch overhead, stay cables stretch down to the deck median.

The first one, Puente del Alamillo, I recall admiring from the car but not from the race. Parallel cables slant down to the floor median from a single massive column on the west bank. The column soars high and leans

Going Down Slow

precariously away from the river, as if falling over backwards. The column's weight pulls up on the bridge floor, putting those two great masses in exquisite balance, tugging at each other in a tensile standoff engineers call equilibrium and poets call a miracle. The taunt cables look like giant strings to pluck. The bridge resembles a harp meant for God.

Twenty-four kilometers into the race the crooked-legged woman quit. She was standing in the rain talking to a volunteer, a tall man. He was pointing down the street to a waiting ambulance.

The sound of wailing sirens spread over the city and joined the race.

Oh, the weather played a joke all right. The day after the marathon the local paper, *ABC*, featured a photograph of Constantina covered by snow. That town, just one marathon distance northeast of Seville, had not seen snow in twenty years, the paper said. So unusual was the storm, *ABC* devoted space on six pages to it. Such rare weather coupled with such rare timing, presents irony to wonder about.

At the Maratón, the material falling on Seville had been not snow but rain with a temperature of 4 degrees C and blowing wind.

The day before the race the weather had been sunny and pleasant, betraying no clue. We had sat outside having coffee on Paseo Colón. Albino, Rafael, María José, their sister, Virginia, Rafael's wife, Angel, a Madrid marathoner, and I sat at a table overlooking the river. Townspeople and

Going Down Slow

tourists alike strolled along the river walk. Albino said he could spot a tourist at a glance. I wanted to not look like one. I knew a few words of Spanish. I told María José her dress was pretty.

So the day before the marathon we sat in the sun relaxing on the street named after Columbus, at the place where exploration of the New World had its beginning. Before us stood Torro del Oro, the tower of gold, the building where Spanish ships off-loaded gold stolen from the Americas and the Indies. Some of it they mined, Albino reminded me. Behind me stood Plaza de Toros, where I like to imagine Hemingway hatched "The Undefeated," a bullfighting story I've read and reread.

Time marched away that sunny day. Albino, Angel and I took a walk around the Cathedral of Seville, the world's largest Gothic cathedral, which dates back to the 1100s. The Christians recaptured Seville and built the Cathedral on the foundation of a mosque begun by the Muslims. Columbus' tomb is inside. One of the double doors was open. It was massive, as wide as a man is tall and twice as high, made of bronze, it appeared. I laid the back of my hand on the edge to gauge its thickness: six and a half inches. Stone saints, cast in relief, high on the wall guard the doors.

We strolled through the castle Real Alcázar and among its gardens. A giant tree spread its crown over us, its trunk thicker than a truck; Albino said it was a ficus tree. We had drinks at a sidewalk cafe where I saw the only SUV I can recall seeing in Seville. Then we drifted past the Cathedral back toward the car.

Going Down Slow

Next day, after some thirty-six kilometers, the marathon returned me to the Cathedral. My circumstances had changed. The wind and rain focused their attack where defense was weakest, my hands and feet. Their pain shriveled my spirit.

What about pain, I wondered? When it comes, where do you hide? When the race wearies your flesh and time grinds and erosion sets in, what then? Can you hold onto your dream?

Questions come: How much farther, what time, why, and so on. But question words are no help. A good runner stays in the moment. Right here. Right now. And knows there's nothing else. A good runner accepts the ache with placid resignation, examines it with professional interest, dwells in the "now" like a Buddhist, avoiding thoughts of the end.

But I am not so brave or wise. Patch after marathon patch, I stitched with nothing but yearning for the end, faith and hope meanwhile slipping away.

I glanced up at the soaring Cathedral. Men worked, and died, on it knowing they would never see it finished. But they had faith it would. Banal lyrics from a Latin rock band ran through my head:

Dáme fe, dáme alas, dáme fuerza
Para sobrevivir en este mundo

Imploring words from Maná asking for faith, for wings, for strength to survive in this world. Thus slopping along the wet pavement I came as close to prayer as I

Going Down Slow

would come—and thereby stitched in yet another tiny patch of the marathon, like a seamstress bent at her work.

Hoping for it or not, the end does, in some manner or the other, eventually come. And so I ran across Puente de la Barqueta, the fourth and final bridge, the only one I can remember—remembering it only because I knew that I must. After the last turn, straight ahead a tunnel gaped open to the stadium where the finish line waited. I decided to shed the plastic bag that had sheltered me the entire way. I reached a frozen claw up to the neck hole and ripped it wide. When I flung the wadded bundle off, the wind drifted it to the side like a weary soul.

Then inside—and it was over.

Someone wrapped a towel around my shoulders. Who? I strode past a tent where I could have gotten help for hypothermia, across the field to the tunnel under the stands on the far side. Someone hung a finisher's medal around my neck. The towel, already wet, draped over the medal.

At least the tunnel was dry of the rain, but a cold wind was blowing through. I drifted around in a growing crowd looking for a place to get warm, a place I couldn't find. I went into a locker room, but it was crowded, and it stunk.

At a table in the tunnel people were picking up their warm-up clothes placed there by race management. But I had made no such provision, my clothes were in Rafael's car, and it was in an enormous parking lot. I wasn't sure I could find it even if I ventured into the rain searching. And I didn't have a car key anyway. Only Angel and Rafael

Going Down Slow

had a key, and I hadn't seen either since the race began. Now I wished I had not thrown away the plastic bag.

Without my clothes, I could only do what I was doing—stand and shiver, drift around and shiver. Or maybe declare an emergency and let medical workers take over repair of my hypothermic self. But language deficiency and fear of humiliation made me hesitate.

I found a wad of clear plastic lying on the floor, the kind used to protect construction supplies. I wrapped the dirty mess around my shoulders and continued as before—standing and shivering.

Suddenly in the crowd I came face to face with Albino. He had run faster and finished quicker than he expected, having recently recovered from an injury. So here he was, cold like I was. I was relieved to see him.

"Let's go get a massage," he said.

"I don't need a massage, I need to get warm."

"It's warm up there."

Ah. We hopped on the elevator and landed in a warm room.

While the massage was pleasant enough, for me, it was mainly a way of stalling in a place where it was warm. And it led to an unhappy discovery—I'd lost my marathon medal. The ribbon still hung around my neck, but the wet towel had dissolved an adhesive joint in the ribbon allowing the medal to drop off.

Back downstairs in the tunnel, we discovered we were still cold, cold to the core.

"I need to go see if they'll give me another medal," I told Albino.

Going Down Slow

The table of medals was at the far end of the tunnel; lots of people were in the way. We stood looking, shivering, deciding. We could take that long walk to where the medals were or we could go the opposite way and catch a van to the car. A warm van.

"Let's not go; I'm freezing," Albino said. I was, too.

"I'd kinda like to have a medal," I said, the idea fading to wistful hope.

"Here," Albino said. He reached out his medal to me.

"I can't take your medal, man!"

"Take it. I've got others." He'd run the race before, he said.

Our friendship may seem unlikely. Albino has half my age. We had met two years earlier, soon after he moved to Kentucky and started running races around Nashville. His job had brought him to the states.

We had made this trip to Spain as partners. He put me up in his Seville apartment gratis. He took me to his parents' house for dinner, to his brother's house for lunch, and guided me around town. Now he stood offering his finisher's medal, too. And wouldn't take no for an answer. So today in my study hangs a medal that holds special meaning.

A man who gives you his marathon medal is a friend.

This story resists ending—there is a postscript, and it starts at the expo two days before the marathon. There they had placed the age-group trophies on display. As I wandered around among the bays, Albino came up to me.

"I made a picture of your trophy," he said.

He'd set his camera on "close up" and made a picture

Going Down Slow

of the first-place trophy for "Category J", as my age group was called. For the trophy to be mine, I had to first win it, and I thought that was unlikely. I expected tough competition from the European runners.

"I don't know, man. I may not win here."

After the race, we had not gone to the awards ceremony. We were too cold. My finishing time of 3:26 was not too bad for a man who ran the whole race cowering inside a bag of polyethylene. But they don't give awards for bag wearing. I wasn't hopeful.

So I didn't know if I'd even placed in the top three until I got back to my Cookeville home. Then a check of the marathon web page showed that I'd won second place, not first as Albino had predicted. Albino called and said he'd ask his brother, there in Seville, to pick up the trophy for me.

When Rafael went to do that, they told him that my second place showing was a mistake. I had indeed won first place! Albino's prediction at the expo that day was borne out after all. Proving his prediction, I have the picture. Proving my win, I have the trophy.

15

THE EDITOR WHO WANTED ME TO WRITE STORIES

The call from Charles Denning had come before breakfast on a Thursday morning, while I was sitting in a rocking chair drinking coffee and listening to the news on public radio the way I always do when I first get up. He didn't know me then, and he had some questions about a story I'd left with the receptionist the previous day, the first piece I'd ever submitted to the *Herald-Citizen*.

"Are you a writer?" he asked.

That question hurled me into the next phase of my life like falling down a rabbit hole. He couldn't have imagined the implications it held. Nearly four decades earlier I had tried to teach myself creative writing; I'd admired that skill above all others I could think of.

But I'd finally given it up with the clear understanding that I had not been born with the knack it required. The knack for engineering, I did have—and it paid the bills. Creative writing was forgotten.

Now years later and resigned from engineering, I'd written a story about the third-annual Country Music Marathon and submitted it to the paper—one that started out as a letter to a friend and then somehow morphed into a full-length feature.

Going Down Slow

And here was the editor asking that incredible question, re-awakening all the old vain hopes. There had, in fact, been some incredulity in his voice. He told me later that he thought a writer had moved to town without his knowing it.

The question came not just from an ordinary writer but from one whose stories I had read and admired over the years, a consummate professional—and an editor, to boot.

And he mistook me for a writer! Until then, I had a successful retirement going. The question came like a hard south wind, blowing me off course, into strange new waters.

That first piece appeared as a splashy feature in the Sunday edition. Several readers called that morning to congratulate me on what they said was a good story. One left a sobbing message on the answering machine, she had been so moved by the pathos.

I soon followed that first story with others. Charles Denning continued to publish them—sometimes to my amazement. At times he allowed me more column inches than he should have. In my narratives he let me skip backwards and forward in time, as I like to do. And he even permitted me to shift to the present tense at dramatic moments. For a newspaper, I thought these were enlightened and generous editorial policies.

I didn't *always* agree with his editing. But I learned from it. The clarity of a story was paramount. It always had to be clear. Sometimes clarifying words he added came at the expense of cadence; sometimes I lost irony—irony,

Going Down Slow

itself, being a discrepancy — and sometimes I lost suspense. But no matter. The *Herald-Citizen* is a newspaper, not a literary magazine. I understood that. As a rank greenhorn, I had no room for literary pretense anyway. I was just glad to see the stories in print — a great thrill for me still.

We were talking one day — late in 2002, I think it was — when he casually suggested I write a book.

"I think you have a book in you," he said.

That gave me the courage I needed to find out. Turned out I *did* have a book in me, and that first book is lying on the desk here beside me now. I'm as proud of it as anything I've ever done. You could say he caused it; he gave me the confidence to write it, and then supported me along the way.

He made the photograph that decorates the cover of *Falling Forward*. We went down to Blackburn Fork, in Jackson County, (he would insist that I identify the county) one Sunday and he shot three rolls of film — trial shots, I thought. But when he saw the print of that particular picture he gave me a call to come look at it. The picture was so loaded with metaphors, I knew it had to be the book cover.

So here is this image that could win a photography contest. And what did he do with this valuable picture? Why he gave it to me — an act of generosity I'd be a clod not to appreciate.

Then there comes the story of how I came to be writing a personal column. He suggested the idea, of course. I gently declined. Trying to publish a book and train for the races I run was all the work an old man needs, I'd thought.

Going Down Slow

A short while after that I gave him a little piece not intended for the paper, just one I thought he'd be amused at, one I'd prepared for a small running magazine. A few days later he called me up; he wanted to publish it! The story was a remembrance of an event from thirty years earlier. I couldn't imagine how it could be printed in a newspaper. So I declined.

"I don't think I want to do that," I said. I'd be embarrassed, I thought. He didn't give up.

"But it's a *good* story!"

He said I shouldn't let naysayers stop me. Okay go ahead, I finally told him. But I still didn't know what he could possibly have in mind for that story.

On August 1, 2004, the Sunday paper arrived at my house and I found out. In the "News Features" section was a brand new column called "Up Front," and I was the author. The title "Up Front," was his, a title I like for its double meaning. He made the author's picture that appeared at the top, too, on the same day he made the cover shot.

So whether I wanted it or not, I got the gift of a column. That's not a small thing. Some writers would rob and steal for such a space.

On the Sunday that my readers read my tribute to him, Charles was already two days gone from the *Herald-Citizen*. After forty years. Gone. Retired. What was lost?

An "institution" was lost. He was embarrassed by the word, of course. He once told me he'd had the word hung on him — by his son Ryan, for one, a man Charles mentions frequently. "Dad, you're an institution," his son had said.

Going Down Slow

Whenever I find cheap sentimentality in one of my stories, I kill it like a snake in the hen house. So the next sentence is not sentimentality; it is, in fact, a fact:

Charles, you changed my life.

I've come to learn in life that I'll be unable to thank some people, that my words are weak and not up to the job. But that's the best I have, and so I wish for more and say the word my momma taught me to say. In my rambling way that's what I'm trying to do in this book now, say the word:

Thanks.

Charles, I hope you catch the Willie Nelson syndrome. Once, when his career was on the skids, he said he thought he had a great future behind him. That paradox turned out to be wrong — his career suddenly exploded. So there's a great future ahead. The fun is in looking for it.

When I set out to write *Falling Forward*, the book you encouraged, I took as preparation the job of reading several running books. Most were pretty boring. But I found one that I treasure, *Meditations from the Breakdown Lane* by James Shapiro, published in 1983. The book is an account of his transcontinental run across the United States, from California to New York's Central Park.

The journey was an extraordinary achievement, amazing even. But Shapiro didn't write about it as amazing; he wrote about the daily struggle of running some fifty miles, about the people he met, about the places he passed through, about his thoughts along the way. He wrote about life — the kind of writing you like.

I have here a second-hand copy of the book. Shapiro

Going Down Slow

penned some words in the front of it to the man who first bought it.

Charles, I'm going to steal those words like a petty thief and hand them over to you like hot property:

"Keep on going, gently, strong, straight ahead."

16

THE MOMENT OF INERTIA

She sings to me. In the quiet moments, a seductive song of speed hums through her slender frame, pleading, *Can we go? Let's go!* I know her. It's a promise of speed, but a promise of pain, too, one coursing through her from the ground to the wind brushing my skin. She is the medium.

It is interval day and we are going to go fast.

Once again my ride and I go rolling up Jennings Creek Road, through Whitleyville, Tennessee, the little hamlet of six houses, a post office, an abandoned store, an historic bank and the Church of Christ. The volunteer fire department occupies the building where long ago the grade school was. That was before the two-room country schools consolidated with those in Gainesboro, the seat of Jackson County.

Our road is a two-lane blacktop. It is narrow. In places there is no shoulder at all. Where there is one, it's covered by fescue and weeds that haven't been mowed all summer long, and it is August now. Occasionally, the very pavement edge has broken off to the white line and dropped into a rock-strewn creek bed. No second chance there. Oblivion begins at the fog line.

But I love it that way. The road lays easy on the land. It

Going Down Slow

winds along the foot of the steep hills on my right, skirting the narrow creek bottoms on the left, barely disturbing either one. In this valley where they'll spread my ashes, the road knows its place.

My little steed does what I ask. When I press the pedals, I can feel her surge. Aluminum joy fills her quick heart. But she demands attention. Neglect her and she will kill you. Send you flying over the edge with cold-hearted nonchalance. I know that; we both do.

She can turn away with shocking quickness, responding to the slightest weight shift. So I am careful when I reach for a water bottle or an energy bar. Why does she veer off so quickly? It is inherent in her thoroughbred design.

Physics lesson: Spinning wheels act like gyros to help stabilize a bike. A gyro wants to keep spinning in the same plane, requiring a force to turn it aside. Its stabilizing ability is higher if a quantity engineers call the "mass moment of inertia" is higher. The inertia of my bike's wheels is lesser because their diameter is smaller, 650 millimeter instead of the standard 700. That seems a small difference, until you consider the math. The inertia depends on the *square* of the distance from the axle to where most of the mass resides, in the rim and tire. Moreover, that mass itself is a linear function of the radius. So, altogether, the moment of inertia varies as the *cube* of the wheel's radius. That cubic dependence magnifies the size difference and cuts back the stabilizing effect of my smaller wheels by maybe twenty percent.

Other aggravating factors pitch in: the light

Going Down Slow

aluminum frame, the shorter wheelbase and the steeper head angle found on triathlon bikes. And then there I am, the awkward rider, laid out on the aerobars, sticking out over the front wheel like a cantilevered gargoyle.

All tends toward instability. It makes for a tense ride, jerky as a squirrel. But that's okay; I've grown used to that.

Now I'm just warming up, rolling along easy, holding the main bars. Behind me I hear this summer's bane coming up, trucks hauling crushed rock. The view ahead is open and the trucks—five small ones this time—swing wide, giving me plenty of room. Usually there's very little traffic on this road, but this summer, trucks hauling gravel to a road job up in Macon County have been passing through here. I'm a pesky gnat to them and, if swatted, would hardly make a bump. But they've shared the road well. I'm glad for that.

The plan is to warm up for ten minutes, grabbing a drink at the last moment. Then the world changes. We will go hard for two minutes, followed by one minute of easy recovery—and then repeat that until we have done ten such intervals. It promises to be hard, and maybe even fast. But one should not expect more than hard.

That's the plan. But who needs ten minutes? At nine minutes I'm approaching my favorite curve and so I change the plan. I grab a drink, get down in the aerobars and watch my computer, waiting for 0:09:00 to flash.

I know what waits around the curve. The view opens to a wide creek bottom that stretches out a mile. The road makes a long sweeping arch around it, hugging the hills. The field's far end is in soybeans, this end in hay. Their

Going Down Slow

colors are different. A heaven tree hangs out over the road. Just past it, mile marker twenty once stood. Bush hog got it. A little farther on and I'll see the red barn where North Fork crosses and mile marker twenty-one still does stand. A mile of road lies ahead in languid repose, measured, marked, and in full view. I like that mile.

Nine minutes flash up, and it's throttle to the firewall. I lean into the curve, dropping low, cranking hard. On the inside the pavement widens a bit past the white border. I cross that dangerous line and hit a sweet groove. Ragweed and Johnson grass swipe past my knee. I crank hard through the curve and roll out in the open on the other side, still pushing.

My heart monitor, slow to rise at first, has zoomed past the aerobic threshold, into numbers I should not allow. But I don't care. Speed is a drug and I'm on a good trip. Let it ride.

I hear the rattle of the big diesel downshifting as it comes up behind me. It slows to an idle. I'm in his way. Without a mirror, without even a backward glance, I know this is one of the big trucks, the kind with three dual wheels on each side. The diesel picks up the cadence again. The way it labors tells me this truck is loaded. He's coming around.

My two minutes are not yet up and I keep cranking hard. The truck lumbers apace just a hoe handle away, the stack blowing black. I glance over as the ponderous wheels grind by, each turning with deliberate certainty. I can almost count the lug nuts. The tires sag under their overburden. Twenty tons of rock press down like death.

Going Down Slow

The two-minute interval expires as the truck pulls away. A scream races after it, tearing the valley's space in a drawn out shriek, racing up the wooded slopes, rushing over the hay field and creek alike to the hollows and hills beyond. The shocking sound morphs into a raw, guttural cry like that of human anguish.

It is my scream. And I know this is going to be a good ride.

17

IRON BILL, MEET QUEEN MAEVE

Thirty miles into the 112-mile bicycle ride at Ironman Wisconsin a badger lay on the shoulder. Victim of a traffic mishap. He looked like I felt. The ominous outcome foretold by the dismal sight led to the most poignant moment I've witnessed in endurance racing. Not my failure—although fail I did—but that of another.

You must have water. You won't get very far without it, especially when the temperature soars into the 90s, as it did that day. The boring old story: hydration.

Leg cramps worried me. They had plagued me throughout my swim training, and by race time I wasn't sure I'd ever solved the problem. I was worried: The night before the race I'd bought a salt shaker so that I could eat salt. A waste, probably. Potassium would've been a better bet. You worry. And do what you can.

In the pre-dawn on race morning we milled about on the fourth level of the Menona Convention Center, a building designed by Frank Lloyd Wright. Our bicycles were waiting there on the fourth level. We had to check in, and make sure the tires were pumped, the water bottles full.

"It's too early," I told the volunteer.

Going Down Slow

"Yeah, it's gonna be a long day."

"Before it's over we'll all be singing 'On Wisconsin,'" I said, and he laughed.

I walked around some more. I'd drunk a bottle of water on the walk over from the hotel, but I wanted another bottle just before the swim—leg cramps in the swim are scary. A young woman with dark eyes and dark hair, long plait running down her back, walked beside me. She looked at me in my racing pants.

"I wish my parents were racing, like you," she said. Parents? She was kind; I was old enough to be her grandparent—old enough but still in the game, going down slow. The unexpected comment by someone I'd not seen until then left me wondering what to say. I just smiled.

To get from the fourth level to lakeside you walk around-and-around down a helical ramp. There is one at each end of the building. After the swim we'd run up one helix to get to our bikes, and then ride out down the other one.

Soon I was going to file down the east helix, and put on my wet suit. But first, where was that second bottle of water I was going to drink just before the swim start? There will be water down there, a volunteer told me.

That turned out to be no help. Two thousand triathletes filed down that helix, creating a crowd at the bottom, inside a fenced area that only opened to the lake. If there was a water station there I couldn't see it, let alone get to it.

Spectators pushed up against the other side of the

Going Down Slow

fence, trying for a view of their athlete. Some of them nearby watched me pick up a half-full bottle of Gatorade sitting on the pavement, watched me drink it down like a homeless man. On a face I saw disgust and fascination.

"I need a drink," I said to her.

And I still did. Soon the sun would rise across Lake Minona, soon we'd be swimming. So I found another bottle, half full of water, used a little to wash my goggles, and drank the rest. Now my preparations were finished.

It was a deep-water start; you first swim out to where the course begins, a rectangle. Once started, you swim around the rectangle twice—if you can.

Bobbing there in the water, waiting, I checked on the sun, and found a salmon disk burning through low haze. I pointed it out to another swimmer. We agreed: It was pretty. It was the last beauty either of us was likely to notice for a while.

The swim was no good—exactly what I had expected happened, only quicker than I'd expected. Just half a mile into the swim, my legs began to pull and draw in that tiresome old way, and I knew what was coming. Before a mile, before a complete lap, full-scale cramps hit. A kayaker threw me a cushion to hang onto. I massaged my legs and then headed out again, trying not to kick at all.

Didn't work. By the time I made the full lap, back to the starting place, hard cramps hit again. A kayaker yelled for me to hold onto his boat. But I couldn't get to it. I'd lost so much time, the fast swimmers were coming through on their second lap, cutting me off. It was like trying to cross a lane of sharks with disabled legs.

Going Down Slow

When I finally managed to reach his boat, I held onto the nose and asked if he had any water on board. It happened he did have a bottle and I was welcome to it. But then twisting his face, he had to tell me something hard: I'd be disqualified if I took it. So I soldiered on dragging cramped legs another mile. So ravaged were they that when I finally made it out of the water, they buckled and I fell down on the way to the bike. I should have stayed there.

Six hours later: I drop the bike in the grass and plop down beside it. My race is done, twenty miles short of the finish line. It's an easy call. My feet won't press the pedals. Muscle cramps seize both legs—from top to bottom—whenever I try.

After two hilly loops here in the country—some ninety-two miles—the stretch back into town is mostly downhill and downwind. Doesn't matter. It's over. I'll not ride those twenty miles. Or run the marathon that lies beyond them.

I sit facing west, my back turned to the road, to the race, to Madison, the place where I was headed, the place where 2,076 triathletes started this day with a 2.4 mile swim in Lake Monona.

Behind me now, Ironman Wisconsin rages.

Before me a grassy lawn falls away to a swale and rises in the distance to a new two-story brick-and-vinyl house, a domestic scene. Scattered trees shade the grass, inviting the exhausted traveler to stop on this hot day.

Another resigned Ironman sits in the grass a dozen

Going Down Slow

feet in front of me, his back to me, to Madison. The man sits with his knees drawn up to his chest, unable to straighten his legs. Cramps got them. Unlike his, my legs stopped cramping when I stopped pedaling.

I sit quietly, looking on. The man is even older than I am—and more severely dehydrated, too. They've called an ambulance.

A tan young woman with a blond ponytail massages the man's legs, trying to ease his cramps. Her job is to rescue stricken bicyclists—her minivan sits on the shoulder. The man, sitting in a stupor, seems to scarcely notice. Despite the woman's youthful charm, he sits staring vaguely across the lawn, occasionally grunting an answer.

The homeowner and his adolescent son have brought water helpfully. They stand looking on with an air of pity and concern, like someone watching a dog die, amazed that a man can push himself past life's ordinary limits.

But this is no ordinary man. His broad back expresses a sense of power, and you can guess he's not a man easily brought down, by heat, wind or hills, all of which have converged on today's race.

The man is Bill Albrecht of Marquette, Michigan. He was seventy-six, a veteran of twenty-five Ironman races. He will tell me these things before he leaves.

Soon a white ambulance arrives. Two young men in their white uniforms very officially walk over and stand around waiting to see what's needed. The moment comes to do something, either carry the patient or let him walk, if he can, to the waiting ambulance.

In all Ironman races, time limits are enforced for

Going Down Slow

finishing the swim, the bike, and the overall race. The inevitable slowing associated with aging eventually insures that, even though still capable of comfortably going the distance, one can't complete all three events within the seventeen-hour-hour time limit.

Bill Bell, an Ironman hero of legendary endurance and determination, is an example. At Ironman Florida when he was seventy-eight, he failed to finish. Today, as Bill Albrecht and I sit in the grass, no eighty-year old man has ever finished an Ironman race. That day will come a month later, at Ironman Hawaii, following twenty-six years since the first Ironman.

Today, Bill's race ends in a whimper rather than screaming success, as does mine. That much is clear. But for Bill, his age pushing the limit, today's failure raises a troubling question, one an aging Ironman, for all his toughness, resists asking:

Can I ever finish another one?

Bill knows the limit is out there. He didn't complete twenty-five Ironman races without learning it. But he's not going to ask that stark question, being more circumspect. He would avoid uttering anything evoking pity—he's an Ironman, and proud.

The question hides in his next statement, maybe unseen even by him. The men in white wait, the ambulance waits. He has to go to it, upright or otherwise. He gathers himself, preparing to stand on ravaged legs. And then he says the poignant words I can't forget:

"I guess my time has come."

The woman helps him. He rises stiffly, turns slowly

Going Down Slow

and sees me, another failure, one eleven years his junior. Maybe that makes him feel better. Before walking on, he steadies himself, and we chat a bit. I recall they'd introduced him to all the athletes at the pre-race dinner the previous night.

"You're a legend," I say, slapping him on the shoulder. And then, "Good luck."

The words sound puny and hollow, but I can't summon better ones. He heads to the ambulance, a man on each side steadying his steps.

The young woman is called Maeve, and now it's my turn—and she is very pretty. But I don't need a massage. All I need is a lift in her van. I want to get away from this race. She opens the back of the minivan and invites me to load up. My bike is slimy with snot, GU, Gatorade and grease, while her van looks new and clean.

"I don't know, Maeve…I don't want to trash your van."

"It's rented. Trash it."

She doesn't pussyfoot around.

Since he had to leave in the ambulance, Bill has left his bike for Maeve to haul. It's a bright yellow job. The color is striking because of the contrasting color of an accidental decoration. An unwrapped energy bar, brown and ugly, is glued along the top bar. Why? I wonder. Was Bill preparing to eat it when he hit a hill where he had to get out of the saddle and use both hands? There were a lot of hills like that. Maybe in a rush he stuck it there. Now, drooping from the heat, road vibrations have welded it tight to the bar. The vulgar material sits there like human stool patted flat.

Going Down Slow

We head out. As she drives, I ask Maeve about her curious name.

"Is that a family name?"

"Actually, it's the name of an ancient Irish queen."

It must take a moment of wild hubris for a couple to name their baby girl Maeve. The ancient Maeve, the queen of legend, was of such beauty she made men sick with desire. A courageous and successful warrior, she assured the loyalty and devotion of her army by granting sexual favors to those soldiers most distinguished by their courage in battle.

So the name Maeve must be a heavy load to carry. But my driver, rises to the task, at least in the aspects of courage, strength and looks. She has just ridden her bike across the U.S.A., she tells me, west to east, from Washington State.

"I felt myself getting stronger along the way," she says.

I'm anxious to get back to Madison, but Maeve gets a call about another stricken athlete. It's a woman, and we soon find her standing beside her bike, nursing leg cramps, like so many others today.

Before the day is through, 398 athletes will drop out, nineteen percent of the total, the highest failure rate of any Ironman race ever held.

In doing two loops, bicyclists rode twice through a small, strung-out town. I never learned its name. That's no loss. But that town is where Maeve now takes the exhausted woman to meet her son. It also is where school buses are waiting to transport failures like me back to Madison.

After dropping off the woman, Maeve drives around

Going Down Slow

looking for the buses, but we can't find them. Finally, someone on the cell phone tells her the buses are parked behind the cemetery. We then start looking for a cemetery.

A cemetery is hard to hide, and we locate it soon enough. As claimed, two yellow school buses sit parked on the street behind it. It's not clear how to get there. That doesn't bother Maeve. She points the van into the cemetery, first on a gravel path. After it plays out, she continues on the grass past the tombstones into an open field, makes a sweeping right turn and jumps the curb back into the street in front of the buses. I just hang on.

"Maeve, you're gonna get arrested! But I like your style."

Like a brave queen, she rode her bike across the country. Trifles don't worry her.

The bus driver heads his big machine toward Madison—total load: me and two bicycles. As he drives, I stand in the stairway and make conversation, passing the time.

He has two boys, twenty-something and thirty-something. He retired from his job with the U.S. Postal Service in Arizona, divorced his first wife and got a younger one. Her family lives nearby. So that she could be near kinfolks, he and his new wife moved from Arizona to here. He likes his life in Madison, Wisconsin.

18

IN MY FATHER'S GARDEN

Mildred Garret is an artist who poured her grief into a painting for her father.

I stopped at the Cane Creek Recreation Center where she works during a routine training run on a winter day. The Center is a normal pit stop on one of my twelve-mile routes. I stop my chronograph, go inside, fill up my bottle, and use the bathroom. If I see Mildred around, we have a little chat. I look forward to it. This run was on a Saturday, when she normally doesn't work. But she was standing outside an aerobics room where they were starting a new jazz dance class.

I'd recently seen Mildred's painting hanging in a local art gallery. I didn't know anything about it. So I asked her,

"Did you sell your painting yet?"

"It's not for sale. It's my father's."

Her father had recently died, and she told me about what a natural he was at growing a garden, at nurturing plants.

"My daddy could drop a seed and it would grow. I can't do that," she said.

The comment grabbed me, and on the run home, I kept thinking about it. I wished I'd found out more about her dad. I called her up a few days later and we met at the gallery. We made some pictures and talked.

Going Down Slow

She calls her painting "In My Father's Garden." Art lovers have made inquires about purchasing the piece, but it's not for sale. She painted it for her father. Growing up she loved her father very much and followed him around in his garden.

"I was a daddy's girl. Some girls are a momma's girl, but I was always a daddy's girl," she said.

Before he retired, Isaac Peake Carver was a chef who had worked for various restaurants around town, including Nick's, a white tablecloth place. Mildred said he'd retired some eight years earlier, but he'd only "supposedly retired." Because he then went to work doing what he loved, working in his gardens and holding barbecue cookouts for family and friends. In his gardens he raised vegetables and flowers, both, and shared them with friends and family.

As Program Coordinator for the Cookeville Department of Leisure Services, Mildred's office was in City Hall then. Isaac Carver made sure the women around that City Hall Office had freshly-cut flowers. The man they fondly called Ike, "...would bring flowers to all the women," she told me. Roses were his favorite.

Isaac suffered a brain aneurysm at home alone on a Thursday in August of 2003. His wife of fifty-seven years, Nina, had been away from the house that morning. She returned at 2:00 o'clock to find Isaac lying lifeless in the bedroom floor and called the ambulance. The paramedics managed to revive his heartbeat. Following family wishes, doctors kept him on life support. Without ever regaining consciousness he died two days later, on Saturday August 23, 2003.

Going Down Slow

It was his 80th birthday.

Isaac had been planning a big family cookout for that weekend. Mildred has two sisters and two brothers. The sister from Michigan was expected in for the celebration. Isaac's sudden death came as a terrible shock. Practically speaking, he'd died suddenly, on that Thursday when Mildred's mother found him.

No one got to say goodbye.

Mildred was devastated. She was accustomed to seeing her father daily. He was raising two gardens that summer, one at her house and one at his place a few blocks away. "I could look out my kitchen window and see the vegetables in the garden," she says. He was raising potatoes, cabbage, okra, onions…. "The next summer, the hardest part was looking out my window and the garden wasn't there," she recalled, her eyes watering.

Mildred told me all about her father's kind heart and sense of humor. She had seen him on that Thursday morning, as she usually did "If it was too hot I'd tell him he shouldn't be working. He'd probably say something like, 'You're not my mother!'" His death made Mildred realize, "Just because you see somebody in the morning you can't take it for granted you'll see them again."

Since he was a chef he took food seriously and frequently bought supplies in large quantities. Then he'd end up sharing that food with people. He once bought a whole case of pink salmon, Mildred remembered. She figured he'd eventually bring her a can too. After a long time passed and he had not brought even one, Mildred, curious and wondering why, asked him about

Going Down Slow

it. She discovered he'd fed the salmon to stray cats in the neighbor, distressed to see them go hungry.

After his death, Mildred wanted somehow to give her father a flower garden, to make a gift, to honor him. But lacking his talent for nurturing plants in the garden's soil, she didn't know how she could.

One night about a week after his death, she couldn't sleep. She got up at three in the morning and started painting. She continued day after day, painting whenever she could find the time. Sometimes that was 11:00 o'clock at night, other times 3:00 o'clock in the morning.

She spread bright acrylic colors across a two-foot by three-foot canvas, altogether working for two months. In the process she struggled, unhappy with the result. "I couldn't get where I wanted to be with just paint," she says. Then she noticed some wall joint compound sitting nearby, the material commonly called "mud" and used to finish sheet-rock walls.

"I wondered what would happen if I use wall compound," she says. "Paper was the first thing I tried. I molded the papers and wall compound on the canvas. I was experimenting. I didn't know if I could get the effect I wanted or not, and after a while I liked what I was seeing..." Encouraged, she continued. In addition to crumpled newspapers and wall compound, she molded in household paint, fingernail polish, recycled grocery bags, fabric and rocks—a bizarre range of mixed media.

She wanted to transcend canvas, painting, mere art—she wanted to make her father a garden! The beauty, the richness of the flowers she'd seen him harvest—that

Going Down Slow

was what she was after. Consciously or not, in seeking transcendence, she ironically sought out banal objects, even rocks.

By nurturing his flowers, Isaac had coaxed beauty from the dirt we walk on. In honoring him, his daughter likewise wrought beauty from the commonplace items of everyday life, constructing at once a suitable tribute to her father and a stirring triumph of the human heart.

Though unexpected, the materials of the painting could be no more surprising than what hit the family when they looked through the papers and records Isaac left behind. He'd innocently kept a secret they'd never suspected. He was a veteran of World War Two—that much they knew. Other things, they didn't know.

In service to his country, he'd earned four medals, his papers showed, medals that had never been presented to him. Isaac had never mentioned the awards. The family never knew he'd served with such distinction.

With proof in hand and with the help of the local veterans, Mildred contacted the Veterans Administration about getting his medals. Too late for Isaac but not for his family, the medals duly arrived. To his family, Isaac had always been a hero. Now his country acknowledged it as well.

Mildred was keeping the medals, along with the flag from Isaac's military funeral, safe for Nina. Soon, Nina would celebrate her 80th birthday, the same milestone Isaac had been looking forward to. Mildred's daughter is also called Nina. She, too, can gaze at those medals and feel justifiably proud of her granddaddy. So can her children,

Going Down Slow

the same on through the generations.

I run past the Recreation Center, I guess, a hundred times a year. Now it reminds me of this story, this memory. How unlikely it was that I ran into Mildred that Saturday. Unlikely, too, that the conversation turned to her father — and that I actually followed up with a call. I wonder that I did that. How unlikely it all was. I surely run past dozens of stories each week, failing to note the tenuous connection, the off-hand remark that leads to another life.

To note those remarks, you must first engage people. Running leads me to do that more than I otherwise would. I'm not selling running, but that fact is true.

I never met Mildred's dad; I wish I had. After this story I felt like I'd always known him. I would've liked him.

While we talked about her painting that day, Mildred gently touched the swirling-colored hills and vales that stand out in relief on the painting's surface and recalled loving stories about her daddy. The painting seems to bring him a little closer to her.

She likes to share her creation. But no one needs bother making an offer. The painting is not for sale. It's her father's garden.

PATHOS

19

I COULD SEE THE MIDNIGHT SUN

Mancha Creek would be a river in most places. Here, it's lucky to have a name. Most of the streams and mountains do not.

Mancha Creek lies in the most remote part of the Arctic National Wildlife Refuge, next to Canada, on the eastern edge of the sprawling wilderness. It drains into the Firth River in Canada, which, in turn, drains into the Arctic Ocean seventy-five miles north of us.

In two flights of three passengers each, bush pilot Kirk Sweetsir had delivered six of us here in his Cessna 185. It was on the sixth of June. He took off and headed west. I watched the plane grow small against distant, blue mountains. He was the last human we would see until he came to pick us up twelve days later and fifty miles to the north, on Joe Creek.

The Arctic Refuge has been called the last great wilderness of North America and one of the greatest wildernesses in the world. Lying north of the Arctic Circle, its abundant wildlife, rugged terrain and expansive solitude are unmarred by modern man, and among one of the last places visited by him. Measuring nearly twenty million acres—the size of South Carolina—it spreads

Going Down Slow

south from the Arctic Ocean for 250 miles, and lies against Alaska's border with Canada. The plants and animals live here in relationship to the weather and terrain as they have for thousands of years.

The unmarred part is important. There are no roads, fences, or power lines. No motorized vehicles are permitted — except for fixed-wing bush planes, which must land on a gravel bar or on the tundra. (An exception is that the native people are permitted to carry out traditional hunting.) All the stuff we've become accustomed to seeing is absent here. You stand on a mountain and see ranges of mountains spreading before you in every direction over thousands of square miles, all doing just fine without the aid of a single blinking strobe light.

"Unmarred" is important, one reason for our trip. My topo map covers an area of 5,000 square miles. It shows only one man-made feature — a cabin on Mancha Creek. It's not there anymore — U. S. Fish and Wildlife Service (USFWS) burned it. But the debris remained.

Our leader, Don Ross, who was sixty-three, knew about it. He was the Assistant Manager of the Refuge from 1976 to 1984, during which time a researcher used the cabin to do a bird survey. Following that, from 1985 to 2000, Don was a bush pilot, flying scientific and recreational expeditions into the Refuge. He then sold Yukon Flying Service to Kirk Sweetsir, the pilot who flew us here.

Our assistant leader, Fran Mauer, who was sixty, knew about the cabin site, too. Over the years, he logged a passel of hours in the back seat of a Super Cub, counting caribou and moose in his capacity as Senior Wildlife Biologist.

Going Down Slow

"I spent twenty-one years working in the Arctic Refuge. I figure I had the best job in the world," he says.

Both retired from their jobs now, these two men may know more about the Refuge than any other two persons in the world. The cabin site offended them. In a trip sponsored by the Sierra Club, four of us joined them in an effort to erase the cabin. There was a husband and wife team from Illinois, a man from New Jersey, and myself.

Plane gone, we shouldered our sixty-pound packs and hiked up Mancha Creek. We were in open country containing a bit of thinning boreal forest. Scattered spruce trees grew in the flats together with thickets of low bushes, generally dwarf birch and willows less than shoulder high. The going was tough, hindered by swamps, potholes and stream crossings.

The closest landing site Kirk and Don had been able to find was five miles from the cabin, measured as the crow flies.

"How long's it gonna take?" the man from New Jersey asked.

"Oh...we'll get there before dark," Don answered. Which was true enough, since, in the summer, the sun doesn't set in the Arctic.

At late suppertime, we camped. Next morning two bull caribou, their antlers in velvet, posed for my camera. Without much stealth, I managed to approach to within forty-five yards. If I'd had my camouflage clothes and bow, I think I could've bagged one.

On the second day, we reached the cabin, a discouraging sight crouched in a dense spruce forest. A

Going Down Slow

good deal of its logs had not burned. A mangled metal roof slouched over the mess. Litter lay scattered about: Two barrels, two bear-proof boxes, a stove, four five-gallon cans, a battery, a set of dishes, a load of tin cans, and miscellaneous hand tools.

The crew went to work. We flattened all the tin cans. Don chiseled the ends out of the five-gallon cans and we flattened the cylindrical shells, to make it all compact. Some of the junk we put in burlap bags for attaching to our packs, most of the rest we bolted shut into the two barrels and the bear-proof boxes. The metal roofing we tied into bundles.

In his work at the Refuge, Fran often fielded questions from journalists. Those questions dealt with the effects of oil drilling on the wildlife. Whenever truthful answers contradicted the position of pro-drilling administrations, Fran couldn't answer freely without placing his future in jeopardy. It was a conflict that troubled him.

"You couldn't even say that, could you?" I said, realizing that he couldn't even tell them that he couldn't tell them.

"No." But he solved the dilemma.

"I referred them to Canadian biologists. They could say any damned thing they wanted to."

After all, the Refuge animals don't recognize international boundaries, and many of the animals in question migrate to and from Canada, especially the moose and caribou. The birds nesting in the Refuge fly to virtually all continents. Fran is passionate about protecting the Refuge from oil drilling—for its own intrinsic value,

Going Down Slow

for the animals. Retirement had not stopped him and Don from working for the Refuge.

It's a pitched fight, bringing nothing but truth and passion against lies and greed. Several times the Refuge has hung by the thinnest of threads. So far the vote has always favored preservation.

"But you can't win; they'll keep trying," I said.

"We have to win every time; they only have to win once," Fran said.

We built a big fire to burn the cabin's scrap wood. One of the five-gallon cans contained a bit of oily material, which turned out to be creosote, probably used to preserve the logs. We decided to dispose of it by burning. Fran poured a little into a pan and threw it onto the fire. A tall column of flame and black smoke roared skyward and billowed for an instant into a dark mushroom. We all whooped and yelled.

"Isn't it ironic to be burning oil in the Arctic National Wildlife Refuge," Fran exclaimed. "We've finally found oil in the Refuge!"

Next day we loaded our packs with as much metal junk as we could carry, and hiked the five-plus miles to the landing site, and then back. Our loads included all the metal roofing. My pack alone contained two big bundles of roofing plus the stovepipe and cap, a weight that felt like well over sixty pounds. We left all the junk in a pile for the bush plane to pick up later.

On that walk we mostly followed the serpentine creek bed, walking extra distance to avoid the brushy flats. That creek bed spread into an ice field a half-mile wide and a

Going Down Slow

mile long. We walked on the ice spaced out in single file so as to avoid what Fran called a "larger statistical sample" of finding a spot to fall through. Breaking through into ice-cold water wearing a heavy pack seemed a poor idea.

A two-inch layer of slush covered the ice surface. Rivulets of ice water ran in depressions across our path. My boots leaked like a sieve, continually bathing my feet in ice water. We returned to camp. Total march time—eight hours. My cold, wet toes looked like albino prunes.

We all carried bear spray, and it was on that junk-hauling hike that Fran lost his—ironically Fran, because he had the most experience working in bear habitat. He thought he'd left it in the pile of junk at the landing site. He was upset.

"How much does it cost?"

"Forty-five dollars," he answered. I told him that the pilot would find it and eventually return it.

"I'm not worried about replacement cost," he said, surprised at my thought. "I don't want to be without protection!"

He went on to explain that at USFWS they'd had two rules: Never go into the field alone—have at least two persons—and never go without a gun (And someone qualified to shoot it.). That gun was usually a pump-action shotgun loaded with slugs or buckshot, or a big-bore rifle like a .375 magnum.

Of course, we had no such weapon, that being against the policy of the Sierra Club, which was sponsoring our trip. After losing his bear spray, Fran carried the flare gun instead.

Going Down Slow

"At least you'll be able to light him up," I said.

After that discussion with the expert, I began carrying my own bear spray in a handy front pocket, instead of in my pack.

Our bear worries worsened. That morning we'd discovered that we'd set up our tents astride a bear's trail. It was marked by deeply pressed tracks we'd not noticed and by ample tuffs of hair hanging on a tree where we cooked breakfast and supper. Too tired to move our tents, we decided to sleep there one more night.

As an expert on the wildlife of the Arctic Refuge, Fran Mauer often got calls from hikers proposing a journey through this wilderness. One guy planned to traverse the Refuge on just the food he could find and wanted to know if that was possible.

"It is if you've got the stomach of a caribou," Fran had told him. Fran said he never heard of him again. Another time there was a solo hiker who had nothing to eat but a bag of Power Bars. Power Bars every day. Power Bars for breakfast, Power Bars for lunch, and Power Bars for supper.

The North Country attracts strange people with cockeyed notions. Alaskans call them "queer ducks."

Fran is a superb storyteller with a skewed sense of humor. But he'd been serious about the caribou. They have the stomach for the food they can find here, which includes lichens I would not want to eat. He showed me some lichens whose names alone are off-putting: elk horn, white worms and dead man's fingers, to list a few. Their

Going Down Slow

names are accurate.

Groups of caribou streamed past us each day, all migrating north to their ancestral calving grounds on the Arctic coastal plain, members of the 123,000-strong Porcupine herd. The cows go first and were already there, Fran said. We were seeing yearlings and bulls headed to join them. It is that coastal plain that some want to drill for oil.

There are plenty of animals here big enough to kill us and eat us—including wolves, black bears, and grizzly bears. Grizzlies, which tend to be unpredictable, especially worried us.

We walked in the season when the sun never sets; the plants and animals work overtime. We kept up a silly line of chatter, which had the benefit of telling grizzlies we were around. On another level, maybe the talk was our way of keeping company and asserting our small selves against the immensity of a wilderness that makes one feel diminished, a wilderness where humans are not needed at all.

Ethel, Glen, Fran and I were hiking along one day—the other two hikers were ahead, out of earshot. Ethel Chiang is a former emergency room doctor. Her husband, Glen Freimuth, is an anthropologist, a burly man with a white beard who looks like Ernest Hemingway. The two world gadabouts are from Illinois.

My hands and forearms were covered by lacerations I'd suffered while climbing two spruce trees to tear down a bear-proof food platform at the cabin site. Those trees are covered with sharp stubby limbs that can puncture

Going Down Slow

and tear skin. I'd put a glove on one hand for protecting the sores while deflecting brush.

"I'm doing my Michael Jackson thing this morning," I said.

"Now there's a queer duck for you," Ethel said.

"We're on the march again," I said.

Fran began singing, *Marching to Pretoria.* Then he asked Glen if Pretoria was in Illinois. They decided Peoria was in Illinois, but not Pretoria.

"Roto-Rooter," Glen said.

What?

"It's the place where Roto-Rooter is."

"Oh, is it there?" Fran replied.

"That's where it got its start." An anthropologist should know.

Fran mentioned how he'd once had his sewer line reamed out.

"Kinda like a colonoscopy," Doctor Ethel said.

Talk turned to forget-me-nots, which Fran said he'd told his Japanese wife were "forgive-me-a-lots." She hadn't believed him.

Thus we repelled grizzlies.

Accustomed to always packing a big gun, Fran was thinking about bears, especially since he'd lost his bear spray. "There's no place we can go where they can't," he said. He told me that when a man and a bear suddenly meet they both have the same thought: "Kill that thing!"

A grizzly had approached our camp just the previous morning. I enjoyed the whole thing—I wasn't there. I watched it from above. We were camped on a gravely

Going Down Slow

flat next to Mancha Creek. Across the creek an unnamed mountain rose up steeply. Its slope was covered by spires sticking up like crocodile teeth.

Bill Curzie, who patrols second base in age group World Series baseball, christened the hill "Cathedral Mountain." "Curzie" rhymes with "Jersey" and so his baseball handle is Jersey Curzie, but I call him Jersey Bill.

Group leader Don, Glen, Ethel and I decided to climb Cathedral Mountain and check out a cave we'd spotted, curious to see if it was a bear's den. Part way up, we paused to rest. We gazed steeply down on the tents—they looked small and fragile. In the brush on the flat to the left, I saw what I at first thought was a caribou, and said so.

"That's a bear!" Don said. Easy to tell once it moved a bit. It was a golden blond grizzly. "That's a big one," Don noted. The bear meandered and then headed toward our tents on the gravel bar below.

There were two people in camp—Fran, who had lost his bear spray, and Jersey Bill, who'd been worried enough about bears to bring a shotgun, until forbidden to do so. They didn't know the big grizzly was coming. We could have yelled down. But we wanted to see what he was going to do first.

The bear came to the creek bank, ready to splash across—after which it would be 130 yards from the tents, as I later paced it. He stopped and put his nose up like a bird dog sniffing quail. Then he suddenly wheeled around and trotted off. Good bear. Bill and Fran were denied some excitement.

Fran had told me how fast a grizzly can go when it hits

Going Down Slow

full stride. "(When he charges) his back feet are scratching his ears," was the way he put it.

Fran had told me about a bear charging him once. The bear stood up thirty-five or forty yards away, looked at him, then dropped down and came fast.

"It was like everything switched into slow motion. I could see the drool or slime coming from the corners of his mouth." Fran made a motion like saliva trailing back.

"How far did he come before he stopped?" I asked.

"Stand here," he said. He took six steps forward and turned facing me.

"It was that far. I know because I dropped my notebook, and where he turned he left hair on a tree."

Fran's partner had been going for the rifle, but couldn't get it in time—they'd put it under the rain fly to keep it dry.

Death by grizzly can be quick, I expect—the animal is so big and powerful, it can tear one's head off. Fran had been within seconds of oblivion when the bear turned, an act Fran didn't expect and doesn't understand. A true scientist, Fran came back with the data: six steps, the distance from the notebook he dropped to the hair the bear left.

Fran risked his life working at the Refuge, a land he loves. He's not inclined to surrender it to oil drilling. His Gale Norton story illustrates the fight, one that continues to this day.

In 2001 after President George W. Bush appointed Gale Norton Secretary of the Interior, Frank Murkowski, then senator, later governor of Alaska, asked Interior for a

Going Down Slow

report of historical caribou calving on the coastal plain in the 1002 study area where drilling was being considered. Murkowski, a proponent of drilling, may have thought he could get a useful answer from Norton, who also favored drilling. Murkowski, who headed the Senate and Natural Resources Committee, needed to show that the plain was not important to caribou.

The U. S. Fish and Wildlife Service (USFWS), a part of the Department of Interior, was given the job of preparing the report. That agency also had the data and expertise.

"I wrote the report," Fran told me. His management reviewed it, making what Fran called "editorial corrections" and approved the report for release to Interior. That was in May 2001. The record showed that for twenty-seven of thirty years, there had been concentrations of calving (excluding lesser-important scattered calving).

In June 2001, Gale Norton visited the Arctic Refuge. Fran was given the job of escorting her about. He spent parts of two days with her, a total of five hours, explaining features of the Refuge.

"We sat on the plane facing each other. The Regional Director sat next to me nervous that I'd say something I shouldn't," Fran said. In a total of five hours with her, "She didn't ask one substantial question."

She appeared uninterested in facts that failed to support her drilling view, and later called the coastal plain "a flat, white nothing."

When Interior released the calving report, it had completely changed. It said that for eleven out of eighteen years there was *no* concentrated calving in the 1002 area — a

Going Down Slow

stunning reversal of the results submitted by USFWS, which said that for twenty-seven of thirty years there *was* concentrated calving.

Someone blew the whistle, making the original report available to the press. The *Washington Post* broke the story in October, 2001, on the very day Norton was addressing a meeting of environmental journalists. Attending reporters, armed with the *Post* story, questioned her about the discrepancies in the Interior report. Her explanation was simple: "typographical errors."

At the very least—given the nature of the changes—that answer lacked credibility. The episode supports troubling doubts about the truthfulness of the federal government, of that particular administration anyway.

On our twelve-day hike through the Refuge we encountered abundant wildlife. We hiked up Mancha Creek, which is in the eastern part—the most remote part—of the Refuge. On the sixth day we turned up an unnamed north fork of Mancha Creek and followed it until we crossed into the Joe's Creek drainage, on the eleventh day, where Kirk Sweetsir picked us up in his Cessna 185 the following day.

The animals we most frequently saw were caribou, since the Porcupine herd was following its spring migration route north to the calving grounds on the coastal plain. Caribou were plentiful each day, traveling in groups ranging from two individuals to a few dozen.

We sat eating our re-constituted freeze-dried suppers one evening. I looked up.

Going Down Slow

"I'm eating Pad Thai and gazing at caribou grazing by," I said, surprising myself with a little poetry and a lot of truth.

Caribou were indeed drifting past our camp, grazing along. And unlikely as it seems, I was eating Pad Thai, straight from its foil pouch. Each hiker carried a variety of freeze-dried dinners, including Santa Fe Chicken, Pesto Salmon, Turkey Stroganoff, Katmandu Curry, and so on. We looked forward to those dinners and gave great attention to the selection every night. Each pouch held a serving for two, and every hiker ate both servings. With all the walking, we were still losing weight.

Besides caribou, the mammal we saw most was the arctic ground squirrel, a mink-sized mammal. One morning one posed like a model. He invited me to photograph him at his breakfast, reaching high to pull down a green stem and munching earnestly. I talked to him softly and crawled close. He struck a formal pose, looking straight into the camera, standing tall and reverent like a deacon. He'd never seen a human. He knew I wasn't fat enough to be a bear.

He has to careful about bears. We saw several places where a grizzly had moved great volumes of dirt and rocks, trying to dig up a snack. In the wintertime the ground squirrel hibernates under the snow in its burrow, its body temperature falling to below 32 degrees F.

We saw a porcupine, two red foxes—one was dead—a white wolf, an impressive golden blond grizzly bear and some twenty Dall sheep, not to mention a multitude of birds. We never saw a musk oxen, although one day we

Going Down Slow

found some of its hair hanging on a bush. I put it in a plastic bag and took it with me. A few days later, I opened the bag and dropped it on the tundra. Take only pictures.

The animal we saw the most signs of, we never saw at all. That's because the moose weren't in the Refuge. They spend the summers at Old Crow Flats, in Canada, a place filled with highly nutritious lakes that produce the aquatic plants they need. Once they get fat enough they drift back to the Refuge and spend the winter. No one knew where the moose went until Fran Mauer did a study where he radio collared several and followed their movements

Their droppings, which look like elongated malt balls, were everywhere we went. We in fact carried malt balls in our packs for energy food; Don referred to them as moose turds. The great palmed antlers shed by moose littered the flats. The willows in those flats look like runty shrubs, perpetually pruned. They are—the moose bite the limbs off.

On our walk, Bill Curzie, the age group baseball player from New Jersey, showed a knack for comedy. Don, Fran and I were talking about a merganser they'd seen, and I was wondering if it was one of the ducks we see in Tennessee. We were rattling off the names:

"Hooded merganser."

"Red-headed merganser."

"Red-breasted merganser," Don corrected.

"Extravaganser," Bill deadpanned. Which ended the duck discussion.

A few nights later I had spread my freeze-dried dinners on the ground like a culinary poker hand. Everyone stood

Going Down Slow

looking down wondering which one I'd pick.

"You want to hear my Jackie Mason story?" Bill asked.

Jackie Mason is a comedian who ends every sentence with an accented word and an exclamation point. In a chance encounter, Bill talked to him in a Las Vegas hotel, mimicking the comic's delivery perfectly. He now did the dialogue, acting his and Mason's part both—both in Mason's voice.

"Are you *Jewish*!?"

"*No!*"

"You can't help *that!*"

It went on, the story of a comedian ambushed by his own shtick. Bill had us all laughing, and before the trip was over, everyone was talking like Jackie Mason.

On another occasion someone said he'd never forget something or the other. Bill, the baseball player, said, "I'll never forget my first home *run*! I'll never forget my last home *run*! It was the same *one*!"

He could also sing in a velvet baritone, and make up the lyrics on the spot. At supper one night, talk turned to lasagna, one of the dinners on our menu. Bill broke out a song: "Some enchanted evening, you may eat lasagna/ It may come upon ya, as you cross the room," and it went on.

A few nights later, Bill surprised us again, telling how he had studied at seminary to be a Roman Catholic priest. He went far enough to be given the name "Albert." But before he became "Father Albert," he quit, breaking the news to his disappointed mother on his parents' twentieth anniversary. He learned appreciation of Saint Francis of

Going Down Slow

Assisi, the patron saint of the environment.

We found our best campsite came on the eight day. It was elevated enough to offer a view east across the valley. A burbling brook of snowmelt ran through our camp from a valley behind us. Caribou continually drifted from that valley past us.

Expedition leader Don, wanted to climb a mountain across the valley that rose up 1,400 feet above us. I went with him. He had a purpose in mind. From the air, he had once seen a collapsed mountain nearby, one that sheared off and fell, filling the valley below with a jumble of rocks. From the mountaintop he was hoping to spot it. We hiked a mile on tussocks across the valley and then started up.

Half way up the mountain, Don stopped to show me a delicate bunch of flowers growing on the mostly-barren ground. Forget-me-nots, he told me, the state flower. They reminded him of his friend, Michio Hoshino, a photojournalist killed by a bear ten years earlier. Don had written a poem titled Forget-Me-Not and read it at Michio's memorial.

Standing there on the mountain, Don Ross, former fighter pilot, Vietnam veteran, bush pilot veteran of Africa and Alaska, and former Assistant Director of the Arctic National Wildlife Refuge, this world-wise man recited a poem:

Forget-me-not where the wind blows free,
Forget-me-not of the frozen sea,
Forget-me-not of a Higher Power,
Forget-me-not of love within a flower,

Going Down Slow

Forget-me-not of a past September,
All of this I remember,
Forget-me-not.

Michio Hoshino was killed by a rogue bear on Kamchatka Peninsula, August 8, 1996. *National Geographic* had featured his photos. Exhibition of his photographic collection continues around the world, Don said.

Once on top, Don and I spotted the collapsed mountain. On our next day's walk we were able to reach it.

We saw lots of birds. My two favorites were about the same size but otherwise completely different. The ptarmigan, a grouse-sized bird, spends the winters in the Arctic. It is almost totally white. One startled me in the bushes one day, flushing with a cackling laugh that fell somewhere between Woody Woodpecker and Clem Kadiddlehopper, the funniest sound I've ever heard an animal make.

The plover is beautifully decorated. Its black back is dappled with shining gold patches like you'd sling out of a paintbrush. A white band starts at its wing and snakes a graceful curve up the side of its neck and alongside its head. It migrates to Argentina.

The birds of the Arctic Refuge affect practically the whole world. They fly to all continents, including Asia and South America, and all states except Hawaii. Snow geese in the hundreds of thousands nest on the coastal plain, the place Gale Norton called a "flat white nothing" — the same snow geese hunters shoot at in Tennessee.

Going Down Slow

Birds have amazing capabilities. They do and see so much more than people. It's a wonder they have any respect for humans.

We stood overlooking the broad tundra of Joe's Creek. The wide valley opened before us. On the other side the craggy mountains of the Brooks Range rose up. Through our binoculars, we could see Dall sheep clinging to the high slopes. Fran turned to me.

"This place deserves to exist for its own inherent value, independent of people — although people can derive benefit from it. It deserves to exist for its own value."

Our last day we broke camp and prepared to walk over to where Kirk Sweetsir would pick us up, past where we'd seen a serene white wolf trot by the previous day. Don and I waited while Bill shouldered his pack — the others had already left.

"Bill, do you want to have a final ceremony and say a few words over our last campsite?" I asked.

Bill raised his arms to the heavens, a hiking staff in each hand, and Father Albert's voice came forth:

"I commend this place into the hands of Saint Francis of Assisi for his blessing and protection from oil drilling forever, amen."

Amen.

Bill and I landed in Fairbanks at 5:55 p.m., and so I reckon the pilot had said fifty-five minutes of flying time instead of thirty-five. But then I wasn't too sure when we'd left Fort Yukon. Didn't matter — we'd be late for supper.

Our little band of six had splintered. Kirk Sweetsir had

Going Down Slow

flown Don Ross, Ethel Chiang and Glen Freimuth out of our campsite, on Joe Creek, at 9:30 that Saturday morning. The last instructions leader Don Ross had given us were that if it worked out we'd get together in Fairbanks at six for dinner at the Pump House Restaurant.

Don, Ethel and husband Glen then left in the Cessna 185 for Arctic Village, where they expected to catch another plane for Fairbanks. That left assistant leader Fran Mauer, Bill Curzie and me waiting on Joe Creek for the 185's return, hanging out near the place where we saw the white wolf trotting along the previous day.

We sat on the ground and reclined against our propped- up backpacks facing in different directions so we could watch for grizzlies. Lacking a gun, something Fran had always had in his twenty-one years of working on the Refuge, we were watchful. We watched caribou from the Porcupine herd drift down the valley. Sub-adults and bulls in velvet streamed north to join the cows that had already calved on the coastal plain.

Kirk Sweetsir returned in his 185 at 2:30 and flew us to Fort Yukon where his flying service is centered, a business he bought from Don Ross. Don himself had bought the business after the founding partners were killed in separate plane crashes—hazard being a cost of doing business. En route Kirk arranged with the airborne pilot of a Cessna Caravan to pick us up in Fort Yukon.

Once in Fort Yukon, it turned out that the Caravan only had two empty seats. Bill and I took them, leaving Fran stranded in Fort Yukon. I'd regretted that. "Don't worry; that's normal up here," he'd told me.

Going Down Slow

He was a veteran of the Arctic. We'd left him there where the sun won't set, as it had not throughout our hike. For sure, Fran wouldn't reach his hometown in time for a six o'clock supper.

Now in Fairbanks, Bill and I grabbed our backpacks and went tearing across the tarmac, heading for the car he'd left there. After being in the wild for nearly two weeks, there were two things I wanted — a shower and a steak. The shower would have to wait. If we went directly, we knew we might make it to the restaurant no more than thirty minutes late. Our other three buddies might still be waiting for us.

I read the map and navigated while Bill Curzie drove. We hit the restaurant around 6:30, to discover that none of our camp mates were present. Wild Bill — as we called Bill Curzie — is not an easy man to defeat. At seventy-one — looking fifty in his dark beard — he still patrols second base in the age group World Series of baseball, playing for a team he organized and manages. Since New Jersey is his home, I call him Jersey Bill.

Jersey Bill soon called up Glen and Ethel, but they were already having supper in another restaurant, group supper plans having fallen through. We then called Don and learned that he'd already eaten at his Fairbanks home. He decided to come over and talk with us while we ate.

You can discover that if you eat nuts and dried food for two weeks, a New York Strip steak looms as the best meal in the world, a craving maybe deriving from a need for protein, like that after running a marathon. The meal your heart desires — especially if you wash it down with

Going Down Slow

Alaska Dark Ale and precede it by a garden salad, all of which I did.

It was coincidence, of course—we'd returned to Fairbanks on the Saturday before the June Solstice. I chewed steak. Don spoke.

"You ought to go see the start of the Midnight Sun Run. It's kinda fun." It happens at ten o'clock, he told us. Shortly after that Don left. Bill and I were alone again.

"You oughta just run it," Jersey Bill said.

Bill's comment seemed to plop down on my plate. I sat, head down, chewing on it like a tough gristle.

It was all just coincidence, of course. There wasn't any of it my fault. And I couldn't do a thing about it. If the weather had been rainy, the bush plane wouldn't even have shown up on Joe Creek today. We'd still be there waiting, not here dining. But things happen, and so there you are—they're having a race in Fairbanks tonight. Don didn't need to mention it, but he did.

Tough gristle—I'd just eaten a big steak with all the trappings, and drunk a beer. And I hadn't had a shower in two weeks.

Coincidence—at 8:30 p.m., ninety minutes before race time, I knew the truth. I looked at Jersey Bill. "Bill, if you'll take me by the hotel, I'll check in and put on a pair of shorts and run that race."

That was like I'd announced Christmas in June. Jersey Bill, always ready for excitement, jumped up and threw down a tip.

"All right!"

My running shorts were dirty, too. I'd worn them

Going Down Slow

under my hiking pants for days. But then I hadn't had a shower either. It all matched.

Twenty-five minutes before race time, we found the start location at the University of Alaska. There was a huge party in progress, people in costumes, balloons waving. Music was pumping, and dancing girls jazzercised on a stage improvised from a flatbed trailer. Let us celebrate the Midnight Sun!

I zipped my wallet and hotel key into the pocket of the rain jacket I'd worn on the trail. I put my glasses in the other pocket, and handed the bundle to Jersey Bill.

"You'll have to find out where the race ends and bring that jacket to me; I may get a chill after the race," I said. Jersey Bill was happy as a clam. There was purpose to life.

I jumped out to register while Bill parked. I held nothing in the world but thirty dollars, which I hoped would be enough to cover the entry fee. Lucky guess, turned out that was precisely the right amount. My wallet, in the rain jacket, held 500 dollars, my photo ID, credit card and debit card.

Without a photo ID, I don't get out of Fairbanks; I can't get back home; I can't get past airport security, I realized. And if someone gets my wallet, they can steal my identity altogether. All I had I'd entrusted to Jersey Bill, a man I'd not met two weeks before.

It was all a mad rush, darting through the crowd, trying to get ready for the start. I needed a drink but saw no water. With fifteen minutes to go I found myself standing in line for the portable potty, number 3146 pinned to my soured tee shirt. I hadn't trained in two months, during

Going Down Slow

which time I'd crammed in two hard backpacking trips, one on the Escalante River in Utah, and the present one to the Arctic. I had not run at all in a long time, or even stretched. So I stretched a bit, as I waited, all the while checking my watch as the minutes ticked by.

I turned to the woman behind me—who happened to be from Hong Kong—and asked the question no one wearing a bib number in the long history of road racing had ever asked before—because I wasn't sure about the length,

"Is this a 10K?"

"Ya," she said. She squinted hard. "Where you from?"

But she'd never heard of Tennessee.

Seven minutes to go; I got my turn at the can. After that I went running toward the street. A huge crowd was shuffling forward. A countdown was booming out over the PA system. I stopped on the walk—there was a woman watching.

"What're they doing!" I shouted.

"They're startin' the race."

"But it's only 9:55!"

"They're startin' early!"

With that a howitzer thundered. And 3,000-plus people started running.

We don't care how they do it in the lower 48.

So I jumped in the street and started running.

I've heard of people having a dry mouth—I've been thirsty myself. But this was different, maybe the results of the salty supper I'd just finished. There seemed to be a total absence of moisture. My mouth was dry as chapped lips. That'll do no harm, I hoped, and then thought, maybe

Going Down Slow

there'll be water on the course.

There was, just after the first mile, which I ran in 6:53. In my only pause, I stopped just long enough to get the drink I'd needed before the race.

It got ugly after that. The energy drained right out of my legs, and the second mile took around 7:14. Then it got worse.

I thought I might puke. That grew more likely. Then outrage set in: *That supper cost forty dollars!* The urge passed.

It was warm under the midnight sun. People had propped their garden hoses to spray in the street. That was some help. But my miles got slower. Finally, I could barely manage my marathon pace.

I wanted it over. I wanted to see the finish line wherever it was. And I wanted to see Jersey Bill.

I *did* see Jersey Bill. He was standing on the sidewalk just after mile 6, as I ran into a place called Pioneer Park. Jersey Bill was pointing his camera, saying, "You doin' good, Dallas!"

Then there was the crowd, the clock, the chute. The usual.

And it was over. My watch showed forty-five minutes and change. I'd won third place in the 60-69 age group, I found after my return to Tennessee. The official time was 45:08. Nothing to crow about. Subtract four minutes, and, on a good day, I could've run the race in the remainder — which I'd already done in setting the Tennessee record. Nothing to crow about. But it doesn't matter. I can live with it, like going down slow.

What does matter — I didn't puke, or soil my pants. Or die. Maybe I should have, for pulling such a caper.

But what can you do? It wasn't my fault. A chance

Going Down Slow

comes. Things happen. It was all coincidence, really. Don brought it up. And so there I was. You find yourself doing something dumb. It happens a lot.

Jersey Bill, good ol' Bill, solid as a rock! He had my jacket draped over his arm, just like he'd promised. When we left Pioneer Park, runners were still streaming in. We climbed a bank beside the course path. A statuesque blond ran by. Bill's eyes followed her along.

"Good form! Good form!" he cheered.

Jersey Bill knows baseball, not running, but any kind of excitement suits him.

I needed a shower. The sun shined on.

20

PORCH IS GONE

Throughout his long happy life he never once snarled, bared his teeth or raised his hackles at a human being. Despite his fierce countenance, athletic build, and warrior lineage, a gentler dog was never born.

When he died my fingernails stopped growing. When growth resumed, the interruption appeared as a shallow groove spanning each nail crosswise. Toenails, too. It took weeks for that reminder to grow out. It's been a few years now, and I still miss him. These were my thoughts that day:

Porch is gone.

The tan Shar-Pei the family had named D. J., but whom I always called Porch Patrol, is gone. It's Monday, and he had a stroke Saturday a week ago. Since then he has gradually lost his strength.

Yesterday he was very weak, and he got weaker throughout the day. He was just limp in my arms when I'd take him into the yard to try to stand. But he could not stand; his legs dangled helplessly when I'd lower him to the grass. He drank only once all day long, in the morning. With help he could still stand then, and I'd put some ice water in his bowl. He wouldn't eat anything, even Kibbles 'n Bits, his

Going Down Slow

favorite treat.

I stayed with him on the back porch last night until eleven. I'd put his bed, a carpet remnant, in the middle of the floor, and I laid him on it. I turned him from his left side to his right side occasionally and back again later. A few times he found enough strength to lift his old head. I stroked the side of his wrinkled face and put my cheek against his.

"You my little buddy, you my little buddy," I told him, my usual saying. In thanks, somehow that good dog would find the strength for a feeble tail wag.

He was breathing awfully hard, trying to get enough oxygen. I measured his respiration rate by my running watch—sixty-four breaths per minute. Yellow mucus oozed out of his eyes; I'd wipe it away with facial tissue.

I thought he'd not make it through the night. But this morning he was still laying there, his old ribs heaving with each hard breath. He'd moved a little—enough that I knew he'd tried to get up during the night. He still managed a faint tail wag when I stroked his head and spoke to him. I felt of his feet, and they'd gotten cold. Circulation to his extremities was waning—his body was shutting down.

Jo Ann and I didn't want him to suffer any more. I called the veterinarian. Dr. Thomas Holt came out. His examination confirmed what needed to be done. He filled a syringe with a pink solution of phenobarbital and shaved a place for the needle on Porch's left front leg.

"Are you ready for me to do this?" he asked.

"I am if you're ready to see me cry."

He pushed the needle in. The dog's blood pressure

Going Down Slow

was so low he couldn't pierce the vein, even after sticking the leg several times. Probing, he wagged the needle back and forth, but couldn't find blood. He decided to try for the jugular vein and stuck the needle in the dog's neck several times. That didn't work either. Finally we turned that patient dog to his left side so as to try his other leg.

"He likes laying on that side better anyway," I said.

Several more sticks, still no success. Finally, Dr. Holt said, "let's try this." We raised his head and chest to an upright position. I knelt beside his limp body and cradled his head in my hands. His tail gave the faintest of wags, little more than a few trembling jerks, but unmistakably a wag.

"Did you see that?" I said, looking up at my wife—her eyes were wet and red. She nodded; she had seen it too.

Dr. Holt pushed the needle in. I saw blood rush into the syringe.

"There it is," the vet said. He emptied the syringe into the leg. Almost at once Porch relaxed the weight of his old head into my hands, and I eased him gently to the floor.

"I'm sorry for your loss," Dr. Holt said. "I'm sorry it took so many sticks." We knew he couldn't help that.

The dog's body rests there on the back porch yet, covered with one of the towels I used during my swim training for Ironman. It's a garish rag, red, yellow and brown swirled together in an African motif. I'd rescued it from the throwaway box, and it became my favorite towel—a canine funeral shroud now.

I have to go dig a grave.

This place won't be the same without him. He leaves an empty space. The empty space will be everywhere:

Going Down Slow

on the cool concrete under my front porch chair; in his corner near the French door on the back porch; around my folding chair in front of the shop when I sit watching the sky at night and eating popcorn; in Jo Ann's garden when she waters her flowers…

Who knows how many times I've laughed because of him, how many stories I've told about him? What is the value of laughter? Of stories?

I spent more time with that gentle dog than with any human. In my day-to-day routine he was a constant presence, watching for me after my morning run, trotting across the yard to wait at the top of the driveway, my simple return being his happiest present. And on and on.

I wrote about him in 2003, in the last paragraph of my book. In equivalent human years, he was at the age of sixty-three then, as I was. Out of pure exuberance he'd run back and forth fast across the back yard each night. He was old but still strong. I imagined in his running a metaphor for mine.

He came to our back porch in May of 1994, a little pup. Twelve years and two months later he lies on that porch. He ended up where he started out.

I have to go dig his grave.

21

THE WAY ANGELA RUNS

What had happened to Angela Ivory came as a rude surprise to me. I didn't know her very well at first. We'd talked a few times at local races. Then I didn't see her for a few months. After I heard her news, I invited her up to my Cookeville home so we could make pictures and talk about a story.

By then she had run over a hundred combined marathons and ultramarathons. That list included a marathon in each of the fifty states plus D.C., a saga that required what seemed to me a staggering amount of travel.

She lived alone in Nashville, but grew up in Memphis. Prior to her marathon saga she had been west of the Mississippi River only twice, to visit an aunt in West Memphis Arkansas, she told me.

She spent an afternoon in Cookeville, answering my questions and posing for pictures. Then she and Jo Ann and I went out for dinner. An astonishing saga emerged. As impressive as her list of races was, it barely began to tell her story.

She'd started out by dabbling—two marathons in 2001, two in 2002, one in 2003. Then things went crazy. In 2004 she began running either a marathon or an

Going Down Slow

ultramarathon every weekend, traveling wherever she had to, to wherever there was a race, crisscrossing the country time and again. When I asked her about the travel, she only said,

"Yeah, it's hard on you. I really believe in jet lag."

She was on a mission then to record a marathon in each of the fifty states. She was doing it the hard way, by not counting some of the ultramarathons she ran along the way. The typical ultramarathons she runs are 31.2 (50k) and 50 miles in length, usually on a trail. Since all ultramarathons, by definition, are longer than a marathon, she could have counted an ultra as a marathon in a given state. There's a reason she didn't count the ultras, and that's part of her story.

With the Orange County Marathon, in Newport Beach, California, on January 8, 2006, she completed the mission, her fifty-first state (counting D.C.). It was her thirty-eighth birthday.

"I went out there scared," she said.

To understand her apprehension, you'd have to know what happened in the December preceding that January race. As she closed on her target, two bogies reared up: her hardest marathon, and her first DNF, the term runners use for "did not finish."

The Kiawah Island Marathon, in South Carolina, was her hardest, despite its flat course. It turned into a seven-hour trudge. She had tendonitis of the iliotibial band, more commonly called the IT band, and had to walk most of the way. That race was her forty-seventh marathon of the year.

Going Down Slow

Forty-seven!

"Yeah, I missed a couple of weekends, but there were four weekends I ran doubles."

Doubles?

"That's where I ran a marathon on Saturday and then ran another one on Sunday."

But her body was wearing down. The crunch came the next weekend at a 50K ultra in Indiana. It was a cold nineteen degrees and the trail was under a foot of snow. Her body screamed its warning. She faltered after the first ten-mile loop. It was her first failure. She went to the car and cried.

"It hurt. You get through most of these races with your mind, and I guess my mind wasn't in it. I guess everything has a breaking point."

So her hardest marathon—the forty-seventh that year—was followed a week later by a failure. And that set the stage for her thirty-eighth birthday, and for that capstone race in Orange County that ended a saga.

That saga is just part of her story. To understand how that part came about one needs to go back to the year 2003. That year changed Angela Ivory's life—and who knows in how many ways?

They cut off her left breast.

They had to. The big C. It was June. They took out twenty-two lymph nodes, too.

The doctors laid out a menu of long-term outrage. Chemotherapy started three months before the surgery, and continued for three months after it. For that, they planted a "port" in her right shoulder, a sort of plastic

Going Down Slow

valve under the skin that connects to a blood vessel via a tube, a handy place to stick the chemo needle. After the chemo ended, five weeks of radiation followed.

Chemo is supposed to be tough, right? Tougher than the Tour de France, Lance said. But Angela didn't whine about it. Only the port drew her scorn—for the reason that it hurt when she reached for the bicycle bars—yeah, she was biking, too. The doctors installed the port in February 2003; they decided she was clean and took it out early in 2004.

Then everything changed for Angela Ivory.

Oddly, I remember talking with her about that time. It was January 24, 2004, at Natchez Trace State Park, just after the five-mile "Race on the Trace." We sat on the steps of the lodge talking about running, as racers will.

I didn't know her secret, and she didn't mention it. I couldn't have guessed the perfect storm of marathons to follow; I doubt she could. That day she seemed a bit wistful and dreamed about running an ultramarathon, something she'd read that I'd done.

Later that year, in June, she indeed ran an ultra, the Star Mountain 50K, in Etowah, Tennessee. Maybe by then she'd learned what she wanted to do, although she doesn't recall a particular moment when she formed her fifty-one states plan; it happened gradually.

You can imagine that a black girl growing up in Memphis during the 70s and 80s faced all the usual pitfalls of big city life. But Angela's parents taught her well. She studied hard and earned an academic scholarship to Vanderbilt University. Once there, she knew she wanted

Going Down Slow

to major in mechanical engineering—this despite the scarce number of women in that program, not to mention black women.

Despite earning the degree in mechanical engineering, she took a job doing a vital kind of civil engineering work—another irony—as an environmental protection specialist with the Tennessee Department of Environment and Conservation. She was working and living in Nashville—between races.

Races, always the races. Somewhere every weekend. And those races had become ultramarathons.

The ultras started another saga, another story, because Angela Ivory raised the ante: She planned to run an *ultramarathon* in each of the fifty states. Already she'd checked off sixteen by the time of our Cookeville talk. And that number was wrong by the time I had written it, for the reason that it was growing week by week.

But why? Why that goal? I wanted to know.

The self-effacing woman was much too modest to give a pretentious answer. In fact, she seemed embarrassed by the attention and preferred to not mention the quest, or her accomplishments. She just laughed at the question and answered with humor.

"Well, I'm not sure. The more I run the less brain cells I have."

Her dad died in 1993.

"What does your mother think about all that running?"

"I don't think she completely understands it, but she's supportive."

Going Down Slow

By its nature, Angela's quest didn't permit great speed. Her best marathon finish came in 2005—the year she ran forty-seven—in, remarkably, the Country Music Marathon, in her hometown, a time of 4:26:49.

Angela is a shy person who dislikes talking about herself, a trait that evinces what you might call character. As a consequence, she completed a marathon in each of the fifty-one states—forty-seven in one year—quietly, without fanfare, almost secretly. And she started the ultra quest the same way.

I wrote a feature story about Angela's running and her battle with cancer for the Sunday edition of the local paper. It was reprinted in three running magazines. The story surprised many of her running friends. Until then, they had not known about her cancer, and had barely known the extent of her running. She'd done the running quietly and endured cancer the same way.

So modest was Angela, she'd initially declined the article. She didn't care about being the center of attention. I didn't want to pressure her; I wanted her to make the decision, yes or no. But I did point out that such a story might inspire someone else, help someone else. That idea—the thought of helping someone else—was what changed her mind.

The story blew her cover. It was time. This brave woman deserved recognition. The inspiration her courage brings to running and to life deserved broadcasting to the most remote corners of human endeavor.

"I'm just a chicken, and a slow chicken at that,"

Going Down Slow

she said.

Chicken? Ha!

There, in admirable humility, she belittled her remarkable courage. In Angela Ivory, humility and courage are complement qualities. Her humility veils the heart of a lion.

22

IRONMA'AM

Ironma'am: she displays the word on her license plate holder, a variation on "Ironman" she adopted as her nom de plume. It fits. Ironman is her life. She will talk your leg off about it, evincing a spirit of enthusiasm and intensity with a twinkle in her eye, talking fast as if her speech has to rush to catch up with her thoughts. Because she is also smart.

Indefatigable, indomitable, that's Susan Ford. When the last ding-dong of doom finally claps and fades, the sound Faulkner's ghost will hear won't be man's puny voice still talking. It will be Susan Ford's.

But she is also my generous and kind friend. She would give you her heart, but if you're between her and the finish line she might stomp yours. You must forgive her: a race is a temporary transformation of ordinary life into a new realm. After the finish line, life returns to normal.

So, yes, Ironma'am is the name that fits. She earned the right, the first woman to do so from among every last hill, holler, ridge, knob, cliff, creek bottom and plateau of the entire Upper Cumberland region of this here state—the whole raw spreading put-together. I was her witness.

Going Down Slow

She trained for months for Ironman Florida, her first Ironman attempt. Time approached; she didn't know I was playing a trick on her. I'd made plans to be a spectator there — she knew that much. What she did not know was that I was hoping to write a story about her experiences—if there was a story. So to avoid raising any expectations and putting even more pressure on her, I didn't tell her my plans. She knew I had other friends in the race that I wanted to see, and so my little secret was easy to keep. I traveled to Panama City Beach separate from her and staked out a fan's position on the sandy beach that morning.

As I stood waiting with my camera, a brisk north wind was sweeping across the beach, plunging the chill factor into the thirties. Even wearing a coat I was cold. There stood Susan at the Gulf's edge with some 2,200 others waiting for the 7:00 a.m. start. She stood and shivered among the throng. But I knew the hope was in her. If she could succeed in traveling the combined 140.6-mile distance she'd become the first woman Ironman from our whole region of Tennessee.

In the end, after all the shivering and fury and misery, she was able to do just that, realizing her dream, posting a finishing time of 15:09:55. The first woman Ironman — from our corner of the world, anyway — was forty-one years old.

In normal life, Susan practices veterinary medicine, and loves dogs. She loves her husband Ivan, too, a medical physicist. He was along on the Florida trip to provide moral support for his athletic wife, to help out with the logistics and to baby-sit their ten-week old whippet pup, Archimedes.

The race started with the 2.4-mile swim. Overnight

Going Down Slow

passage of a cold front had churned the sea and breakers were forming 100 yards offshore. Their sight made me shudder. The rough water was likely to hinder visibility and control, favoring a swim more chaotic than normal. I dreaded it for her.

I watched the anxious faces of swimmers as gun time approached and marveled at their courage, and I had the brief stupid thought, completely in sympathy, "Will they actually go in there?" But, of course, they would. I've done it myself, and I know there's no turning back, even if you suspect catastrophe waits.

Susan later told me how it was.

"…scary and exciting all at the same time. I also got a lump in my throat, but I had to choke that back because I can't swim with a lump in my throat. The sand was cold…. Our feet were numb; we were huddling to keep warm."

The gun fired, and I watched the stirring mass march into the froth like a doomed migration. Swimmers jostled for position; collisions became ordinary.

Susan: "I was hit in the nose—an elbow!—twice in the lip, kicked in the face. I had people go over the top of me."

She saw stingrays and jellyfish—one stung her on the foot. She saw lights in the water, bioluminescence, she said it's called.

Her swim took on an element of survival. "I remember thinking, *all the months I spent working on my swim form have nothing to do with the way I'm swimming now.*" (Divers recovered an unconscious swimmer. He had a pulse but died three days later. I never learned if an autopsy determined the cause of death.)

Going Down Slow

Susan finished the swim in a time of 1:18:52, a respectable performance despite conditions. But then the second crunch hit. She raced in wet clothes up the beach to her bike, running into the teeth of a north wind forecast at ten to twenty miles per hour.

I was waiting to get a picture of her exit from the water, but all the swimmers in their wet suits looked so much alike, I missed her.

She describes it. "...it was sooo cold. When I pulled off the wetsuit—everybody was cold! —when it came off, it was just unbelievably cold. I was in shock." Shock or not, she had to jump on the bike.

The north wind was unlucky. The first part of the 112-mile bike course went generally north into the wind, which further chilled her and killed her speed. And it crushed her spirit. Susan expected to average 16.5 mph, but as the grueling headwind wore on her, she realized she was only achieving 14.5 mph. Finally the course turned away from the wind, giving relief for a while—until she reached a turnaround.

Then the wind again: "They headed us back into the wind and I thought, *Oh no, the damned wind again.* And there were cracks in the pavement that went thunk, thunk, thunk, and each time it did that my neck...oh my God, my neck hurt!"

I know that feeling. For aerodynamic efficiency, a triathlete leans sharply over the handle bars, a position that puts severe strain on neck muscles as you lift your head to see forward.

Waiting in the crowd back in town, Ivan and I could

Going Down Slow

only guess and wonder. We wandered around and stayed in touch with each other by cell phone. I was trying to find a good spot for a photograph. After missing the swim picture, I hoped to catch her on the bike as she returned to town. In the end, I failed that mission too, she blew by so quickly.

Waiting for her, Ivan and I couldn't know it, but Susan's right calf was cramping as she pedaled. "The anterior tibialis," the veterinarian later called it. She believed she would not be able to run if the muscle cramped hard. So she favored the right leg, adding more pedal load to the left. Of course, that produced the unhappy results of a cramp in the *left* leg.

So when she finished the bike ride and started the 26.2-mile run, she had no control over her left foot.

"Basically it just flopped, and I ran six miles like that—step, flop, step, flop." Then it got better.

But the worst was yet to come.

Late the morning after the race I called her up and then went up to her hotel. Her room was a shambles, triathlon gear scattered on every horizontal surface. Ivan and Archimedes shuffled around in the narrow clearings. Susan and I decided to leave Ivan in charge of the dog and retire to an outside table at the pool. There she told me about her run.

Night had fallen while she ran. With night the mercury plunged. Darkness drew in around her. She was cold. The long distance stretched ahead. Each mile yielded grudgingly, bit by bit, to her aching struggle.

She'd trained years for just this moment, the last

Going Down Slow

eighteen months working under Nashville coach Robert Eslick. She followed his biweekly instructions for biking and running. Swimming, perhaps her best sport, she worked on separately, grinding out the laps and miles at the Cookeville YMCA.

The problem Robert had was preventing her from training too much, from inducing an overuse injury. Susan will tell you she obsesses about Ironman. Ultra endurance requires ultra obsession. Her tendency is to over do it. "I'm always training," she says.

She's not kidding. I recall a conversation with Robert. I told him I thought Susan was the most intense, dedicated, enthusiastic… He cut me off.

"She's crazy!" That response was loaded with grudging admiration.

For Ironman Florida, specifically, Susan trained twenty-four weeks—twelve weeks of base training and twelve weeks of building speed and peak distance. During that training cycle, she incorporated several shorter triathlons as training exercises. During her peak training, on one weekend alone, she rode 105 miles, ran twenty, and swam two.

Now out on the marathon run, descending into night and deeper into misery, she needed all the toughness her training could bring. She was determined to stay positive, "…but the ongoing power of the wind, and cold, and fatigue…" She trails off, trying to tell me that. Her silence expresses the mental anguish she'd faced.

Because a problem loomed—a huge unknown for her: she'd never actually run a marathon before, let alone

Going Down Slow

one preceded by a swim and bike ride. Overuse injuries had prevented it. Now her outraged body was forced to go beyond all the limits it had ever known.

I'd known Susan since just running a 10K was an adventure for her. In those early days running injuries nagged her and hindered her progress. She'd climbed a high mountain in training, but she couldn't be sure it would be enough.

Someone has described a marathon as twenty miles of hope and 6.2 miles of seeing God. Reaching that last six miles, Susan confronted a crisis. Overcome by fatigue and no longer able to run, her only chance was to walk. If she could. Walking violated her principles and drove her further into despair.

Most of all, she feared failure.

Help came in the form of a gentleman from Virginia who was making his third try at becoming an Ironman. They walked together, leaning on each other, urging each other on. "Just go with me to that next light pole," he said.

She painfully needed to go to the restroom. Though portable toilets were stationed along the course, she dared not sit. She knew she'd be unable to get up. She couldn't simply wet her pants as some do; it was too cold to be wet again. She strode on.

"If there were a thousand dollar bill on the ground I don't think I could bend over to pick it up," the man said.

"I know I wouldn't pick it up. It might kill my chance to get the finisher's medal, and that's more important to me than a thousand dollars," Susan answered.

I myself was standing out in the cold and dark during

Going Down Slow

those moments, waiting for her about a mile from the finish line. When she and the man strode out of the dark, she was confident by then she would make it. Finally, I got a picture. Despite all, she was still wearing a smile, as my picture shows.

Finally, slightly past 10:00 p.m., the two approached the finish line. The crowd's roar, the thumping music, the announcer's voice filled their ears. Joy filled their hearts.

"Let's run across the finish line. I'm at least going to cross the finish line running," the gentleman said.

"Not me. I'm going to walk across, and proud of it!"

Barely able to walk or even stand, she *knew* now she'd finish. Despair and fear gave way to overwhelming joy. She used her last ounce of energy coming down the stretch, slapping hands with fans, and marched across the finish line in celebration.

Then she collapsed.

Race officials held her upright. Ivan rushed to her side. "You gotta get me to the bathroom," she pleaded.

Next morning she was too sore and stiff to get out of bed. She called a masseur to her room. It took two hours of massaging before she could stand.

"I've always heard that it was going to hurt, but I was unprepared for *how much* it was going to hurt. There was not a spot on my body that didn't hurt. It was excruciating."

"Ironman is the supreme challenge. And it's part of what I am from now on."

Sitting there at the patio table that day after the race, while she was still barely able to walk, I had one more question I wanted to ask her, although I knew the answer.

Going Down Slow

"Was it worth it, all the training, all the pain?" Her answer was pure Susan, more convincing than anything else she could've said.

"I signed up this morning for next year's race," she said. She leaned forward, eyes flashing. "And you know what? If I don't finish, I'll still be an Ironman!"

Yes, she will. I agree. Having once earned the medal, the title lasts forever. So do the memories. For Susan, the Iron Life lasts, too. Since that morning in Florida, she's finished ten Ironman races, and cut three hours off the time of her first one.

My subsequent story about Susan's first Ironman was written for the local paper, but it eventually appeared in two papers and in two running magazines. Susan framed the paper's story and hung it on her wall.

23

THE HUNTER'S MOON

I read this story in the Halloween edition of the Sunday *Herald-Citizen*. I read it there because that's where I published it. People thought it was true. They even thought the young boy Will was the alter ego of a young me. I didn't deny or confirm it. I'm still not talking. I only write them. The reader decides.

The old people say that...

...on that warm October night the young boy Will walked in the dark across the backyard, heading to the shop. He was a hunter, and he always carried his knife, a two-bladed barlow. He opened the big blade and raked his thumb across it as he walked. It needed sharpening, and he was going after the whet rock.

The shop was a three-sided shed with a sloping flat tin roof, its front open to the west. The family called it the garage, because it had once held his grandfather's car. Now it was full of the tools of farming—shovels, hoes, hammers, welders and wrenches—things used to build fences, make gates, cultivate crops and repair equipment. The whet stone would be setting on a two by four runner just inside the opening, and he knew he could put his hand on it, even in the dark.

Going Down Slow

Over the hills west of Smith Bend—the loop of the Cumberland River where he lived—the crescent moon hung near the horizon, just left of the big hackberry tree that stood below the barn. The moon was waxing, setting a little later each night, and near the end of the month it would be full, a moon called the Hunter's Moon.

Will glanced in that direction, at the moon, at the big hackberry. The family referred to the tree just that way, as the "big hackberry tree." Its thick trunk lifted a huge crown into the sky above the setting moon. The leaves had begun to die and fall, thinning the crown, giving it a shabby, tattered appearance.

Will didn't much like the big hackberry. The bark was scabby and knotty. The leaves were rough and ugly, pocked by warty growths; they turned a dull, dead brown in the fall, not a bright color like the maples and hickories. The berries were no good to eat either, each one just a seed covered by thin orange paste and a red skin, tasteless as raw pumpkin. But the birds liked them, and that made for good hunting. It was a mean tree, save for that one good quality.

As he reached the shop he heard a sound coming from the barn. He stopped and cocked his head, listening. Then it grew louder, a nervous squawking coming from the chickens on roost in the lower shed of the barn. At once, he knew:

Something's after the chickens!

He took off running toward the house, went in the back door, dashed across the kitchen and into the hall where his .410 leaned in the corner. He shook out a hand

Going Down Slow

full of shells from a box sitting on the chest, grabbed a flashlight from the top drawer and snatched the gun. As he sprinted back across the kitchen he heard his mother calling from the living room, "William!" But the screen door slammed behind him about then, and he kept going.

Once through the gate and on the lane to the barn, he walked slowly and carefully. The squawking talk of the chickens seemed more urgent. As long as that noise kept up, it meant the intruder was still there. That was good. Will didn't want to scare off whatever it was, until he could get a shot at it.

He was making plans as he approached the barn. He'd have to hold the flashlight and the shotgun forearm both with his left hand. It would be hard to aim both, he knew, but that was his only chance. The light was off now and he wouldn't flip it on until he was in shooting position. The shed was open at the front except for a gate low enough to shoot over. He had to reach that gate without detection.

He walked slowly in a slight crouch. The crescent moon traveled with him, creeping behind the big hackberry, outlining its skeletal-like crown against the sky. The moon winked through its openings as Will crept toward the barn.

Will had learned to hunt a couple of years earlier with a slingshot, when he was eight and nine years old. He made several slingshots, cutting the rubber straps from scrap inner tubes made before the war, using a leather shoe tongue for the pouch and a fork from a small tree for the stock. Eventually he found the perfect fork, one where the limbs made equal angles. It was an elm, a

Going Down Slow

tree locally known by two syllables, pronounced EL-lum. Recording his kills, he'd already cut four notches in that fork when one day he shot an indigo bunting, a beautiful little blue bird. The hue of its feathers seemed to radiate a blue aura, a color like electricity, he thought, having felt a spark plug's shock.

He'd been walking toward the tobacco barn that day. The bunting sat on the electric lines that crossed the pasture. He drew and shot. Instantly, he knew he'd made a perfect shot. The stone hit the bird with a dull thud, catching the rib cage and wing. The bird fell straight down, its life knocked out. A blue wing feather, floating softly down, landed by it.

He'd been sad about the little bird that reminded him of electricity and wished he'd not shot it. He cradled the tiny warm body in his hand. Its head dangled and flopped. The feathers on its back shined a blue radiance that seemed alive. Will stuck the blue wing feather back in its wing, lacing it in with the other feathers.

He forgot about going to the tobacco barn and, instead, headed toward the other barn where the hackberry was, carrying the bird. He passed through the barn hall and turned toward the big hackberry tree. The soil was soft and moist under the tree. Runoff crossed the hog lot, picking up silt, manure, and corn cobs. Some of it settled out as the water spread and slowed to go through the fence at the hackberry. That made the soil rich. Will could count on finding red worms there when he needed fish bait.

He dug a grave with his knife under the big hackberry, put the little bird in and covered it over. Then he cut a half-

Going Down Slow

foot section of dead horseweed and sharpened one end. He made a short split in the weed and threaded a smaller section through that split, forming a cross, and stuck the cross in the moist ground at the bird's head.

On his way now to save the chickens, Will was glad he held his .410 instead of the slingshot. He tried to put the slingshot with the perfect fork out of his mind. But he remembered.

He'd decided that day he didn't want the slingshot anymore. On his way back to the house, he'd pulled the perfect slingshot from his hip pocket. He cut the pouch from the rubbers and threw it aside, and then cut the rubbers off the perfect fork and threw them into the Jimson weeds.

At the house, a door hid the stairs that went to a dark attic. Will opened the door and climbed half way up. The tongue-and-groove siding stopped near the top, a few inches below the attic floor, leaving a dark opening there. Will reached through that opening and down inside the wall to his elbow. He felt a horizontal brace there, like a shelf inside the wall. He laid his perfect fork on that brace in the wall, and never disturbed it again.

He never told anyone about shooting the electric blue bird, about regretting it, about its grave under the big hackberry tree, or about dismantling his slingshot. His father wouldn't approve of such tender feelings, and his friends would have laughed. He was ashamed and didn't want to think about the slingshot.

That was a long time ago; he hunted with a shotgun these days, for bigger game. As he approached the barn

Going Down Slow

now, the urgent din of the chickens filled his ears. He could see them in his mind, sidestepping on the tier poles where they roosted, jostling and flapping for balance, mouths open, wild eyes blinking. He hoped the intruder would be a wildcat. That would be something—shoot a wildcat. He could feel the pulse in his neck. He was stalking the barn carefully now, bent forward into a slight crouch, although he was not aware of it.

He remembered Mr. Reeder. A wildcat had jumped on him from his barn loft. Although in his sixties, Mr. Reeder was stout. The cat had knocked him down twice. He finally killed it with his bare hands. Once he got his fingers around the cat's neck, his hard thumbs pushed in its throat, crushing out that fierce life. But the cat had fought with fury and left deep cuts to prove it. Mr. Reeder carried his bandaged arm in a sling as he told Will and his father about it.

Will edged along the front of the barn now, quietly approaching the shed opening. The thought "wildcat" ran through his mind, merging with the squawking din into a single shrieking turmoil. He paused at the shed corner, the last cover, tensing for action.

Something's about to happen.

He swung into the opening, shoved the gun over the gate and switched on the light all in one action. There was a flurry of motion at the far end, a rushing toward the double doors there. Will's .410 boomed loud enough to ring the tin roof.

But it was gone. Will climbed over the gate and rushed to the double doors. At their junction, the bottoms

Going Down Slow

of the doors were rotted away, leaving a hole big enough a hog could run through it. He couldn't find any blood on the doors. From the sleek motion he'd seen, he believed it'd been a fox. But it had not left any hair on the door to prove it. He couldn't see any birdshot in the door planks either. He pointed the light at the hay-littered ground and couldn't find birdshot evidence there either. It was as if he hadn't shot at all, he thought dismally. He'd missed, he decided. That made him angry. He wished he had a 12-gage instead of the puny .410.

He walked back through the shed, flicking the light beam up at the restless chickens, safe on their poles. There was no bunch of feathers on the ground. No chickens had been lost at least.

He climbed the gate, straddled the top plank and swung his trailing leg across. In that precise moment of precarious balance there was a sudden commotion he had no time to understand. A booming whack came like a hard slap on his ear, accompanied by what seemed like flapping and hitting, and Will knew he was falling. He thought, "feathers." Then he didn't think.

After a while his eyes opened. A light was shining. He lifted his head. It was the flashlight, lying just ahead. The beam swept across the hard manure-soil and lighted a sprig of dead crabgrass at his face. He spit out some dirt absently. He'd fallen on the shotgun and his ribs hurt. He was confused and unsure for a moment. A thought was trying to come, but he couldn't think what it was. Then he scampered to his feet, remembering, and ran hard toward the house.

Going Down Slow

In the living room, his mom was peeling apples she planned to dry, catching the peelings first in her apron and then piling them on newspaper spread in the floor. She cut the apples into wedges and dropped them into a white enameled dishpan. She was a slender woman with white teeth and dark hair. Will flopped unhappily on the couch.

"What was it?" she asked.

"A fox in the lower shed. It got away."

He didn't mention the rest.

Next morning he returned to the barn before daybreak to milk the two cows standing in the main hall. Dawn came and sunlight angled into the hall while he did the milking. After letting the cows out, he returned to the lower shed to look around.

Standing at the gate where he'd fallen, he inspected the ground. He picked up a nondescript feather, mostly gray, some brown. Could be a hawk or an owl, maybe even a chicken feather, he thought. Undecided, he let it drop. Then he saw something bright partially hidden under the bottom gate plank, and picked it up. It was a small curved feather, like a wing feather. In the morning sunlight it seemed to radiate a blue aura. It reminded him of electricity. He twirled the feather slowly in his fingers, lost in thought, gazing toward the big hackberry tree.

24

ADVENTURES IN PARADISE

Adventure is discomfort recalled at leisure, a wit observed. This, then, must be an adventure story.

Sixteen Sierra Club members met at Cruz Bay, St. John on a Saturday in February for a service trip to the Virgin Island National Park. I was one of them. We stuffed ourselves into a rented Ranger pickup and Ford Explorer for the ride to the Virgin Island Environmental Resource Station (VIERS), a facility belonging to the University of the Virgin Islands.

From Cruz Bay it is eight miles east across the island to Coral Bay, and then six more meandering miles south to VIERS. Since the National Park takes up three-fourths of this hilly island, it is less developed than the other two major islands. The roads are about as winding and steep as any you will see, even if you grew up in Jackson County, Tennessee.

Six of us rode in the back of the Ranger. The truck's bed was equipped with two opposing benches and a cloth canopy. Our assistant leader, Carol Marty, from Maryland, drove, joined in the cab by leader trainee, John Doidge, from California. So there were eight of us in the Ranger, eight in the Explorer. Starting, we were strangers,

Going Down Slow

but not for long. The overloaded Ranger dragged its body on a wheel gratingly each time Carol bent it around a switchback.

She remembered to drive on the left most of the time. The U. S. vehicles configured for right-side driving made it harder. Once when she drifted over to the right, an outcry from us brought her back. Then on a climbing switchback, the Explorer, driven by trip leader, Peggy Hepburn, from Maryland, together with our Ranger, locked into a logjam-like standoff with a tractor-trailer. Everything stopped on that steep hill. It took a while to untangle, before we could go on.

Sitting directly opposite and bumping knees with me was Pete, a retired professor of anatomy from New York, elder of our group, out pacing me by two years. He would end up being my only roommate at VIERS. They wisely put the two professors together, figuring otherwise we might talk someone's leg off — a matter of protecting the party.

Sitting next to Pete was Brenda, a fiery redhead from New York. Her outspoken demeanor makes Bette Davis in the old movies look timid. She enjoyed badgering me about my Tennessee drawl. Far from being a bother, that only provoked thicker cornpone. It helped that I was the South's only son.

"Well, it's not standard broadcast English," she announced one day, referring to my speech. I doubt she knew I'd lived a scholar's life. I used the quaint word "passel" to describe a large number of sea urchins one day. That brought a hoot. I suggested looking it up. It was great fun.

Going Down Slow

On the bench next to me sat Meredith, who was twenty, a rock climber and college student from Indianapolis. Lithe as a snake, she wore a piece of metal through her tongue, and hair under her arms. She was missing a week of classes to make the trip. "You gonna have a lot of work to make up," I said. "I've already made it up," she corrected me smartly. You had to like her.

VIERS turned out to be a remote collection of nineteen wooden cabins squatting in the jungle near Little Lameshur Bay on the island's southeast side. One cabin was equipped as an office and library. Another was kitchen and mess hall. Still another was a classroom. The bathrooms were in a separate building, as were the showers. Various groups come to VIERS for workshops and short courses.

Sometimes we heard lectures. The president of Friends of V. I. National Park described his organization's efforts. We sat outside in a circle of plastic chairs permanently arranged around an unneeded fire pit. Palms trees heavy with coconuts together with an immense rain tree spread their shade over the scene. At the end the president was responding quietly to questions. The scene was peaceful as a garden club.

I remember a brief rustling from something overhead. Then something hard and rude slammed my face. I shoved away a rough rustling weight. The circle sat in shock. I jumped up, stunned. Scott, the camp manager, rushed over, squinting hard at my face.

"Are you hurt?" he asked.

"I don't know. You can see better than I can."

I touched my cheek and pulled back bloody fingers.

Going Down Slow

"Oh, my God!" a woman cried.

"Go with Scott," Peggy said.

We headed to the bathroom. Scott had a first aid kit. I bent over the sink and washed away the blood. It was coming from a cut one inch below my left eye. An inch higher and I might have lost a peeper. My upper lip had taken the hardest lick; the bruise penetrated to my teeth roots. An inch lower, without my lip for a cushion, and I might have lost teeth. As it was, I just had a fat lip. There was a three-inch bruise and laceration on my left shoulder and another bruise and laceration on my neck.

"What hit me?" I asked Scott; I still didn't know what had happened.

It was a coconut palm frond, he said. My question made him wonder about my noodle. He asked me to state my full name, which I was able to do. Then he wanted to know the current date. The display on my Ironman watch may have helped me out on that one. He was satisfied.

I wasn't addled, just lacking information. The frond turned out to be fifteen feet long, later examination showed. It weighed several more pounds than any fish I've ever caught. It fell from a height of maybe forty feet, gaining a good load of energy and dumping it on my face. It fell like an arrow, the blades acting like vanes. The butt end was hard woody material close to a foot wide, like a plank, which explained how it managed to hit me in so many places.

It was all very lucky. Pete later told me that my reflexes had helped, that I'd put up my hands, which helped slow it down. I have no memory of that, but it must be true

Going Down Slow

because the insides of both my wrists were scraped. I have no memory of looking up either, but I certainly did because the thing cut my cheek without hitting my cap bill. Looked up at the perfect angle, too, so that it landed between my teeth and eye, missing both.

A couple of Band-Aids later and I returned to the circle. Everyone applauded. I raised my arms in celebration — the marathoner was home.

Ruins are abundant in paradise. Our purpose was to help clear vegetation away from some of those ruins needing archeological study and from areas around the VIERS Station itself.

We soon learned that water is scarce, rain collected in cisterns being the only source. The island was currently suffering through a drought. Peggy, said it was the driest she'd ever seen it. We were limited to one three-minute shower per day. Scott, the Station's manager, instructed us to not flush the toilets unless "absolutely necessary." Exactly what that meant was left delicately unexplained.

On a Sunday, our first full day on location, we took a hike out to Ram's Head, a high rocky hill guarding the entrance to Saltpond Bay and looking south over the Caribbean. The terrain is reminiscent of the deserts of Arizona and South Texas. Organ pipe, Turk's cap, century plants and various thorny trees grow in hard rocky soil. Some of the trees had turned brown from the drought.

As in the desert, some of the plants can painfully stick the unwary. Some are capable of greater evil. The Manchineal tree, the one Columbus called the "death

Going Down Slow

tree," bears a crab apple which is poisonous. The leaves and bark alone can cause massive outbreaks of a rash on the skin, like over-zealous poison oak. It only grows near water, so you don't have to worry about it all the time.

Kyle and I sat resting at the water's edge, looking into clear, shallow water at a different hazard. Kyle was an engineering student at Purdue. He was also in the Army, where he drove an eighty-ton Abrams tank—he knew how to make it bunny hop. We saw black blobs scattered about on the submerged rocks.

"Sea urchins," Kyle said. The dreaded sea urchin, bane of snorkelers, we already knew about. It looks like a jet black tennis ball full of finger-length black needles. Step on it and the needle-like spines go deep into your foot and break off under the surface. The needles are venomous and thus cause a painful sting. Another charming feature: barbs prevent their removal. People go to the emergency room.

Kyle told me an amusing story about a young woman who had suffered a hard encounter with one. The pain was excruciating, he said. She called the doctor. He told her to put urine on the needle wounds, to go to the shower and pee on her foot, as Kyle put it. Something about chemistry, the urine neutralizes the toxin and makes it quit hurting. Not a folk remedy, the doctor prescribed it.

In snorkeling I always gave the sea urchins plenty of room. They were on the rocks everywhere, an evil crop of pincushions.

In September of the past year an AP story indicated that forty percent of the coral around the U. S. Virgin

Going Down Slow

Islands had died due to record high water temperatures of 2005. Another source said fifty percent. I wondered about that, and wanted to see for myself. Although we went snorkeling at several places, I never saw the massive amounts of dead coral I expected. Perhaps I was in the wrong place, or perhaps the coral has recovered. The issue has important implications. Coral is like the forest of the ocean, and sea life depends on it for shelter and food.

I also wondered if the warm temperatures contributed to an infestation of sea urchins. Pete, the retired professor from New York, answered that. He said a few years earlier the sea urchins died off, and the present population, in fact, represented recovery to a normal number.

Our service work consisted of grunt labor. On four mornings we removed unwanted vegetation. Call them "weeds" if you want to. One of the most obnoxious weeds stood upright like a waist-high wall of green blades. Each blade was pointed at the end, and it had come to stay. It's called mother-in-law's tongue. It had to be pulled out by the roots or cut off at the ground. At the VIERS campus itself the plant had invaded in two dense stands. We removed and carted away each stand, burning not being permitted.

At Little Lameshur Bay near our camp the ruins of a bay rum and sugar plantation sprawls down the mountain side down to the sea. The jungle has overrun the buildings, except for the plantation's great house, which sits high on a hill overlooking the bay and is used as the park ranger's residence. The park is considering making the ruins into an interpretive center. First, archeologists must study the

Going Down Slow

site. The dense vegetation was a hurdle repelling their efforts.

For two days we worked in these ruins removing the omnipresent mother-in-law's tongue, century plants and brush. The archeologist, Ken Wild, who happened to be from Chattanooga, told us about the importance of the site.

During the 1700's and 1800's the Danes owned what is now the U. S. Virgin Islands, and there were close to 200 such plantations on St. John. In those days most of the land was cleared for the cultivation of sugar cane. The work was carried out by slaves imported from West Africa, racked like cordwood in the holes of ships.

On one of our hikes, five of us sought out the remote great house of a past plantation. Defunct and decaying, the opulent structure sat shrouded by the jungle, high on a hill overlooking a broad bay. Its remains suggest its past splendor.

A courtyard surrounds the main entrance. Twin concrete stairs lead to a landing at the door. Beyond lies a great hall, now inhabited by bats. On both the north and south side, porticos with arched openings extend the length of the house.

One can imagine a cool breeze wafting through those verandahs at sunset, imagine the owner sitting there gazing out over his spread, all of it framed by the Caribbean's turquoise waters. On this splendid estate his family lived a life of privilege and luxury. They lounged on the bones of slaves.

Now trees improbably catch hold of the lintels

Going Down Slow

and eaves, sending roots inching into cracks and joints, crumbling the walls. With the old force of time's steady ooze, the jungle creeps through the building, eating away its secret heart.

As we left, I photographed the proud date cast in tall numerals on the masonry of a courtyard gatepost: 1844.

Marathon plans? Ha! laughed the harsh sea.

The road soars into the blue Caribbean sky. I'd like to run it, is what I'd like to do, all the way to the top. Sure I would. But the hill resists with all the Newtonian elegance of gravity's old steady sway. Against it I bring nothing — can bring nothing — save the frailty of human endurance.

And hope, which is part of frailty. The grade is steep and knows it, pushing back harder than any hill I've attempted. Stairs without steps. I put my head down and get up on my toes, taking tiny chops against the concrete. The gentle percussive pats of the shoes blend with my panting, the only sounds I hear.

Here's a distinction I'm trying to make: run, don't walk, stay in a running motion, however feeble it becomes. Don't stop either. Keep it honest. We want the truth.

This road goes to our camp. It's made of dirt. Except this hill, which has been paved with a strip of concrete, a hedge against torrential rains washing the whole track to the bottom.

Here is the switchback; it's so sharp every time we bend our rented Ranger around it, the truck growls a death rattle, the rear wheel rubbing a body appendage. You think the little truck is going to die. Then it finds another

Going Down Slow

gear, gets down to a slow grind and crawls nervously over the top.

I'm in a slow grind too, going down slow, even as I climb upward. But like the truck I finally trudge across. The hill has two sides, and on this four-mile out-and-back jog, I've got to climb it again. But the other side is merely steep, not impossibly steep.

This casual jog came in mid-February, when I'd taken a one-week break from my training for the eighth Country Music Marathon. By some hubris I'd managed to install myself on a tropical island with five men and ten women, Sierra Club members from across the U.S., all strangers to me. But my racer's heart doesn't mind strangers.

Volunteer service to the Virgin Islands National Park was our main excuse. In addition to grunt work clearing weeds and brush from archeological sites within the park, the trip schedule allowed ample time for recreational activities — hiking, snorkeling, sightseeing and even some running.

Four of us decided to go sea kayaking one day. A half-mile from our cabins VIERS maintains a small lab building at the edge of Great Lameshur Bay. There were two kayaks there. One of them leaked, we'd heard, but we ignored that hearsay.

Pete, the retired professor from New York, and Karen, a traveler from Milwaukee, took one boat. Lynn and I took the other one. Lynn owns kayaks back in Minneapolis. She's a dermatologist too. It's always good to have a doctor around.

Being a greenhorn, I paddled from the front seat,

Going Down Slow

Lynn in back. We followed Pete and Karen out of the bay, skirting a steep, rocky shore.

Our kayaks were plastic shells having a molded depression on top where paddlers sat. Essentially you sit on top of an enclosed void. In front of me, ours had a six-inch opening capped by a lid. I took the lid off and looked down in the hole to discover water sloshing about. I reported the water to Lynn and put the cap back on.

We reached the mouth of the bay, and the waves hit us harder. The boat kept listing to the right. I wondered if Lynn was causing that. It was quite annoying.

"It's leaning to the right," I complained. We shifted and got straight again. Soon it started leaning right again. Attempts to correct it caused a listing to the left. We couldn't keep it straight. It listed either right or left, ponderously so.

Our boat was filling with water.

We'd already turned the rocky corner at the mouth. Waves pounded us. We yelled to Pete and Karen that we had to turn back. That suited them. Both boats turned back toward the dock, Pete and Karen in front, Lynn and I plodding along behind.

Our boat was leaning far to the right, toward the waves. Once again we tried to correct. We rolled to the left. The waves helped. We kept on rolling.

"Whoa," I heard Lynn cry. Then the water smacked my ears. And we were bobbing in the waves beside the boat.

"Now we swim," Lynn said flatly. The doctor was right.

We swam, swam in our sandals, which we were both wearing. Lynn pushed at the back of the boat and I pushed at the side. Meanwhile Pete and Karen, unaware that we'd

Going Down Slow

tipped, paddled happily on toward the dock, far ahead. There was no use yelling. Waves crashing made too much noise.

The waves pushed us closer and closer to the steep rocks. Finally we saw Pete and Karen turn back, realizing our plight at last. Meanwhile, I was caught between the boat and the rocks, trying to keep the hull from crashing against their sharp edges.

We drifted dangerously close as the rescue boat approached. For a moment, I gained footing on a submerged rock, and pushed against our boat. To no effect. The waterlogged kayak probably weighed a thousand pounds by now.

As Pete and Karen arrived, the waves knocked me off the rock. In deep water again, I started kicking hard, pinched between the boat and shore rocks.

Then disaster! Just as Pete got a hold on our floundering boat, it happened. It was that close. If he'd only arrived a minute earlier....

The pain shot through my right foot.

"Dammit!" I screamed. I started to yell some richer invectives, but realized there was no use; the sea didn't care.

It was done now. I'd kicked my foot into a sea urchin, an evil prickly animal like a pincushion radiating porcupine quills, all black, mean and sinister. The venomous needles had gone deep into the top of my foot and toes, where my sandals offered no protection.

Pete and Karen took our crippled boat in tow, leaving Lynn and me behind for still more swimming. My foot

Going Down Slow

was on fire. But pain wasn't my problem.

In an instant, I'd seen my training for the Country Music Marathon blown to shards. That was the problem. The needles break off under the skin and their barbs prevent removal. How could I run with a foot full of needles?

Lynn and I swam on to a cove in the rocks and finally dragged ourselves out. We walked. My foot hurt. Lynn and I discussed the treatment Kyle had previously described to me — applying urine to the stings.

"If you need to stop and pee [on your foot] go ahead," Lynn said. What could I lose? Lynn was a doctor after all. I told her I would, that I could wash up at the dock, which was maybe a quarter-mile away. She discreetly drifted out of sight on down the trail.

My foot had four black tattoos on the top, where the needles had embedded. Another needle had centered my little toe precisely in the red spot where my running shoe rubs. Another needle had gone into the side of my big toe near the front and out the other side. I massaged all those spots with urine.

It helped. After I washed up, helped stow the boats and walked the half-mile trail back to camp, my foot felt better. That didn't improve my marathon prospects though. The stickers were still there. Their barbs guaranteed they'd stay there.

Vinegar was the answer, Lynn thought. She found some at the camp's laundry room and soaked my foot in it. Gloria, a medical malpractice lawyer and former nurse, sprang into action with the best treatment of all. She read

Going Down Slow

in a first aid book words of pure joy to my ears. She read out loud to the whole group how the needles dissolve in a few days, and that vinegar helps them dissolve.

The needles dissolve!

Then she read the most amazing statement of all, something like: "Rum taken internally speeds the process."

We had rum! But I didn't need it, I decided. The needles dissolve, the book says. That was all I needed to know. Dead no longer, my marathon plans roared back to life.

Nevertheless, Dr. Lynn decided on surgery. She held my foot on her knee and went to work with tweezers and scalpel. Pete assisted.

I sat in the same circle of chairs where the falling palm frond had bloodied my face three days earlier. The crowd gathered around to watch, staring in fascinated horror at the black needles in my foot.

A sea urchin was everyone's nightmare. Campers imagined I was in terrible pain. How could I stand it? First a falling palm frond brains me. Now this. I was picking up a reputation. Guy asked me if I wanted a piece of leather to bite on. But I could have gone to sleep.

"Do you want that bottle of Jack Daniel's," leader Peggy asked seriously. I gently declined.

Brenda, a hard-mouthed New Yorker, was touching in her frantic concern. She plopped at my side and grabbed my hand to comfort me, talking fast and loud.

"I know you're a man and supposed to be tough and all that! But you don't have to worry about that here!"

I just smiled and glanced at what the scalpel was doing.

Going Down Slow

"No! Talk to me! Talk to me!" Brenda shouted. "Don't look! Don't look!"

Lynn dug around with the scalpel, made a little blood and finally gave up without getting out a single sticker. Good medicine means do no harm.

I went and took a shower. My foot never bothered me again.

25

COUNTRY MUSIC CONTRARIAN

History: There it sat like a fat boy in the middle seat, squeezed between the Boston Marathon and Strolling Jim.

I'd never run either of those two races, and as their dates approached they sat scotched on my calendar where they'd been for months. The first Country Music Marathon wedged itself between them, twelve days after Boston and seven days before Strolling Jim, the forty-mile race that all veterans know is really 41.2 miles long, thus precisely fifteen miles longer than any race I'd run at that time.

Stolling Jim was not to take lightly. It demanded my respect for its implacable distance and for my inexperience at it. I didn't want to jeopardize it by running a marathon just a week before.

I'd taken up running competition just two years earlier, at age fifty-seven. Within a year I'd moved to marathons and, despite a broken ankle, notched eight in the twelve months preceding Boston. I was fascinated by experiences that at once astonished and shocked me.

In other words, I was ignorant, always traveling alone, training alone, knowing little about what I was doing. Just running.

But I knew not to stick Country Music between Boston and Strolling Jim.

Going Down Slow

There were other reasons, maybe less compelling, I think. Don't you always disrespect anything near home? It just doesn't have the panache of something far away. I'd traveled to Alaska for one race, scheduled another in Hawaii. By comparison, traveling to Nashville seemed dull.

And then, too, there was the awful name they'd hung on it, "Country Music." Why didn't they call it "Music City Marathon," a name that better embraces the capitol city? Despite the country music exported by the town, Nashville has a rich blues heritage which was omitted by the "Country" moniker.

I'd grown up in the hills and gone to sleep with John R whispering in my ear, as Don Williams says in one of the most remarkable lyrics ever penned by a country singer.

Clear-channel WLAC spread Howlin Wolf and Muddy Waters across the East, the Southeast, the Heartland, reaching into city taxi and country truck alike, share-cropper shack and city slum, both. It made no difference.

John Richburg—way down in Dixie, as he said—straddled the fat part of the night. These were the days before playlists. He played exactly what he wanted to play. And what he wanted to play was the blues.

Radio stations that shared their frequency with no other station were called clear-channel stations. Nashville had two such entities, mammoths, both, and they blanketed an immense area. WSM had the Grand Ole Opry, WLAC had the blues. These two giants shaped a postwar generation, brought us Hank Williams and Bo

Going Down Slow

Diddley both.

"Country Music Marathon" denied half the music, I thought. But, then, there the name was. And there the race was. And its time was approaching.

It was from that well of vague misgiving and generalized dismissal that I then happened to be talking to a clerk in a North Carolina triathlon store where I'd phoned in an order.

"You gonna run that Country Music Marathon?" he asked.

"Nah, don't think so."

"Well, it looks pretty interesting, being the inaugural race and all."

Then I hung up and thought about it. The man in Carolina had seen the race as attractive and glamorous while I had dismissed it like a charity cake walk. He was right, I realized. I'd been running marathons everywhere. Except at home, like a geographic chauvinist. And here was one in my backyard. I had to go, I suddenly decided.

But I hedged my bet. The day came for the first Country Music Marathon, as I had well known it would, just twelve days after the 104th Boston Marathon, a brutally hard race in a cold wind that blew away my performance, left me hypothermic and lost like an idiot wandering the streets of Boston and clutching my Mylar blanket and knowing not the whereabouts of my hotel or how to get there until, improbably, I encountered twin young women on the sidewalk, one of which I'd met by chance at O'Hara Airport, and she told me where to catch a cab.

So twelve days after that I hedged my bet. I wouldn't

Going Down Slow

run the Nashville race; I'd just jog it, something I'd never done in a race before.

I didn't bother to put on my racing flats that morning and showed up in corral number 1 wearing my old trainers. Take it easy, just get the medal was the idea.

But a strange thing happened: The race started. And I ran fast. Too fast. The miles raced by, and I could see I was running too fast. *You will blow up*, I thought. Then I thought: *So? Who cares?*

Nobody cared, of course. *I'm just messing around here.*

But I didn't blow up. At the then-age of fifty-nine, I posted a time of 3:20:10, nine minutes faster than I'd ever run, twenty minutes faster than I'd just run at Boston. It was good enough for 2nd place among the 145 finishers in the 55-59 age division.

After that I grew older and my division grew smaller. Despite that, year after year, *my runs at Country Music continued to improve.*

Many runners have complained about the Nashville race—unfairly, I think. Runners know the rap: the weatherly weather, the hilly hills and so on. They whined enough that race management modified the course—in 2004, I believe it was—to eliminate some of the climbing. They didn't do it for me. I didn't care. Because here is the empirical reality:

Six years in a row I ran a personal record at that race. This was despite the fact that during that period I ran a lot of marathons in a lot of places, some with flat courses. But I always performed better at Nashville, and each time in the Nashville marathon I set a PR, hitting 3:12:12 in 2005 at

Going Down Slow

the doddering age of sixty-four.

It was a trend that had to end, no doubt. It reversed in 2006 for the first time, when I posted a time of 3:20:04. I bounced back the following year with 3:18:02.

The Country Music Marathon has been a lucky race for me, magic even. I've run all eleven races, to date. Since that first race where I took second, I've won my age division ten consecutive times. My runs have shown—amazingly, to me—remarkably consistence, especially when one reflects on the vagaries inherent to the marathon distance. During the string of first eight races, the total time-spread between my best performance, 3:12, and my worse, 3:20, was only eight minutes. I finished race number 11 in a time of 3:21:11, just a minute slower than when I was eleven years younger, in that first race. So I'm showing down, as my age dictates I must. But, so far, anyway, the change is gradual. Going down slow, that's the idea.

Country Music brings pain and passion aplenty.

The twenty-mile mark comes on the east end of the Woodland Street Bridge. That's a benchmark. That's where the real race begins. Marathoners know the first twenty miles are just preparation. The finish line is only a couple blocks to the right, at the Coliseum—so close your heart breaks when you look that way.

But I know I can't go there yet. I have 6.2 winding miles through East Nashville that will finally bring me back to that Coliseum. It is time to race now. I am here thirty seconds late. But my goal is still doable; I have 6.2 miles to make up the thirty seconds.

Going Down Slow

The story of this marathon, the fourth Country Music Marathon, seems egocentric and was hard to write. The race somehow became a story about me in a way that I did not expect and had not experienced before. I prefer to write about the *experience*, not about *myself*. But if I am going to write about it, I have to write what is there.

The theme started shortly after I entered running corral number 1. There stood Tommy Kell, who was age forty and hailed from McMinnville, Tennessee. He was saying what he had first said a few months before and had said again as recently as just six weeks past: "I'm running with you."

I had run the whole Tennessee Running Tour without ever talking with Tommy, although I had seen him at the turnarounds a dozen or more times. He is a fast runner and was always in front of me. We were at different levels of speed and age and just never happened to talk.

But at the Country Music Marathon the previous year I had already finished the race and was standing in the recovery area chatting with a runner when Tommy came across the line. We suddenly came face to face in the crowd. I remember the look of shock on his face when he looked up and realized I had finished minutes earlier. "You beat me!" he blurted out before he could think. His surprise and complete lack of guile was amusing. Losing to a guy a whole generation older is a hard thing, I guess.

A marathon is about maintaining the right pace. Tommy decided he would run with me this year, so he could be on the right pace—and keep an eye on me. "Okay," I told him, "if you think you can go that slow."

Going Down Slow

In the corral Tommy began telling "Dallas Smith" stories to others. Here came Shawn, an Ironman I know from Daytona. Tommy set in, briefing him about my running adventures. Soon Jesse, forty-five, from Shelbyville, showed up. Tommy and I both know Jesse, a superb athlete who had retired from the marines. Jesse has the highly conditioned body of a middle distance runner that must be seen—a tiny waist rising to wide shoulders, flanked by lats that spread like a cobra's hood. He has a wide Magic Johnson smile that could disarm a stick-up man. Tommy told Jesse how he was going to run with me. We were making our plans.

Tommy kept his word. When the race started we ran side by side down West End Avenue with me setting the pace. Soon Tommy started telling runners in the race—rank strangers—how I had beat him last year and that I was running for a 3:15. The general theme of his remarks was that I was some kind of running hero—and he was sure glad to be running with me. Two other men joined us: a man named Mike, thirty-seven, from Lake Placid, New York and Bill, thirty-three, from Peoria, Illinois. I've forgotten their last names. They were all much younger than I. Anyway, I became the pace runner, the leader, of the little group. In addition to the ones I actually met, there were others hanging back, following my lead.

I didn't ask to be the leader of anything. Now, here I was, some kind of marathon guru, the duke of a whole pace neighborhood. I wasn't totally comfortable with that role. And it got worse. Along Demonbreun, Seventeenth Street and Music Row I had friends among the fans who

Going Down Slow

called out my name as we passed. With a name like mine there's not much doubt who they mean when they shout, "Go, Dallas!" My little group noticed that immediately, and began talking about my "fan club." I overheard Mike, the Lake Placid runner, tell another marathoner, "This is Dallas. He's the Man. Three fifteen!"

Well!

I began to feel responsible for *their* success. "I better do good in this run—you guys put all this pressure on me," I said. The trash talk rolled on. All of it was good-natured fun, of course, but there was indeed a serious vein in it. They actually *were* depending on me to keep them on pace—they weren't timing their own miles, depending totally on me. And, too, Tommy was running with a man twenty-two years older than he was out of respect, not disrespect. I knew that, but at the same time, all the chatter was distracting.

"What happened to Jesse," I asked Tommy.

"He took off."

I wasn't surprised. He was fast, and already far out in front, I figured.

At the five-mile marker, I was nineteen seconds behind schedule. I speeded up—slightly I thought—to get back on schedule. But my concentration was broken. We went through the next mile in 6:47, not the 7:15 I wanted. Putting my foot in the carburetor like that wasted energy and I wasn't too happy about it.

None of them knew my secret. They were all thinking 3:15, passing that number around. I just let them keep thinking that, even though it wasn't my goal. Actually 3:15

Going Down Slow

was very important to Mike—it was his Boston qualifying time. What I *had* told them was that I ran 3:16 last year. Somehow the "sixteen" morphed to "fifteen. But 3:15 was not my goal.

Actually, I was shooting for 3:11:30, the state record for my age group. The mile pace I needed to average was 7:19. Under good conditions I was capable of a time of 3:10, based on projection of three shorter races. But I wasn't about to predict such a time. I was hopeful, but didn't expect it. There are many factors beyond a runner's control in a marathon. A record for me would take a near-perfect run under good conditions. Already my pace had been erratic, less than perfect.

I turned some of Tommy's flattery back on him. I told the group he had run a half marathon recently in 1:23, much faster than I could go. But he put me right back in the spotlight.

"Yeah, but that was because of Dallas," he said. "I thought, 'I can't let Dallas pass me,'" he said.

Then he uncorked a Dallas Smith story I didn't know. It was about the first time we raced—we would race ten more times before I ever talked with him. "I only beat him by ten seconds," he said. "Then I found out how old he was, and I thought, dadgum!" So apparently Tommy had known me since our first race. That fact was a surprise.

A course photographer was ahead. "I'm getting up here beside Dallas, where I can be in *Sports Illustrated*," Tommy said. He did, too. We ran abreast while the photographer snapped the shot.

"I want to be in the picture with Dallas, so I can tell

Going Down Slow

people that's how I want to be when I get old." That was part baloney, part truth—but all in fun, Tommy's way of making time go fast, as you want it to in a marathon.

Alas, I dropped them all in mile eighteen. There was a steep uphill, and suddenly they weren't there anymore. I never looked back. It's my policy.

So I crossed the Woodland Street Bridge and arrived at the marker that said twenty miles. I was finally alone, the last survivor of our little pace group—thirty seconds late, but ready to run. A gradual one-mile climb was ahead. In that mile I passed Maureen Manning, the first American woman of the previous year's race. She was having a bad time—otherwise I wouldn't have been in sight of her. The pain in her face was frightful. I looked away.

Trouble started gradually, somewhere around mile twenty-two—little cramps playing up and down my right calf like electricity. Who knows why? I had passed up water at the last two aid stations, maybe a mistake, maybe reckless, even for a cool day. Dropping into Shelby Park, the trouble spread—the left calf started cramping, too. Then cramping into my feet and hamstrings, as well.

My race was crumbling.

The cramps were still controllable, so long as the strides were smooth and I didn't try to push. But I needed to push. Well, that was too bad. When my foot landed on an uneven place or I tried to push off too hard, well look out! The pinpricks of electricity had become bolts of lightening. Finally my toes curled tight in the shoes. I ran on curled toes—for a while, until they relaxed again. The cycle repeated a couple more times. A record run faded as

Going Down Slow

a possibility, a dream lost quickly.

A larger question loomed: would I finish the race at all? A hard cramp of the big muscles could slam me to the ground, writhing like a worm. The run might end on the bank of the Cumberland River in Shelby Park; I might not finish at all—or if I did, only by walking and limping the last three miles. I ran on eggs, being as gentle as I could.

I slowed down to eight minutes per mile and drank more water. Mike, the Lake Placid runner whom I'd left at mile eighteen, suddenly passed me, then Bill, the runner from Peoria, too. The two disciples now led their former leader.

The cramps seemed to relax a bit. In the last mile I regained ability to push again, and I overtook Bill. Gradually I picked the pace up to maybe seven minutes a mile by the time I turned the corner to head down the stretch-—a hundred yards to go.

Fans were pushed up against the fence lining that stretch. The race clock was mounted high over the finish line, yellow digits showing 3:14, plus seconds ticking, ticking. The world dissolved and fell away. Nothing remained but those yellow digits, the implacable distance and my determination to salvage every second I could in a final push. They say the announcer called my name. I have no memory of it. My eyes were hard on the finish line. I *do* remember one thing, running along the fence—fans calling my name, "Dallas! Dallas! Dallas!...."

Then I was across.

My official time was 3:14:33. It was good enough to win my age group by a margin of twenty-five minutes. It

Going Down Slow

was good enough to place in the top 100 overall. But it was not a state record.

Mike was standing there holding his hand out, smiling broadly--he had qualified for the Boston Marathon, running 3:13 something, finishing eight minutes better than his previous best. My pacing was the reason, he said, and he wanted to thank me.

I know his feeling—you never forget the moment when you qualify for Boston. Bill crossed, twenty seconds behind me. He was happy, too. Our little group was home, except for Tommy, who showed up a few minutes later, delayed by cramps, just like the previous year. Despite my pacing, he stood whipped by the old man again.

In Shelby Park a good outcome for me had been in jeopardy. My thoughts flew back to there, and to the shirtless man I was running behind then.

Even with the leg cramps, I am slowly gaining on the man. I should not be in sight of him, like I should not have been in sight of Maureen either. He has bonked, run out of carbohydrates. Weakness has seized him. Now he runs beyond the wall, something that takes great effort—even to go slow. Nevertheless, his stride is still smooth, springy, owing to the superb strength his musculature shows.

It is Jesse. I'll pass him soon. For all his strength and wonderful physique, he is too weak to hold me off. I doubt he could hold off a butter cookie right now. I decide I'll say something snappy, like, "Okay Jesse, let's take it to the house." But I know the pain, and when I pull even I don't have the heart to be clever. Instead I say, "Hey, man, are you okay?" But I know the answer. Any fool who runs

Going Down Slow

marathons knows the answer.

Passing, I reach back and touch his hand. I have to go; I'm fighting a battle, too. Emil Zatopek, the Czech gold medalist, reportedly said, "If you want to run, run a mile, but if you want to experience another life, run a marathon." Jesse is experiencing another life, one never glimpsed by most people—seeing God in every step was the way Ironman Scott Tinley put it.

Road racing is a primal sport played outside, in whatever weather the day offers. The outcome is unaffected by referees and lucky bounces. The racer's only equipment is muscle, bone and sinew in a contest that does not lie— whoever crosses the finish line first is the winner. The hurdles are implacable—the arrow of time goes forever forward and 26.2 miles is the same as it ever was.

A runner stands frail and alone in a face-off against the two most terrible entities known to physics—time and space. He brings against them nothing more than himself. And somewhere down the road he finds his truth.

In this race five men found their truth.

I love my marathon colleagues. I'd cross muddy water for them. Jesse and Tommy won't quit; they'll be back—stronger for the experience. The next time we race they'll pound me into the pavement.

Or maybe not.

26

COME HOME, HOKIE

The time for the Boston Marathon rolls around each year on the second Monday in April, Patriots Day in Massachusetts. It's unfair to that storied race, but its arrival triggers a different kind of memory for me—the murder of thirty-two students and instructors at Virginia Tech. Both events occurred on the same day in 2007—Monday, April 13.

Today, a semi-circle of thirty-two "Hokie stones" guards the stone reviewing stand in front of Burruss Hall on the Tech campus. Buses stop there and unload tourists. They walk around taking pictures of the memorial, just as I have done.

When tragedy brushes close you pause or stop, or maybe you make a turnaround. But then you go on. Because that's what humans do. You go on, but you don't forget. Going on is required. Forgetting is not part of the deal.

So I go on, but I remember. This was my tribute to the fallen Hokies then. This is my memory still.

When the gunman carried out the bloody massacre that Monday, his shots pierced the hearts of Hokies everywhere. That grieving community included me.

Going Down Slow

But you don't have to be connected with that university to appreciate the enormity of the tragedy. The gunman snuffed out thirty-two of the best and brightest, plus himself, and injured several more. Scan the list of the fallen. You only have to look at the photographs of their engaging smiles, reaching out from a time now snatched away, and read their biographies to see that these fallen were extraordinary. Their energy, talents and accomplishments are humbling.

Exemplary, like this student: In high school he ran track, played football and basketball, played the trombone and was valedictorian. To mention even one is to unfairly omit the others. Nonetheless, here is another: Due to graduate in a few days with a triple major and a 4.0 grade average, he was a leader in the Virginia Tech band, and he spent his summers working at a camp for special-needs kids. And then…. But you have to stop. There's no room. So many, so many struck down.

The list stretches out, including a number of staff members, as well. Some, like the two professors from the Engineering Science and Mechanics Department, had drawn international attention for their research.

All snuffed out.

The loss! Our country can never replace such gifted persons. Their university can't replace them. And their stricken families and friends could only mourn their passing. It was a loss the whole nation felt. One of the e-mails pouring in to VT said simply, "We are all Hokies now."

I myself dug out an old hat I hadn't worn in a few

Going Down Slow

years. I wasn't sure I still had it. But there it was, mashed flat at the bottom of the stack. I smoothed it out and pulled it on, a white hat with the familiar maroon VT on the front. It's the hat I wore when I first qualified for the Boston Marathon, at a race in Alaska. It's the hat I wore when I subsequently ran that famous Boston race, which, by coincidence, was held for the 111th time on the very Monday of the tragedy at VT. With more reasons than ever, I pulled that hat on again.

We are all Hokies now.

That morning I had just finished my last track workout before the Country Music Marathon, the hardest workout I attempt, running 3x800-600-600 intervals at 5K pace. I walked into the snack area at the Tennessee Tech Fitness Center, and the TV was on. It showed a squad car and police running with weapons drawn. A shooting had happened. This time it was at Virginia Tech.

"That's where I went to school!" I said to the only person present, a young woman student sitting at a table watching. Then I left. It is a sad measure of how familiar such scenes have become that I don't even remember if the TV reported one or two dead.

Just another day in the U.S.A.

When I got home, I decided to check the story again, and switched on the tube. I watched incredulously. The fatalities climbed past twenty, heading toward the eventual total of thirty-three, the number we all now know.

A shaky video a student had made with his cell phone showed Norris Hall even while the shots were ringing out. Prominent in the frame was the corner windows on

Going Down Slow

the second floor, I suddenly realized. Those windows belonged to the office I occupied when I was a professor there. The shots were coming from the classrooms a few steps away. I watched in disbelief.

Most of the slaughter took place in those second-floor classrooms. I knew the rooms so well. I had both taken and taught classes in them, taking graduate courses toward a Ph.D. while teaching undergraduate engineering classes. Eventually I earned the degree, accepted the professorship and moved from my graduate student cubicle to that corner office.

The student's video yanked me across the misty stretches, back to that long ago time and place, back in spirit to Virginia Tech, to Norris Hall — now transformed into a scene of unfolding horror. Time and again the shots rang out. I sat in my study sobbing.

Altogether I'd lived out three and a half intense years in that building, afraid I'd never master the arcane mathematics of continuum mechanics, pursuing what seemed at times impossible dreams — dreams no different from those snuffed out with each student the shooter cut down. Madness honors no dream.

Norris Hall sets adjacent to Burruss Hall, the main administration building. In front of it the stone reviewing stand looks out over the drill field. On Sundays when the campus was quiet, I'd take my son to that place. He was old enough to be in grade school then. From that stand, we'd launch our rubber powered model plane out over the field. The little plane sailed across an expansive view of sunshine and grass.

Going Down Slow

And peace. The timeless stone buildings stood silent guard, speaking not one word about the horror fated to unfold there one future Monday, or that spirits of the fallen would fill that space in the days following, buoyed by the students' defiant cry "Let's go Hokies!"

The peace has returned. The memory endures. And thirty-two silent stones guard the reviewing stand.

27

I'LL TAKE MANHATTAN

The U. S. flag draping the front of the New York Stock Exchange was big as a lawn. The Market was closed for Memorial Day. I stood looking up for a moment and then walked on, glancing down.

Something shiny lodged in the joint between the sidewalk and curb caught my eye. I picked it up. It was a stainless-steel sheet-metal screw, inch-and-a-half long, Phillips head. I walked a few more steps and found something else shining on the walk—a Roosevelt dime, minted 2001, the year the twin towers came down.

Clutching my treasure, I rushed to catch up with the twenty-three other Sierra Club members with whom I was touring Manhattan. I held the two objects out to Marianne, a quick thinking woman from Chicago.

"Look at the souvenirs I found back there at the Stock Exchange. I wonder what it means. There must be some symbolism…"

She glanced at the shiny objects in my hand, pointing first at the dime. "It means that if you invest this"—then pointing at the screw—"you get this."

Maybe so, but you'd be lucky if you lost no more than one thin dime.

Going Down Slow

Sierra Club? High desert plateaus, soaring snow-shrouded peaks, deep forest glades, such wild places are the usual haunts of the Sierra Club. So what did two-dozen Sierra Club members mean prowling the concrete canyons of Gotham?

The idea was the brainchild of Jerry Balch, Brooklyn native and son of Ukrainian immigrants. His concept was the same as other service trips sponsored by Sierra: go some place, see the sights and, for good measure, do some volunteer work. Except that in this case the location was anything but the usual wilderness setting; it was New York City.

Our task was to provide some restoration and maintenance for New York's Riverside Park, a sliver of land hugging the bank of the Hudson River, an area of some 323 acres, four miles long by an eighth of a mile wide.

Me? I had my own secret reason for being there, one having nothing to do with the Sierra Club and one my Sierra colleagues didn't need to know about: I'd signed up for the New York City Marathon. It was slated for November 4th, and I was there in May to figure out where my lodging was going to be, and how I was going to travel from wherever that was to the shuttle buses on 42th Street the morning of the marathon, the kind of stressful logistics that can wreck your performance even before the race begins.

Co-mingling my race objectives with Sierra service, I marched happily along. We did landscaping work: building and seeding a berm; pulling, digging and cutting weeds; and spreading gravel inside a dog run, a fenced

Going Down Slow

area where dogs are permitted without their leash.

Each day we met Debbie Sheintoch, Director of Volunteers for Riverside Park Fund, to get our assignment for that day. She and her assistant, Kimberly Green, supplied a pickup truck loaded with the hand tools needed: wheelbarrows, shovels, rakes, and so on.

The work was hot and hard. One woman broke her wrist. Debbie skewered her hand on a honey locust thorn.

We worked by day, but the nights were ours. Our lodging was in the International Youth Hostel on the Upper West Side. We slept dormitory style, four strangers to a room, a tiny space not much larger than a walk-in closet. After work we'd return to the hostel for a shower and dinner. Then it was showtime!

A couple of Broadway plays, the Emerson String Quartet at Carnegie Hall and ballet at the Lincoln Center were some of the shows we took in. Two other campers and I opted out on the ballet and went instead to Shea Stadium where we watched the Diamondbacks thump the Mets, 5 to 1.

On two afternoons before going out on the town, I squeezed in a run through Central Park. The first run circled the upper park, the second explored the lower part of the park, wherein lies the marathon finish line, a location of some interest to me.

Our first day in town, Memorial Day, in lieu of work we took a 16-hour tour of New York, a walk Jerry calls his "Grand Tour." What a walk it was. The man ought to be a marathoner. He wore our legs off. We started in Brooklyn, walked across the Brooklyn Bridge, past Town

Going Down Slow

Hall, Ground Zero, Wall Street, Chinatown, Little Italy, Greenwich Village...

One camper carried a pedometer that showed a total of sixteen miles for the day, not a bad training distance. And I think its mileage was low. Jerry went fast and, among the crowd, he was hard to keep in sight, a concern for those of us who didn't know the town.

"I've never seen anything like this [town]," Eugene DeMine said. "I feel like if I get lost here, I'll die here!" Eugene was no country hick; his day job had been in downtown Los Angeles, and he lives in a suburb of that city now.

We finished the day with cheese cake and coffee at Veniero's on East 11th Street and then ambled through Washington Square listening to a collection of street musicians jamming away the night.

Occasionally a coincident smacks you that seems too remote to be possible, as one did on this trip. On Wednesday we saw the play "Inherit the Wind," starring Christopher Plummer and Brian Dennehy. The play is based on the Scopes monkey trial in Dayton, Tennessee in 1925. Schoolteacher John Scopes was found guilty of teaching evolution in his science classes. Although I grew up in Tennessee, I'd never seen either the play or the movie.

Next morning we reported to work at Riverside Park, near 86th Street. There Debbie introduced us to Charlotte Mayerson, a park volunteer. Charlotte maintains a large flower garden inside a fenced area of the Park. Irises, the Tennessee State Flower, were in full bloom. Our job

Going Down Slow

that morning was to help remove the weeds and rake the leaves from her garden.

Something about the woman's friendly demeanor and community spirit intrigued me. I hauled out my notebook, an object I'd discreetly kept out of sight until then, and began asking questions.

She has lived at her present location on Riverside Drive at 86th Street for fifty years. In addition to her gardening she organizes a series of concerts in the park.

She motioned toward a plaza down the hill. "I run concerts here on Sundays. [This] Sunday we have a brass quintet. Next week a soul group, C. Phineas. And the next week a jazz band called the Jacob Rodriguez Family Project."

First wonder: Denying retirement, she said she was a writer and editor. She had been Executive Editor at Random House. The woman had presided at the top of the publishing world. She still dips her fingers in that pie.

Here is what a reader may not know; I know it in my marrow, from having sent out seventy-five-page book proposals time and again:

An unknown author has a better chance of gaining an audience with the Pope than talking with a New York editor.

Yet by the wildest improbability there I stood, notebook in hand, talking with one. I never once said, "I wrote a literary book about running and may write another one or two." That would have been rude, I thought.

Second wonder: I mentioned seeing "Inherit the Wind," innocently unprepared for what would come from her next.

"John Scopes was a friend of mine. He wrote an

Going Down Slow

autobiography...and I published it."

Working on the book, they had become friends; she knew him well. Then Charlotte Mayerson told me this: "He said, 'if you were twenty years older I'd marry you.'"

It was a history lesson, I guess. I'd managed to live close to the biblical three score and ten without ever seeing "Inherit the Wind." Then the very morning after seeing it, I met John Scopes' friend—and publisher.

There on the Upper West Side, in Riverside Park, standing next to the Tennessee State flower, I met Charlotte Mayerson.

Our last night in town, a Saturday, we had a supper of ribs and chicken at a Harlem soul-food restaurant called Miss Maude's Spoonbread Too, on Malcolm X Boulevard at 137th Street. On the way we stopped at the Apollo Theater, home to legendary soul and R&B acts. Jerry had recruited a Harlem expert to tell us a little about it.

We stood in front of the Apollo, and the expert compared it to the Ryman Auditorium in Nashville, a place he'd visited. His comparison was apt, I thought. The two theaters are similar in a way. Each stands as an historical musical shrine where music bubbled up from the people—country music in the Ryman, R&B in the Apollo.

There was in our group a woman named Jill Gaster, who made her living as a pop singer until age thirty, when her daughter was born. She sports a quaking frizz of red hair, the kind of unabashed woman people used to call a rounder. So as we walked away I asked her,

"Did that view of the Apollo Theater make your rock and roll heart skip a beat?"

Going Down Slow

"You know what?" she answered. "Growing up in North Carolina, I used to stay up on Saturday night to listen to a program from the Apollo. I figured I was the only white girl in the state listening to that show."

Jill is a nurse now. She also attends college on a music scholarship. She applied for the scholarship not knowing an audition was required. She sang a song anyway. It was good enough to win the prize.

Around the first of November I was scheduled to once again be in New York City, either running, preparing to run, or recovering from having run the Marathon. That's the plan. There is the rigor of training. Nothing is certain. The families of nearly 3,000 who went to work in the twin towers that last morning will tell you that.

New York is a kinder and gentler place these days, a running friend told me, somehow sobered by that tragedy of September 11. At lunch one day, I sat in the grass by the river with Kimberly, the park assistant. She is a willowy black woman who looks thirty but claims fifty. I asked her why she works for the Park. Was it to be outside?

No, she just didn't want to be in the tall buildings anymore. She'd worked for a bank as an administrative assistant.

"The Empire State Building and the twin towers, those were my views. I saw the towers come down. The antenna stayed straight all the way down. That stuck in my mind. My last two shots [photographs], it was coming down."

She tried to get home. "I went into a subway that was still working. Then I heard two loud explosions, and I

Going Down Slow

went running out of there like a bat out of hell."

She was shaken. For the next year and a half her daughter had to walk her to work each day. So she changed jobs to get out of the big buildings. She still tries to understand what happened in 2001.

"Why did they do that?" She asks. "I mean, we don't hate anybody because of their religion. We're just working, trying to pay the rent."

Her question searched through the wind out over the Hudson, finding no answer.

They will scarcely notice if I go running, I figure. The twenty-three others are like strangers. I only met them Sunday night, and now it is Thursday. Lee and Willard, two of my roommates at the hostel, know I'm going. They'll hardly raise a panic if I don't return, none of their worry.

"Screw it! He's a grown man, he knew what he was doing," they'll say.

Willard is an educated bubba from Arkansas. He despises Republicans and defies anybody bossing him around. "Let me see your supervisor's licenses," he demands.

Lee, a Navy retiree from Pensacola, is given to blurting out strangely irrelevant statements in a rapid-fire mumble nobody can understand. "I don't know what the hell Lee's talking about half the time," Willard told me one day. "I think, 'What was that Lee said! Man, I need to clean out my ears.'"

Brad, my other roomie, is from Utah. His hobby is dirt

Going Down Slow

bike racing. He combines motorcycles with cardiology, his day job. He sports a shiny pate on top and a ponytail in the back.

He never talks. It's hard to guess what he knows. Damned if I see how he finds his way around anyone's heart—he barely finds his way down the sidewalk, always holding the group up one way or another: showing up late, forgetting his subway card, wandering off to nobody knows where.

"I'd leave his ass," Willard says. He would too.

Presenting, then, the cast and setting: four misfits stuffed in a tiny room on New York's Upper West Side, all, more or less, trying to be agreeable.

For now, the day's work is done, and I'm going running. So I stuff my credit card, room key and four folded $100 bills in my key pocket and set out. Except for the key, I don't need those things, but I can't leave them in the hostel for roving thieves.

From Amsterdam at West 103rd Street I head east, through Frederick Douglass Houses, a high-rise project spanning two blocks. I hit Central Park West and duck into the park itself.

I run past the bench where I'd lunched Sunday, just after arriving in town. I didn't have a room then, but I'd stowed my bags in one of the hostel's lockers, two bucks for twenty-four hours. I'd walked over to the park, stopping at a bodega for a candy bar and a Gala apple, and picked up a hot dog from a street vendor.

I sat on the bench wielding my K-Bar folder, slicing wedges off the Gala, the only apple suitable for human

Going Down Slow

consumption in my book. Woman from New Jersey walks up. "Where are the restrooms?" she asks. I swear. I hadn't been there twenty minutes, and here comes a woman asking directions. Did I look like a bored New Yorker dawdling away his Sunday?

"I just got in town," I said. "I don't know where they are. If we were in Tennessee, I could point you to a tree."

Restrooms? I couldn't advise her. I'm a stranger here. I didn't even know what I was going to do next.

Remembering, I run past that bench now and head on across the park, passing baseball fields. A rock outcropping rises up from the grass. Young woman with a laptop sits on top, practicing an expression of languid boredom. Pretty, young and alone, perched on a rock, like a bluebird on a stump.

It's not a long jog across. The park is only half a mile wide. I hit Fifth Avenue and hesitate, wondering whether to exit the park, or stay on a path. After all, my secret is I know where I'm going: I plan to circle the park's upper side. I can do that within or without the parapet wall. I decide to stay inside the park, on the paths.

Helen will notice if I'm not back for supper, I bet. "Where's Dallas?" she'll ask. Ours fates entwined strangely that first day, last Sunday.

Two dozen of us arrived at the International Youth Hostel, planning to bunk there and do some work on Riverside Park. Our leader, Jerry Balch, had made room assignments, four persons to each room. He hadn't known me except through correspondence.

He thought I was a woman.

Going Down Slow

Something I'd said in e-mail. I noticed his reply had been quite friendly. I discovered his error Sunday when I asked him why I was assigned to a room with three women.

"I thought you were a woman," he said.

Well, I'm not. My white beard helped convince him. But he didn't know what to do about the room. He dreaded changing everything.

"Just make out tonight…" he told me, and then trailed off, suggesting he'd think about it later.

I lugged my bags up the stairs to room 425, dropped my key in the slot and let myself in. The surprised women in the room saw their new bunkmate and started laughing. They thought it was so very funny. I didn't know how to take that.

We talked. They told me Helen's sad story. Before my *de jure* sex change, Helen had been an extra female, and Jerry had assigned her to bunk with three men in 410. That suggested a swap. I skedaddled around to 410 and knocked on the door. There I found Willard and Helen unpacking their bags.

I made my proposal—that Helen and I swap rooms. A wide smile spread across her face. It was deliverance for her. She had already resigned herself to bunking with three men.

"You could tell Helen was nervous, but she was determined to suck it up and make the best of it," Willard told me later.

That night at supper we put on name tags so we could learn who everyone was. On her tag, Helen had written:

Going Down Slow

"Helen, 'friend of Dallas.'"

If I fail to return from this run, Helen will notice.

Skirting along the upper park border at 110th Street now. Given that I started at 103rd Street this won't be a long run. Three miles will be O.K., and it looks like that's how it might work out once I return.

A lake on my left, two little kids squatting at the edge squinting at something on the ground. Maybe they caught a fish, or maybe it's just a tadpole. Kids love messing around water.

Tadpoles, fish, turtles, frogs…I remembered seeing a bucket of bullfrogs at a fish market in Chinatown. There were a dozen or more sitting quietly in two inches of water at the bottom of their jail. They couldn't remember how to croak. They sat silent, like church was going to start.

There are fish here in the middle of Manhattan. My jog takes me past another small lake. I know bass live in there. I saw one on top a few days ago. Guy was pointing it out to a passerby. A few casts of my ultra light… But, no, that bass should be left for little kids who squat at the edge and dream. I can remember doing so myself, many years ago in a very different place.

Before the waters of Cordell Hull Lake drowned it forevermore, there was Billy White's Slue, a shallow two-acre lake standing in the bottomland of Smith Bend, in Jackson County. It could have been called a lake or a pond, even a swamp, but we always called it a slue. Each winter the floods of the Cumberland River filled it with backwater and fish. Then the floods receded, leaving the

Going Down Slow

water and fish trapped.

Brush and trees lined its banks. River bottoms stretched beyond, fields of rich, black dirt strewn by flint chippings and stone tools left by ancient humans. The bottoms grew corn and soybeans, and dropped steep sandy banks down to a languid river. Plowed cropland abutted woodlots, thickets and canebrakes. In the branches muskrats and raccoons caught crawfish, discarding pinchers and shell fragments on the bank. Lowlands oozed oily water and grew dense stands of swamp grass where cottontails and quail took cover.

When I was young, the slue belonged to Joe Myers. When he died in 1949 the farm passed to his son, Billy White Myers, who farms and lives there yet. He has always been called by two names. We dropped his last name and simply called the slue Billy White's.

As a boy, I prowled that slue and all the land surrounding it whenever I could. Everything was there—squirrels, fish, turtles, snakes and, sometimes, ducks. I'd sneak up on the waterfowl with my .410 single-shot. They always flushed out of range of the little gun.

That patch of earth had everything an eleven-year old boy needed. It had always been there. He could not have known it would one day be gone.

It sustained me until I grew up and left the Bend. In 1973 it slipped away, sinking beneath a cold flood that had come to stay.

Before then, though, it was the location of the great carp adventure. I think Carson Givens gave me the idea that led to it.

Going Down Slow

Carson and his family lived in the three-room house near the bottom of the hollow on our farm. He rented the house for half of whatever he and his mules could grow on the farm, a typical arrangement for farmers lacking their own land in those days. "Sharecroppers" is the rude term, but we called them renters, and there was no shame in it. A man did what he had to do.

What Carson had to do was fish. It was a calling and a gift. He could catch fish better than anybody I knew. A place where he couldn't catch fish was a place with no water. I admired him very much. Fishing was important.

He kept trotlines and funnel-shaped nets called fish baskets strung out in the current of the Cumberland River. Each morning and night he checked his lines and baskets, cranking up an old Ford sedan and bouncing a mile over the farm road that wound along the fields and across the spring branch down to the river.

The fish he caught he stowed live in a cage suspended in the river. Thus he always had fresh fish on hand when people came wanting to buy some for supper. He caught buffaloes, catfish, drums, jacks and carp.

His wife and kids helped with the fieldwork. That arrangement gave Carson time to fish. He made money from fishing, and it helped support his family.

This gave me the inspiration to cabbage the carp in Billy White's slue and to sell fish steaks.

Carson's son Harold and I threw in together. Harold was eleven years old, the same age I was. He brought along his young brother Pee Wee, not big enough to help much, but his presence increased Harold's share.

Going Down Slow

It was a hot summer, and the slue was drying up. When we got there, all that was left of it was a yard-sized puddle of roiling gray water surrounded by two acres of cracked blue mud. You could see the hemmed-in fish as they sloshed and churned, their backs slicing though the gray water. We had a fish bonanza.

But we could not reach them. The mud near the water was worse than quicksand. The waxy sludge grabbed our feet and would not let go, and the closer we got to the water, the deeper we sank.

We solved the problem by finding a rotting flat-bottomed boat resting against the bank at the slue's normal edge. We dragged it across the cracked mud, then got in and poled across the slime until we arrived in the middle of the gray puddle. There we sat surrounded by a swarm of agitated carp.

My frog gig was no help. The fish were so big, their scales so tough, the prongs of the gig bent each time I tried to spear one. Did not need it anyway. The direct approach was better. We simply reached over the side and lifted the sagging fish into the boat. Soon the boat bottom was full of flopping carp.

Getting our haul home was the next hurdle. We strung the fish up in three bunches, a small one for Pee Wee. To do that, we slipped a cord through their gills and out their mouths. Their lips would open and close in gasps, kissing the air. We each slung a string of limp fish over our shoulder and starting walking. The fish hung down our backs, nearly dragging the ground.

The weight was too great. The cord cut into our hands

Going Down Slow

and shoulders. We had to stop and rest every few steps. Two miles seemed a long way. Finally, half a mile from home and just past our spring, we lightened our load, throwing some of the fish in a cornfield for the crows.

I arrived at the house with a lightened but still heavy haul. Harold and Pee Wee walked on with their share. I started cleaning fish, squatting in the backyard, working on a board. I figured that if people buy whole fish from Carson, they would give even more if the fish were already cleaned and sliced. Somebody would.

The fish scales were big and coarse, and scraping them off was hard work. My pocket knife was not big enough, and I had to borrow Momma's butcher knife. Even with her big knife, it was slow going.

I put slabs of coarse, white meat into a pan. The pan filled slowly. I worked until nearly suppertime and still had fish left to clean. After working so long I was tired. I gave up on cleaning the last few fish and flung them over the fence, a present for the hogs.

Nonetheless, I had managed to build a hefty stack of fish slabs in the pan, and Momma agreed to fry some for supper. The rest I stored in the refrigerator until I could find buyers. I was hungry and ready for the payoff.

It did not come. The fried fish tasted just like the mud they had lived in, impossible to eat. I think Momma expected that. I had to throw away all that fish, all my hard work. A mouth full of that fish was like a mouth full of mud.

* * *

Going Down Slow

The sounds of the city jar me back to the present moment, back to Central Park. So dismissing fish, I finish my jog in time for a shower, supper and a ride downtown to catch the Emerson String Quartet.

Friday rolls around, and we quit Riverside Park early. Which fact causes me to once again find myself jogging across Central Park, this time intending to circle the lower park, a longer route than yesterday's was.

I jog across the park, like yesterday, hit the east side and head south. That is, I get close to the east side. As before, I decide to stay on the park paths, rather than stepping outside and running down Fifth Avenue. But I don't find that easy. There are many paths and—the greenhorn stranger I am—I keep making choices that threaten to take me back toward the west.

Finally I work my way past the reservoir, and decide to take the direct route south: get out and run the sidewalk on Fifth.

But now time becomes my problem. Reluctantly, I decide I'm not going to the southern end of the Park. My crazy zigzag course has taken up too much time.

I have obligations. Helen, Willard and I are planning to catch a Mets game. It will be a seven-mile run by the time I circle back. Must keep my promise.

So I cut through the park at East 65th Street, six blocks short of my goal. That cutoff takes me close to the Tavern on the Green, near the NYC Marathon finish line. But I never see the line. I suspect the reason is the same one that's dogged me on this whole run—jogging the wrong path.

Going Down Slow

In November I shall surely find that line. And I'm going to stomp on it hard, with all the fierce energy my 142 pounds can bring. That's my pledge. I'm going to stomp that line.

And so…eventually I did. The NYC Marathon came on November 4th that year. I found that line after running for precisely three hours, eighteen minutes, and fifty-five seconds, arriving ahead of anyone else in the M65-69 age group.

28

ONE DAY IN FUNKYTOWN

We sit on Madrid's Plaza Mayor drinking beer and eating blood sausage, Albino and I. My overnight flight into Madrid arrived this Saturday morning. Albino drove down to meet me from his home in Burgos, a city in the mountains 150 miles north of here. After walking around Madrid a bit, we've landed here. It is a little chilly but pleasantly sunny this February afternoon. We sit at a table outside, the busy plaza spread before us.

Sharing our table are Belen and Yeya, two young women Albino called a few minutes ago. They are his age, which is half my age. I'm too sleepy to care about that, having missed a night's sleep on the plane. We order another round of beer, another plate of tapas. Belen puffs Marlboros, Ducados for Yeya. The marathoners abstain.

You could argue that Albino and I ought to not be here. We are scheduled to run the Barcelona Marathon. We should be resting, saving our energy for the big show. But then that's not until next weekend. Meanwhile, we have business here.

Tomorrow is the third annual Media Maratón de Latina de Madrid, a half marathon, a race 13.1 miles long. And we plan to run that, too, whether I wake up or not.

Going Down Slow

After two rounds of beer and tapas we quit Plaza Mayor and wander narrow cobblestone streets, ending up at Sanlúcar, a bar that plays flamenco music Albino discovered a few weeks ago. We order another round of tapas and beer. I opt for Coke, playing it safe.

Lacking castanets Yeya claps her hands to the flamenco, little quick pats. Two men and a striking blond woman sit at the table next to ours. A toddler, a little girl, dances beside them. Yeya encourages her. The air is dense with smoke and fast music. Yeya strikes up a conversation with the blond woman, the toddler's mother. Albino tells me that she is an actor on Madrid TV.

More beer comes to our table, more Coke for me. Yeya keeps clapping. The toddler gets tired of dancing and stands looking up at Yeya through dark, baleful and earnest eyes. Yeya gets up and shows her how to dance, swaying her body, feeling the music. She tosses her hair, pulses her lips and cuts hooded eyes at us, clapping to the music.

The party rages until I lose count of the rounds of beer—maybe six, maybe more. My suppertime comes, and I realize I didn't have lunch, just the tapas. Anyway sleep trumps food. My jet lag shows. Albino leans over and says, "We need to get you back to the hotel so you can rest for supper." Belen's car is nearby and she offers to drive us. We amble along, looking for the car.

Yeya sides up to me and asks in English, "How are you, Dallas?"

"*Muy Bien.*"

"*Bien.*"

Going Down Slow

It's a lie; I'm not very well.

After the long drive to Arturo Soria Suites, I feel indebted to Belen. I take her hand.

"*Tú eres tan amable,*" I say. "Thou are so kind."

I turn to Yeya to tell her too. She beats me to the draw. "Thou also."

"*Tú tambien,*" I repeat.

I hug Yeya and brush both cheeks, the same for Belen, then turn away, likely to never see them again, and follow Albino into the hotel.

I hit the sack at six o'clock, skipping supper. Albino leaves to meet friends. Down on me crashes the paradox of jet lag: an overwhelming fatigue capped by an ironic inability to sleep. I lie wide awake, awake. Albino returns around midnight and I am still awake. We chat. Soon he is quietly asleep. I continue my sleepless night.

Morning comes. At 7:30 a.m. Albino raises up. I am already awake.

"It's late," he says.

He's right, if we plan to make the 10 o'clock race start.

I sit on the bed, knees propping elbows, miserable all over. No real sleep two nights in a row, and no lunch or supper yesterday. I hate the very thought of running and sit wondering if there's an honorable way out. But it's hopeless. I know that. My sport admires misery, and rewards suffering.

To win, you have to suffer, and to run as hard as you can takes great suffering. You try to out suffer the next guy. He knows how to suffer too. If you are fast enough, and if you suffer enough, you will earn the first place

Going Down Slow

award, a trophy that honors suffering.

Hoping to skip this race is vain fantasy. You can't quit in the face of misery. If there was any doubt, Albino squashes it like a scurrying roach. He opens the window and samples the air.

"It's cold and it's raining."

More misery. That cinches it. Suit up. One step at a time. I pull on running shorts, a long-sleeved tee and grab gloves, and I slip on a warm-up suit for the subway ride. Then I mix some powdered skim milk in a hotel glass and choke down a Snickers Marathon bar. Thus goes breakfast.

The subway trip across town to the Latina District takes twenty stops and one transfer. We ride along. Time drags on. Albino sits opposite me. He glances at his watch.

"We're not gonna make it."

That opinion stirs me none at all. There is nothing to be done. The train will reach our stop in time or it won't. If it does, there'll be another step. Until then I ignore my watch.

Of course the train arrives in time, with thirty minutes to spare. Disembarking, we follow other runners who had accrued to the train.

We search for Angel, one of Albino's Madrid friends. He has his car at the race site, and that's where we plan to lock our warm-up clothes, wallets and keys during the race. We not only find Angel but also Jorge and Eduardo, two more friends. We all lock our stuff in Angel's car. Streets are wet, light rain falling, and the temperature is forty-five degrees. You hate giving up the warm clothes.

We are bandits. The race reached its 3,000 limit of

Going Down Slow

runners before we applied, and so we couldn't get an official bib number to compete. We will run it like thieves, shamelessly stealing the volunteers' work, the gifts of water and food, traffic control, all.

Banditry becomes a blessing. I don't have to run hard; I use the race for training. Albino and I decide to stay together, and I settle into my marathon pace, which is naturally slower and easier than my half-marathon pace.

It's fitting that Albino and I run together today, a sort of commemoration. It was this month five years ago when we met. That was in a different half marathon, not here in Madrid but in the little town of Burns, Tennessee. He pulled up beside me. I was running too hard that day to talk, but we chatted briefly. He said he was from Seville, Spain. I wasn't sure I'd heard that right, but I had. He'd been in the U.S.A. then only a month and was living in Hopkinsville, Kentucky.

He was thirty-one and I was sixty-two at the time. Despite that age difference we became friends, a rare friendship spanning two generations. I wanted to help him make friends in his new home. After the race that day I introduced him to a couple of pretty women. I needed not worry. Soon he developed a circle of friends around Nashville, a town that became his spiritual home.

Three months later he invited me to his thirty-second birthday at his house in Hopkinsville. The tables had turned. It was now I who met new friends, including the beautiful Luz Maria and singer songwriter Stan Lawrence, who brought his guitar and sang for us that day.

Four years later Albino's job took him to Michigan.

Going Down Slow

After a year there it moved him again, this time to the mountains of northern Spain, far away from Seville, much further still from Nashville, the two cities he loves.

This day we run side by side in the cold drizzle, through crowded wet streets and along curving roads through green parks. I have no idea where we are. On a hill Albino gets tired. His job has kept him from training well.

"If you need to speed up, go ahead," he says. I laugh and hug his shoulders.

"Speed up? Speed up? Man, I don't need to speed up! I'm staying with you."

A mile from the finish line Angel stands on the curb. He has finished the race already, and jogged back along the course to find us. He runs beside us just long enough to pin his bib number on Albino's chest. Now Albino can cross the finish line, wearing a number nobody will know is not his. To theft, add fraud and conspiracy. We only laugh.

After the race we converge on Angel's car, Jorge, Eduardo, Albino and I. Angel holds a bundle out to me. "For you," he says. It is the red tee shirt all official finishers receive. Somehow he has wrangled one for the bandit. Printed on the front is the logo: *3 a Media Maratón de Latina*. I didn't officially cross the finish line, but I ran the distance. I'll wear the shirt all right.

A bar is just a few steps away. A bar is *always* just a few steps away. Today is Angel's birthday; following custom, he buys a round of beer for everyone. Except that I have coffee. I can't get warm, even with my dry clothes

Going Down Slow

on. My hands are in shock, a condition called Raynaud's Syndrome. The fingers go numb and turn the pale color of death. Only the application of heat can reverse the condition. Through my gloves no one can see the unsightly pallor. I sit with my fingers wrapped around the warm coffee cup and hold my secret close.

We were cruising through the mountains of northern Spain in Albino's BMW. It is 379 miles from his home in Burgos to Barcelona, and we were headed there for the marathon, Marató Barcelona, which would happen two days later.

My running watch thought it was already tomorrow, showing March 1 as we drove along, having forgotten that it was leap year. I scrolled up February 29, creating myself an extra day.

Albino had brought along a couple of soft cases filled with CDs for our listening pleasure during the long haul. He sat with a case spread open on his lap and flipped through the choices, occasionally minding the wheel while we rolled along at the sensible speed of ninety mph, burning up the road to Barcelona. He has an eclectic taste in music and we listened to everything from Andre Segovia to Miles Davis to Etta James.

That last one was on a CD called *Night Train to Nashville*, which Albino bought at the Country Music Hall Of Fame during an exhibit highlighting Nashville's blues heritage. He held the CD up for me to see.

"You wanna hear that?"

"Sure, why not? Plug it in."

Going Down Slow

The very first sound to come out blasted me backwards fifty years. It was disc jockey John Richburg—John R his own self!—introducing his blues show from Nashville's WLAC-AM clear channel station. At night that station ruled the airways over two-thirds of the nation during the 1950s and 60s, days before FM radio. The sun went down, WLAC jacked up its power and all stations with the same frequency blinked off. It didn't matter if you lived in a holler in Appalachia or drove a taxi in Chicago, you listened to John R advertising Ernie's Record Mart, White Rose Petroleum Jelly and Silky Straight.

"...John R in Nashville, Tennessee, smack in the middle of Dixie!" John R was saying on the recording.

Damn! I swear I hadn't heard that voice in nearly half a century. They'd captured his voice from that long ago time and stuck it on the CD. It was as if the space-time continuum stretched and twisted and folded back on itself. No longer was I hurling through arid mountains in northern Spain but instead lying on a feather bed in the unheated room of a farm house in Jackson County, Tennessee listening to an old white AM radio that sat beside the bed. John R talked me to sleep at night.

I never saw a picture of John R, and I hope I never do. I didn't know if he was black or white, and I didn't give two hoots which it was. What I have left is his voice. And I'll have that until they take away my drool bucket.

That's how we drove 379 miles to a marathon—listening to obscure musicians that most people never heard of. Albino knows that old music from the 50s and 60s even though he grew up in Seville, Spain and wasn't

Going Down Slow

born until 1971. He collects vinyl records and owns 500 CDs. After he moved to Hopkinsville, Kentucky, he quickly fell in love with Nashville. Today he fetched along a bit of Nashville for our trip.

At ninety mph you can drive 379 miles in four hours and thirteen minutes. So says kinematics. Practically speaking it doesn't work out that way. You lose time. We had to stop and buy gas, and eat lunch, and pay tolls. Three times we paid the toll takers. Two times it cost 26 Euros ($39 US), non negligible, we thought.

The driver got sleepy, too. I suggested we pull into a parking area because I wanted to make a picture. Albino stretched out for a nap and I took a little hike to get my picture.

What picture? Of something that had bothered me a bit—the way the landscape is changing. We were traveling through a scrubland of brown rocks and badlands reminiscent of Wyoming, terrain familiar to fans of early Clint Eastwood westerns. Now and then we saw a compact town huddled on the slopes, some cropland.

And across the ridgeline marched rows of metallic invaders, tall aliens stalking the land, now facing windward at rigid attention. Legions of wind turbines turned lazily. The unearthly-looking machines provide clean energy all right but, in their imposing strangeness, they completely alter the value of landscape for the human spirit. As global oil production diminishes, their numbers will grow. Spain, as well as all the nations of the world, will need their help to meet energy needs. I made my picture, and photographed the future.

Going Down Slow

When we finally reached Sunotel on Gran Via in Barcelona, our nerves were whacked. It had all worn us out: Trying to find our hotel in traffic worse than New York City, getting the strap on my backpack caught in the car's hatch so that it wouldn't open while traffic backed up behind us, a guy insistently blowing his horn. Albino: "That's why I don't carry a weapon; I would have shot him!"

Albino asked a surly red-faced clerk for a late check-out time for Sunday, the day of the marathon, so that we could take a shower before starting our 379-mile drive back to Burgos. Hotels usually comply happily with that request. Yeah, he could do that but it would cost us 30 Euros extra. Sure. Another insult. Albino fumed, but we had little choice.

And then Angel arrived, a friend from Madrid, a generous *hombre* and also a formidable one. He had made our reservation. He dismissed our fear. Don't worry, you won't have to pay that, he assured us. He was as good as his word, we found out when we checked out that Sunday.

Eduardo and Jorge, two more Madrid friends, arrived. Jorge was escorting Alejandra, his *esposa hermosa*.

We all went to the marathon expo the next day, the place where you confirm your registration; pick up your timing chip, bib number and other miscellaneous stuff, a place where you can also shop for all sorts of running gear. It was crowded; about 8,000 runners had registered for the race.

The men's water closet was crowded too. A woman worked to keep it orderly — *while men were there*. Men did

Going Down Slow

arrive and men did go right in front of her, including myself. I was squeamish about that but overcame it.

In the words of Robert Jordan, the protagonist of *For Whom the Bell Tolls*, a book I was currently reading, Ernest Hemingway said, "There are no other countries like Spain." I believe that's true, and in many ways. Barcelona is maybe an example.

As far as the rest of Spain is concerned, the town is perhaps too proud of having its own language. Catalan, which is spoken by its seven million citizens, is distinct from Castilian, the Spanish language. The reality then is that people of Barcelona must be able to speak several languages in order to talk to anyone. Nevertheless they cling to their history and culture as people are wont to do. As we made the rounds of the various counters, booths and tables at the expo, Albino came up to me.

"Did you notice that nobody will open their mouth until you start talking? They don't know what language to speak. There are so many languages here!"

Angel has refined taste, and he had made lunch reservations for our gang of six at Seven Doors, *Siete Portes*, a white tablecloth place where the waiters wear black ties and dinner jackets. It's been in business since 1836 they claim. We had *paella* – good race food, rice based – and wine and beer. I abstained from those last two, in abeyance to race needs. The tab for six came to 220 Euros, around $330 US.

That night I passed up a visit to still another white tablecloth place, opting instead for marathon snacks, rest and television: professional basketball, the *ACB*, Europe's

Going Down Slow

answer to the NBA; and, maybe better, the Miss Espanya contest, a gaggle of gorgeous women in tiny Bikinis. One by one, they did prance, each gliding the runway like a walking horse hitting its gait.

I was pulling for Miss Tenerife, but Albino came in around midnight and we turned in. I didn't find out who won. Come 8:30 next morning we had a marathon to run.

Morning comes to Barcelona.

The window in our seventh-floor room faces south, overlooking dark patios and balconies of apartments below. The crescent moon hangs low and a pale glow washes the eastern sky. It'll be daylight soon. Our time is near. The marathon Albino and I've long aimed at will start just two hours from now. I open the window and stick out my hand, the old anxious question about the weather. Barcelona hums and answers: perfect, calm and warm.

Albino and I meet our bunch in the lobby for the walk to the race. Alejandra, Jorge's gracious wife, who is not running today, carries my camera to make pictures for me. We drift up Gran Via, a loose collection of six warriors. Morning is creeping over the city. There's no sense of rush. Eduardo, who is the youngest of us, strolls with me, the oldest. Today he makes his first marathon attempt.

"How do you feel, Eduardo?"

"Pretty good. A little nervous."

"Don't worry. That will fly away as soon as the race starts."

"I know."

Going Down Slow

I would go into battle with this bunch. A man could do worse. Angel, talking with Albino at this moment, is competent and tough, a natural leader, continually showing generosity to the others. Jorge is a big man with ample muscle strength for strong-arm jobs, an engineer and problem solver. He has a booming laugh that keeps everyone in good humor. And who could guess the depth of quiet strength in Alejandra, the lone woman.

Look at Albino and Eduardo — two smart young guys, bold and successful, intimidated by nothing, Eduardo serving in the economic office of Spain's president, Albino managing the finances of a multinational company.

A good team all right. We have to split up today though. Each has to go separate and alone. At the Placa, the five marathoners line up and pose for Alejandra, all smiling bravely.

The race starts on Avenida de la Reina Maria Cristina, a short street stretching from Placa de Espanya to Museu Nacional D'art Catalunya. I find my place and stand with 8,000 marathoners, among the "blue" group, up front due to my projected finishing time. The Plaza lies 200 meters straight ahead, an ornate monument anchoring a traffic circle flanked by two tall, elegant towers. Behind us on a hill sets the Museum of Art, a palatial building fronted by Font Montjuic, the Magic Fountain. A more glorious place to start and end a race would be hard to find.

The Magic Fountain, asleep until now, starts up behind us. A soprano's voice ascends high in the morning light, then swoops and soars over us, the Fountain choreographed to her singing. Some 3,600 jets, articulated

Going Down Slow

and synchronized, create water acrobatics of myriad forms.

The central jets shoot founts of water higher than a tree while peripheral founts dance and waver like ballerinas. Suddenly the central founts sweep gracefully outward, forming a giant water blossom of hurling water. The whole display trembles and collapses into a frothing cloud of angry mist and chaos, then recovers its coherence and rises to dance again. Meanwhile the fountains lining both sides of the Avenida beside us begin spraying white founts into the morning sunlight.

It's a glorious send-off. I stand facing backwards and watch the Fountain, looking over the anxious faces of scowling runners behind me. They appear oblivious to the water ballet. Why are they so worried? I wonder. Thus I am when the race begins, and I know we are under way when the throng surges forward, pushing me along like flotsam on a wave.

The race has started.

The first three miles it's all elbows and heels, and body odor of visitors from countries unaccustomed to deodorant. I want a fresh breath.

At the end of the first 5K, I check my watch and discover I've fallen one minute behind my planned pace, due mostly to the crowded conditions and twisting turns, I figure. During the next 5K, I make a point of fighting off the feeling of lost time and run no harder than before, monitoring my breathing to keep my effort in check. Even so I gain back half the lost minute.

Aided by the thinning of the crowd, the running

Going Down Slow

becomes quite easy. The markers pass me by: 10K, 15K, 20K.... My speed holds with little effort from me, varying only a few seconds from my planned pace of 23:17 per 5K, 7:30 per mile.

A couple of male fans see an old guy cruising along, white-bearded but still trucking. Their surprise shows. They lean in, clapping hard and shouting.

"Muy bein, senor!"

This marathon is the most scenic urban race I've run. Barcelona is a complex city, a mixture of crass and sublime, sacred and profane. Ancient buildings and monument-filled plazas scatter themselves throughout the city. On top of that—which you expect—Barcelona boasts several architectural icons that are singularly unusual. The course takes us by some of them.

Catedral de Sagrada Familia, Church of the Holy Family, is a religious shrine like Las Vegas is a summer camp. Dark, imposing and forbidding, it squats before us, shooting spires of curvilinear taper high aloof. Its front is covered with statuary of saints and drips all sorts of scabby relief I can't quite make out. No place looks plain. It is all busy, like a cave turned inside out. Pale salamanders would not surprise you.

A cathedral's purpose is to cause a fear of God. Fearsome is a word to fit this temple. So gloomy and morose, it strikes me, paradoxically, as downright sinister. The Dark Lord of Mordor hatched his evil plans in a place like this. The church was designed by architect Antoni Guadi, who died in 1926. It's still not finished.

Three miles later we come to a new addition. Torre

Going Down Slow

Agbar is as unusual in its shiny and garish way as the cathedral. This 474-foot tall structure of curving sides and round nose sets on the Plaza of Glories like a spent bullet plunked down and clad with tinsel, a phallic paraboloid thrust bluntly into the helpless sky.

Not actually tinsel, the second skin is assembled from glass sheets, some 59,619 of them, which open and close under command of the building's climate system. At night its 4,500 LED lights glow brightly in myriad colors. The water company of Barcelona, Agua de Barcelona, innocently owns this gaudy shaft.

The marathon fans are as friendly as the city is picturesque, helping me along with their shouts.

"*Vamos! Venga!*"

"*Animo!*"

This race transports me. We head across a cobblestone plaza where a drum corps bangs away. I fall in step. My foot slaps down smack on the beat. They're playing my 7:30 pace! How did they know?

"Ba-boom, ba-boom, ba-boom," goes drum.

"Left-right, left-right, left-right," goes me.

The music merges with me and me with it. We become one.

"Left-boom, left-boom, left-boom," goes Me-Drum.

We run conjoined. Barcelona plays the root rhythm of my marathon soul, the canonical cadence of my Barcelona being. I race on, the sound fading, my eyes filling with water.

Oh. Trouble begins. I spot a grey-headed man in a yellow tee shirt thirty yards ahead. He looks to be in my

Going Down Slow

age group, over sixty-five. I have to go after him.

It becomes hopeless. He's going too fast. After a half mile I give it up, unable to gain a whisker. To stay with him would take energy I will need later. I might ruin my race down the stretch. It is a tricky business to meter out as much energy as possible, but not enough to go busted.

I let him go and put him out of mind. You don't always win. You shouldn't expect it.

Four months ago in New York it had felt different. I did win there, although four runners led me at the halfway point. But the race wore on them. Ended up, I ran them all down, passing a German and a Portuguese in the last four miles, beating the man from Portugal by just under two minutes.

Maybe I was lucky. You don't always win. You shouldn't expect it. This is Europe.

Around the 19-mile mark we come to the ocean front and follow it a couple of miles. I glance dully at the water. *Water.* Suddenly, I realize, *the Mediterranean!* wind-rippled, sun-dappled blue water I've never seen before.

Meanwhile, sharing that view, the marathon sound track rolls on, pulsing from speakers unseen, surging in hot waves like the heartbeat of the city, its blood coursing through streets and down narrow alleyways. I know that song: Donna Summer, gettin' down on "Funkytown."

If I'm wrong about the singer, it doesn't matter. Donna Summer lodges herself in my head anyway. I run along thinking about the meaning of it, the song ringing in my ears. And I can't connect the two, first view of the Mediterranean with Funkytown. Is there a link, some

Going Down Slow

lesson of philosophy? The race has made me crazy. Some things just *are*. The Mediterranean just *is*. Donna Summer just *is*. Funkytown? Yes. Boogie on, woman!

Two miles to go, suddenly right in front of me is the man in the yellow tee shirt! He'd seemed so strong before I didn't expect to see him again. I assess his new situation: His juice is gone. He's not dangerous now. No need to wait. I sprint around his right and don't bother to look back. He won't challenge; he's finished. I know that story.

That was the moment, I believe, when I took the lead position for the over-65 age group. I never gave it up.

That night Albino and I were back in Burgos, having driven the 379 miles home that same day. Next day we cranked up his laptop. I checked my email to find a message from Marato Barcelona informing me that I'd finished first in my age division, hitting the finish line in 3:17:05.

That was thirty-five seconds slower than I'd meant to run.

The apple sailed past my ear, struck Margarita on the shoulder and fell bonk on our table. Albino exploded angrily out of his chair, glaring at the table of thugs. The smoky air hummed with menace. I sat quietly, dreading the idea of a bar fight.

Assault by apple aside, Burgos is a friendly town. Setting in the mountains of northern Spain, the Chattanooga-sized city straddles the mountain stream, Rio Arlanzon. Founded in 884, the town is the birthplace of the national hero and king "El Cid." The old quarter

Going Down Slow

is centrally located, and well preserved, containing monuments and plazas, the cathedral and the city gate. The 13th century Gothic cathedral, Catedral de Burgos, is large and magnificent, and holds the tomb of El Cid. The city gate, Puerta de Santa Maria, opens to the cathedral plaza, and dates to the 16th century.

I hung out two winter weeks there, living like a spoiled prince. Albino would slip away quietly to work each morning leaving me the run of his new apartment, including his stash of food, CDs and DVDs.

I'd sleep late and get up around 9:30 a.m., have some coffee and breakfast, stretch and then go running. Burgos sets at an elevation of 2,300 feet and so it is usually cold in winter.

A paved path along the river took me past a small dam and lake and its seasonally empty beach; past the bullfighting arena, Plaza Toro, to the center of town, a distance of three miles. Approaching downtown the walking path gave way to busy brick walks and wide plazas. Several pedestrian and vehicular bridges cross the small river. Pairs of ducks looking like ordinary mallards I see in Tennessee dipped for food in the quick, clear water.

After the jog and a hot shower, a light lunch always hit the spot. I'd have a ham and cheese sandwich with chips, followed by a cup of green tea and a cookie from Albino's pantry. Thus I eased pleasantly into each day.

The afternoons I spent listening to the stereo and reading Hemingway's For *Whom the Bell Tolls*, or maybe watching a movie. I caught "The Blues Brothers," "1941" and "The Road to Perdition;" and the music films, Chuck

Going Down Slow

Berry's "Hail, Hail Rock and Roll" and "Ben Harper and the Blind Boys of Alabama: Live at the Apollo."

One day when I finished my run, the local radio station I listened to was by coincidence playing the Rolling Stones' "Start Me Up." Appropriate maybe, but I was, of course, already started up. I also listened to the late classical guitar virtuoso Andres Segovia play "Son de Andalucia," which includes the adagio Miles Davis used so prominently in his "Sketches of Spain."

Balancing Hemingway, I spent one afternoon rereading some twenty old stories I had myself written for the Nashville Striders' *Funrunner*, which issues Albino had saved on his bookcase. Running down memory lane in Burgos, Spain.

Photos of such a picturesque town are required. Some afternoons my camera and I took little walkabouts. Medieval buildings, heroic monuments, elegant plazas and the river itself posed patiently for us. Statuesque women, on the other hand, tended to angle away. *Que va?*

The park-like environment along the river, before one reaches the busy downtown, reminded me of rural Tennessee at times. Pictures I made there could pass for home. One day a sudden snow storm hit, quickly painting trees and grass white. I rushed out to make photos before it melted. They show scenes of peaceful, snow-covered countryside, although my excursion was surrounded by the town.

Townspeople were friendly and helpful to the foreigner. I went into a café and bar for coffee near where I was making photos one day. If you don't want espresso,

Going Down Slow

you need to order American coffee. Even so, it will still be strong as Drano. If you don't want to clean your pipes, a separate cup of hot water is needed to cut the hard brew.

The bartender listened carefully while I explained in deliberate Spanish what I wanted. He turned without a question and fixed exactly what I'd requested. The barmaid stood by, looking on.

Next day I went into the same place and walked up to the bar again. The bartender was absent. The barmaid turned her back and went to work without speaking. Then she set a cup of American coffee and a cup of hot water on the bar, exactly like I'd ordered the previous day. She'd remembered.

Maybe you wouldn't call her pretty. The stringy brown hair, the gapped, yellow-stained teeth didn't help. When she coughed phlegm crackled, signaling a smoking habit. No matter. She was a friendly soul, and kind to me. I handed her a good tip.

"*La propina está para ti.*"

"*Gracias.*" She made a wide smile.

In such a friendly place what then explains the apple throwing insult?

Margarita is a friend of Albino, a Burgos resident and a generation his senior. She had recently helped him decorate his new apartment. Touched by her kindness, he wanted me to meet her, and for us to honor her with dinner.

The restaurant he had chosen was closed when we arrived. Burgos has lots of restaurants. We walked barely a block and went into another. A dark-skinned young

Going Down Slow

woman wearing jeans and a stud in her lower lip showed us to a table against the wall in the back. We walked past a group of young toughs in dark clothes drinking at a round table. Albino saw their eyes following us and knew instantly we'd made a mistake.

Albino and I sat with our backs to the men, Margarita on the other side. We began looking at the menu, speaking part of the time in English. Then we waited for the waitress. That's when the apple whizzed by my head, missing the *Inglis* but hitting Margarita. The front of her shoulder took the blow, a bit of luck. She wears glasses. Had the brushback been higher it could have broken a lens and ruined her eye.

The apple lay on the table in front of me. It looked like a Granny Smith, an apple too hard and sour for anyone to eat, I'd always thought. Two small bites had been neatly sliced from one side. So, at the least, they had a knife.

Albino jumped up ready for a fight. But where I sat blocked his exit. Margarita shrugged at the insult and begged Albino to let it go. But his eyes were hard on the men. He stood, we waited, Margarita pleaded. Reluctantly he honored her wish, then slowly turned and sat down.

The use of English had marked us as foreigners, I figured. Albino was agitated and insulted. He fumed. Who can blame him? The men had actually struck his friend, a woman. By God, he couldn't let it go! He jumped back up to face the crummy bunch. Again Margarita pleaded. My chair still blocked his exit.

Maybe I should have helped him, and maybe we should have fronted them together. But I had no stomach

Going Down Slow

for it, to get knifed or thrown into a Spanish jail either. I've had my scrapes. Shouting matches can spin out of control, and even turn tragic. Albino probably knows that too. Maybe everybody knows it, knows it in their bones, excluding the drinking bullies at the round table.

Finally, Albino, sat down again. I was glad. He held the charge of being our leader. It weighed on him. He'd made the right decision. But it wasn't over.

Suddenly, one of the dark men stood looming over us. He picked up the apple, talking fast in my face. He had a round face and a round head and, therefore, probably snores. He was wasting his breath. I couldn't understand a thing he said. He looked serious and frightened. He talked at Margarita and Albino, too. I thought he was apologizing.

Wasn't so. He left with the apple, our evidence, and the only food I'd seen so far. Albino looked at me.

"Let's go."

"O.K."

We walked past the men. I ignored them as before. The dark-skinned waitress stared, wondering. We walked past her, too, and out the door. Nobody spoke.

Albino knew more than I knew. The man had been mocking us in the guise of an apology, he told me. Staying would have invited more abuse. And it wasn't about language either, English versus Spanish. Spanish was not the man's native language. He spoke so poorly Albino had barely understood him.

"They were immigrants," Albino explained. Probably shift workers whose hangout was that bar. Our appearance, our clothes, marked us as outsiders who did not belong on

Going Down Slow

their turf. They resented us. Albino summed it up: "They were monkeys."

The irony smacks you: Albino and Margarita are Spanish subjects by birth, citizens of the men's host country. As such, they belong anywhere in Spain with more authority than the thugs who'd run us off.

The next restaurant we walked into was called Daleboca, it gives you mouth. We had a simple supper of solomillo, papa fritas and ensalada, sirloin, fries and salad. The meal was tasty and indeed delighted the mouth. I felt so good I drank two beers, and told Margarita I had four grandsons. The people were very friendly.

29

SUMMER HEAT REVEALS ARTIFACT OF MARATHON MAN

A brief nap following a training run has etched the runner's outline in sweat on a concrete slab. The drawing reveals a tiny head and huge upper arms, scarcely any feet at all. Hardly archaeology, you say. Yet one clearly sees a grotesque artifact of Marathon Man, his self portrait of sorts. The figure, at once somber and absurd, lies quietly waiting in the shade.

He looks out from a prison of concrete and sweat like one of the ancient petroglyphs etched into the red-rock wall of a Utah canyon. Unlike those enduring portraits, Marathon Man is doomed and ephemeral, fleeting and soon to depart, just like those ghostly Utah figures say the Anasazi, their creators, did.

We rush forward while we can, and wonder: Are we doomed, too? Does Marathon Man say that? If not, what *does* he say to us? And what shall we in turn say about him?

Gazing at the concrete, its dappled-gray, sweat-receptive porosity, we see a piercing coolness beckoning from beyond, a comfortable firmness that like bedrock can be counted upon, even if we aren't sure upon for what. "Lie here," the figure says. "Let the weariness drain away." The waves of heat rolling over the cold surface are

Going Down Slow

thus soothed and quieted, like a sweet red sunset. And he speaks again:

"Do you see now...do you see what a marathon is?"

Paradox: In order to contest a marathon in the cool air of autumn one must train through the withering heat of summer.

Run twelve miles in July. Rest on concrete. Dream of October's race. Increase understanding. Produce a portrait.

A portrait in mixed media, to be sure, an image rendered in sweat and concrete. Every artist should know his materials.

We shall address that topic now. Let us consider concrete's properties: its density, specific heat and porosity, its modulus of elasticity, its twenty-eight day compressive strength and so on. The properties of sweat must not be neglected either, especially the viscosity and surface tension, quantities blithely ignored by apparel makers, thus leaving runners with blistered toes and bloodied nipples despite the millions those makers spend developing advertising claims.

But artists have little interest in materials science, seeking instead an intuitive, more transcendental (they would say) kind of knowledge. Very well, we shall eschew technical handbooks and their dreary data-filled tables. Experience is the artist's best teacher, says the empiricist.

To know sweat, he advises following this procedure: Run fifteen miles in August. After stretching, sit in a wooden chair on a deck under the sun. Note the sweat-saturated shorts and how the liquid runs from them onto the chair bottom and drips from there steadily onto the

Going Down Slow

wooden floor planking below.

Sit very still. Note the growing puddle size underneath, how it resembles a glistening low dome, the beveled edges bulging with a curvature shaped by the forces of surface tension and gravity working in concert with the fluid's viscosity and density. Each force plays its part in exquisite and elegant harmony, obeying precisely the commanding baton of Sir Isaac Newton.

It is best if, for drainage purposes, the planking has a sight slope. Puddle diameter is thereby limited. Soon, once the puddle becomes hand-sized perhaps, gravity overpowers the ability of surface tension to corral all the fluid. A bulge forms on the puddle's downhill side and gradually takes the shape of a tongue creeping forward like molasses. While sweat continually drips into the reservoir, the tongue — one-and-a-half-inch in width now — grows ever so slowly outward from the puddle, like an amoeba dividing.

A new phase thus begins, the problem passing from one of quasi-statics to the case of fluid dynamics. Engineers, no doubt, will insist on computing a Reynolds' number. But we shall not. No, we remain faithful to empiricism, content to observe the tongue crawling forward, fascinated by its growing length, reminded of the blob oozing under the door in the old Steve McQueen classic.

To eight inches it grows, to a foot, to two feet...

Finally, at a tongue length of thirty-two inches we conclude our exercise in sweat flow and wander off in search of a cold drink, having developed a powerful thirst.

An explanation, if not outright apology, may now be

Going Down Slow

in order, we realize. During our rather tedious discussion of the chosen materials—in which, of course, we only scratched the surface and barely included enough data to suggest the complexities of material selection—during this, the reader may well have concluded that we had forgotten altogether about the image that began this discussion. But, no, like a good story, we shall now return to the beginning, to the image of Marathon Man itself.

The perceptive reader may well object to the grandiose name given to our image, claiming, after all, to see nothing more than a sweat angel. But we reject that simple slander, noting a distinct lack of "angelic" qualities in the image and detecting in their place a trace of sinister overtone. If "sinister" is too strong a word, then at the very least, could one grant, say, a "severely stern austerity?"

Very well then. Consider first the feet of M.M.—nonexistent, owing to the head-on perspective, perhaps. Turn your attention to the calves, however. Note, in the rendering, how huge they are. A marathoner needs strong calves for a vigorous push off and for hill climbing. Our running man exhibits calves to envy.

Ascending further, we encounter a small mystery: The over-developed hamstrings that give the legs of most runners their evocatively curved taper are nearly absent in Marathon Man. Why, one wonders? Moving a bit higher, the riddle solves itself. We realize the cause of the imperfect impression: the hamstrings were held high by the lofting effect of the powerfully developed gluteus maximus muscles, a muscular trait often prized in mate selection rituals.

Going Down Slow

Without doubt, the most astonishing feature of M.M. must surely be the absence of forearms and hands. But of course! — those appendages being totally useless for running. All the runner needs in their place are swinging counterweights. M.M. meets that requirement with his adaptation of massive upper arms, a mass quite sufficient for counterweight purposes, it seems.

Kindly accept, if you will, the tiny head of Marathon Man. He needs only a small portion of a normal brain, the part concerned with speech that repeats over and over in a continuous loop the stupefying phrase familiar to marathoners everywhere: "Keep going forward, keep going forward, keep going forward…"

30

THE MYSTERY OF WATER

It should be no challenge for a writer to fill a page; he should be able to fill a page writing about filling a page. And a page is what editor Peggy Stanfield needed for the *Funrunner* when she faced a lean content one month. The *Funrunner* is the newsletter of the Nashville Striders, the running club I belong to. I'd been donating a story to it each month for years, just doing my little part, when her request for a page arrived.

I thought about it and remembered some images of running I'd stored away. A poem seemed a good idea, since I already had a regular story scheduled in the issue. To avoid my byline appearing twice that month, my alter ego Jargo Fotcher submitted the poem. Also, he could be as silly as he wanted to be. Who does he think he is?

> Everybody was waiting for me to die
> I kept falling asleep, then waking up
> It was trying all around
>
> I arose from the dream
> And bolted out the door
> Running, running, running

Green plastic penguin
Fat with water
Flaps its arms
Fingertips shooting jets
Swirling, flapping, swirling
Little girl squealing, runs away
From the cold sprinkle
Comes back dancing barefoot
Daring the water
The mystery of water

Rusty circle on the road
Marks the dog's end
Used to chase me
Belligerent little wiener
Screaming invectives
Loudmouth: "Don't come back!"
Belligerent little wiener
Rusty stain on the fog line

Bulldozer scraping bushes away
He won't wave
But I know the smell better than he
Anybody would know sassafras
Who does he think he is?

Storefront window in the town
Full of glaze and curved buildings
White bearded ghost flashing by
I taste salt on my lips
    — *Jargo Fotcher*

PILGRIMAGE

31

SHE THREW OPEN HER GOLDEN GATE

On the Embarcadero at 5:20 a.m. it is dark, but not quiet. Four thousand-plus marathoners mill around and gather behind the starting line. Seven thousand half-marathoners further swell the ranks on this August 3. The Bay Bridge arches overhead, lights on its cables tracing their sag.

Running buddy Josh Hite stands with me among the "third wave," runners who will start at 5:35 a.m. Although the temperature is a cool fifty-four degrees and a brisk wind stirs, he stands shirtless, vulnerable and open to the uncertainties of the 26.2 miles.

"I'm not nervous," he says. "I used to get nervous, the first one or two, but not anymore."

He takes a few swigs of water from a bottle I've just finished with, and hands it to a third guy who wants the dregs. It is a grave blunder to start a marathon while needing water.

The first wave—for the elite runners who can run the marathon faster than two hours and fifty-nine minutes—starts out at 5:30 a.m. It is a small group. The second wave goes at 5:31 a.m.

Little disadvantage attaches to being in a later wave.

Going Down Slow

Each runner's time will not start until he crosses the starting line, activated by a tiny computer chip we wear on our shoelaces.

Josh and I wait in the third wave. The race announcer stands ahead in silhouette against the lights and addresses the third wave and the whole stirring thong of humanity stretching beyond. His libertine welcome is worthy of The City by the Bay.

"We don't care what color you are, we don't care what language you speak, we don't care who you look up in the sky or down in the dirt and pray to. All we care is that you are in the race—the human race."

She'll let no stranger wait, and when we came she threw open her golden gate.

5:35 a.m.: runners of the third wave cast our fate to the streets of San Francisco. Along the Embarcadero, past Fisherman's Wharf, we run in the dark. Some are running stern and intense. Others, less so. Some even stop to take snapshots. One guy runs holding a video camera against his face and narrating the footage.

Through Presidio, it becomes light enough to see the Golden Gate looming ahead and high above, its towers snagging the overhead scud. We begin a hard climb to reach the bridge's elevation. Some walk.

"The steep little hill up to the bridge…," Josh later calls it. What came after that was running across the bridge itself, and Josh, who was well ahead of me, remembers that well.

"The wind was so hard from the left side [ocean side] and it was so strong that when I got off the bridge and we

Going Down Slow

were running into the parking lot [Vista Point] to make the turnaround I realized my whole left side had gone numb. I was dreading going back across the bridge because I knew my right side would go numb too."

On the return route, when he came off the bridge for the second time, his wife Martha waited. Martha, who loves sports involving running, such as soccer, does not love running itself. Yet she nearly always accompanies her husband. This day she stood shivering in the wind, wearing a long-sleeved tee shirt and pointing a camera. Her picture shows her shirtless husband running comfortably, scarcely evincing the annoyance of a numb body.

"The view was so nice, I didn't really think about it that much," Josh told me later.

Together, Josh and Martha, who are both natural athletes, operate two Karate schools for kids, one in Cookeville and one in Jamestown.

Josh's path to marathon sport is a complex one. Prior to college and an M.S. in English at Tennessee Tech, he went to high school in Elizabethton and Oneida, where he was a cross-country runner, the only one the school had. He completed his first marathon in 1996, the Walt Disney World Marathon, after the cross-country season was over and just three weeks after turning eighteen. With hubris typical of youth, he did no training for that race, and finished it in a time of four hours and twenty minutes, ten minutes per mile. That humbling time denies his true speed capability.

The prior September Josh had been the overall winner of Cookeville's Fall Fun Fest 10K, finishing in a time of

Going Down Slow

41:37. He will eventually run faster than that. To convert 10K speed into equivalent marathon performance requires specialized training, he has learned.

In today's run, the San Francisco Marathon, Josh's goals are modest, and he is not trying to run a competitive speed. Because he has another problem—he is addicted to marathons. He can't stop. The addiction costs. He runs too many marathons to run them well. Elite marathoners run only two or three marathons per year, going through specific training and recovery cycles. Josh, by contrast, has run ten marathons in the prior twelve months.

Today's run carries us through more than six miles of Golden Gate Park, past bright flower gardens and giant redwood trees with trunks thick as a bus. Significant climbs lurk in three of those miles, climbs which eat up energy and run the clock, and defeat the tired runner, this one, anyway, enduring his nineteenth mile.

Little wonder, that breaking out of that rough patch leads to what Josh says was his favorite part—the route through Haight Asbury, former home of 60s flower power and hippie culture.

"It was up and down, up and down and then you come up on Haight Street and it seems like that was the longest flat stretch...."

In that stretch, we were spaced apart and strung out. Fans were sparse, explaining why Hell's Angels seemed more prominent here. San Francisco Police provided security for the marathon, closing streets and blocking cross traffic at all the big intersections.

At small street crossings, members of the Hell's

Going Down Slow

Angels Motorcycle club drew that job, parking their black motorcycles in the cross street, lounging around in their dark leather clothes and looking fierce as bad boys. Bad girls, too. Some of the riders were women. They looked like the men except for lacking facial hair and having a softer voice when they called out encouraging remarks to passing runners. Their motorcycle barricades effectively barred the traffic.

Hell's Angels, my eye! They were docile as fox hunters.

Vignette on Haight Street: A woman stands quietly beside a man, watching runners file by. Her face twists into a mask of pity as an old marathoner approaches. So old is he, it seems his strength must surely sag to a puddle, leaving him writhing on the asphalt. Her heart goes out to him, watching his failing struggle.

But no, appearances can be deceiving. In passing, the old marathoner catches her eye and smiles. Nothing could've surprised the woman more. She erupts into whoops and applause, and continues clapping and yelling at the old-timer's back as he pads on down the street.

Her cheers touch him. She can't see the old man's eyes watering. But water they did; I was that old man.

Across the range of who-what-where-when-why, the last is the hardest to answer.

Why?

Josh doesn't say exactly. He will recount deeply etched experiences, or talk about goals. Like the Country Music Marathon of '07:

"I was hoping to qualify for Boston at Country Music, and I exploded." He had been "shooting for 3:10," his

Going Down Slow

Boston Marathon qualifying time. So total was his collapse, his run took over four hours.

"After Country Music, I was so upset with myself I signed up for a real hard one." He refers to one of the hilliest marathons around, the Ridge Runner, in West Virginia. He ran it shortly after the Country Music fiasco, in June of '07, finishing in 3:41, a good time for that tough course. He earned himself a bit of redemption there.

Maybe it is not fair to expect any marathoner to answer "why," to tie it up in a box. Why suffer the misery of it? Not only the misery of the race itself, but the long weeks of training, too, running in the heat, or rain, or cold. Or whatever God brings.

Maybe running is nothing more than natural—like love, hate, anger, fear.... Maybe so. Who tries to explain the "why" of those instincts?—natural and normal as they are. And don't people go through plenty of misery for love? Humankind evolved on the African savannah. Running was essential to get food, to survive, to live. To live was to run.

Living is running. Maybe that instinct is still etched into the ancient genes of people like Josh. And me. Maybe there is nothing we can do about it.

"You finish a marathon and you don't even want to think about running another one, but the next day you're already planning one." – Josh Hite.

Josh Hite finished the San Francisco Marathon in a pedestrian time of 3:52, well below his capabilities. I asked him what enduring image dogs his days?

I was glad to see that Bay Bridge," he said.

Going Down Slow

Toward the end of the 26.2 mile course, the Bay Bridge looms ahead, and we pass under it just before hitting the finish line, near the place where we started that morning.

Josh remembers returning to where he started.

32

THE OLD SLUGGER REMEMBERED THE LONG BALLS

You see them at funerals, elders of the community you hardly knew. When you were growing up they were older and you knew who they where but you never knew them in a personal way. Your parents did, and through them to you the thread was spun.

My Aunt Lexie McCormick had died. I liked her very much. She'd worked hard her whole life without ever gaining much property. Her wealth was in the love she held for her children. She was a kind and patient woman. Long-suffering seems to run in the family. I think it yet finds expression in my endurance pursuits. I'd mailed her a copy of my first book, as a complete surprise for her. A voracious reader, she read the whole thing very quickly. The book was about endurance racing, an entire world that must have seemed strange to her. But that didn't matter. Although she could barely hear well enough to have a conversation on the phone, she called me up to tell me how much she liked it and how surprised she was. No one could have given me a better review. A final gift, her wake led me to a story I would never have otherwise found.

I walked into the funeral chapel at Carthage where her family was receiving friends before the funeral. There

Going Down Slow

sat Kaiser Reece in an armchair against the back wall next to the door. The funeral director greeted me, motioned at Kaiser and said, "Do you know this man?"

Kaiser lived in Smith County on Salt Lick Creek up creek from a community called Gladdice. I had grown up on Salt Lick Creek down creek from Gladdice, in the Smith Bend community of Jackson County. We'd been neighbors in that long ago time when I was a kid.

Kaiser stood medium height, stocky and as sturdy as a hickory stump. Although he was pushing eighty, you would take him as a formidable man, and as much younger. We shook. His hand was thick and strong. It had swung a bat like a sickle. A life of farm work had added rough calluses.

I sat in an armchair at right angles to his and we talked. Being fourteen years younger than he, when I was growing up I'd barely known Kaiser. But there was a question I wanted to ask him.

"I know you were a good baseball player when you were a young man," I said. "I heard someone say—I don't know who it was, I think it was when I was real young—that Kaiser Reece hit the longest home run they ever saw at Gladdice."

"I hit one that went sixteen corn rows." He was talking about the corn rows beyond the outfield.

"Next time I came up I hit one that went eighteen corn rows. Both times the bases were loaded."

"Bases were loaded?"

"Yeah. They walked Carl and loaded the bases."

He was referring to Carl Smith, a strong hitter who

Going Down Slow

later played professional baseball. They'd been afraid to pitch to him. Kaiser continued.

"Jargo was playing center field. He said, 'You've messed up now. He's a good hitter.'"

Jargo Flatt was a loud-talking outfielder raised in Gladdice, but he played for the visitors. He knew Kaiser and knew he could hit the ball out. And Kaiser had, going sixteen rows into the cornfield behind the outfield.

Next time Kaiser came up, the visitors, still ignoring their center fielder, pitched around Carl Smith again to bring up Kaiser. This time center fielder Jargo Flatt must have looked on with a mixture of outrage and disbelief. He'd tried to tell them. He could only watch as the ball flew over, heading back to the cornfield and going eighteen rows deep.

"It was in the playoffs. We were playing Rock City."

Rock City was a community west of Carthage, near Rome. Kaiser had hit two back-to-back grand slams against them. His dingers crushed the snakebit team.

"After that, they quit and went home," Kaiser said.

Sitting there in the funeral chapel that day, I failed to ask Kaiser what the score was at that point, or even in what innings he had hit the homers. With two swings of the bat he alone had put up eight runs for Gladdice. Little wonder Rock City went home.

The incident happened during the late forties, I figure. My dad was a baseball player, too, a pitcher. I was born in 1940 and I can barely remember him playing. Daddy was around eleven years older than Kaiser, and so Kaiser's peak playing years would have come correspondingly later.

Going Down Slow

In those years, neighboring communities like Difficult, Defeated, Gladdice and so on fielded baseball teams. Baseball playing was important to a young man, a way to prove his worth. Families turned out to watch the games on Sunday afternoons. That was their entertainment.

My question had started Kaiser remembering long balls. "They may have been talking about that one I hit up at Celina. It was long." At Celina there had not been corn rows to count. Kaiser looked away to the front of the chapel as if still seeing that Celina ball sail away.

"That ball… That ball… Left there," he said finally.

"They said I struck out fourteen," Kaiser continued, revealing his position as pitcher. "I beat Don Cook three to two."

"Don Cook!"

"He was pitching…"

"I know Don Cook! I still see him around Cookeville. He played basketball at Tennessee Tech. He played baseball, too?"

"He was the pitcher," Kaiser said.

"His family, you know, came from Gladdice. Pete Cook, you know," I said.

"Yeah, Pete Cook," Kaiser said, nodding.

Then he drifted away from Don Cook and the Celina game, still pondering long homers.

"Billy Armistead hit the longest ball I ever saw at Monterey. He was playing for Baxter. You remember Billy Armistead?" he asked.

"Uh…yeah. They lived where Carl Smith used to live," I answered.

Going Down Slow

That house in Smith Bend somehow engendered baseball spirit. Two outstanding players had lived there. It stands yet, a quarter-mile east of the Smith Bend Methodist Church and Margie Agee, a high school classmate of mine lives there.

"That's right," Kaiser said. "Billy hit the longest ball I ever saw hit there (Monterey). There was a light pole in centerfield. It hit two-thirds of the way up and bounced back in."

"Yeah, they lived where Carl Smith used to live," I mused. "Carl Smith was a pretty good baseball player too, wasn't he?"

"Yeah, he played professional ball. He and [Unknown; I forgot this player's name] went up at the same time. [Unknown] stayed, but Carl came back. They played in that league...."

Here, Kaiser couldn't remember the name of the league but told me it had included Nashville, Atlanta and Chattanooga.

"I think it was called the Sally league," I offered. I seemed to remember a league called the Southern-something that had had the nickname "Sally." Undecided, we dropped the name quest. Kaiser continued.

"Carl was a good player, but he came back. He was such a hothead they couldn't do anything with him."

I remember him vaguely, a big, intimidating man, all the more fearsome because he was totally bald. Kaiser reflected on Carl's hitting strength, the man Rock City had twice walked to get to Kaiser. He told me this about Carl Smith's brief pro career:

Going Down Slow

"They said every time you hit a home run you got a new pair of shoes. I heard that when Carl came back he had fourteen pairs of new shoes."

New shoes for a home run, a modest bonus—these were old times, old ways. Baseball was different then.

Don Cook, the pitcher Kaiser was so proud of defeating at Celina, was elected to the Tennessee Tech Hall of Fame. You can see his picture lined up with all the other honorees overhead in the concourse of Hooper-Eblen Center, hanging there today. He forever holds a basketball, poised to shoot.

In fact, you can see Don Cook himself. Go to a basketball game and check the first row behind the Tech bench. You'll find him there still enjoying the game he played so well. We know now he also pitched baseball.

The mystery man, who played professional ball with Carl Smith? His name slipped by me that day when Kaiser told his story at Aunt Lexie's wake. I'd planned to ask Kaiser who it was, but I didn't bump into him again. Now it's too late. Kaiser died a short while later, at the age of eighty-one, in March, the season of spring training.

33

NOBODY WANTS TO CRAWL

The video clip from Fox News shows a runner collapsing within a few feet of the finish line at the Chicago Marathon I'd just run. In the video, the runner braced himself on the side wall and gingerly pushed himself back upright. But his knees buckled and he crumpled to the pavement again. Standing appeared no longer possible. The fallen man seemed dazed for a bit, casting around for what to do. He sat there.

Then a decision came. He leaned over on his hands and started crawling toward the goal, smartly closing the distance. All the while, other runners streamed by, ignoring the man, "dashing to the finish line," as the announcer said. The crawler ignored everyone.

Soon two male runners stooped down, lifted him by the arms, and swept him across the line. Their kindness was presented as a good deed and the two runners were hailed as heroes. The men acted from the best human impulses of compassion and pity. The incident was both "heart wrenching and heart warming," one TV anchor said.

A marathoner sees the men's action differently: it was wrong.

Going Down Slow

The runner had not sought help and did not need it. When the two men jerked him up, they snatched away the challenge he had set himself—just when victory was near. Equally wearisome, they disqualified him. With their aid, the stricken runner managed a better finish position than those behind him who ran with no help. That is unfair; it violates a fundamental rule. Namely, no runner is allowed to have help from anyone other than race officials.

Runners disabled by various ailments—exhaustion, digestive upset, leg cramps, etc., even death—are hardly rare in a marathon. In fact, one runner died and scores landed in the hospital at this very marathon in 2007, due in part to unseasonably warm temperatures. At the big urban marathons, I've read that directors expect a death every two years.

In the present case, medics, trained and equipped, stood nearby ready to help the exhausted runner as soon as he needed it.

Running the San Francisco marathon just two months earlier, I'd seen a man on the pavement a half mile from the finish. Medics had covered him with a blanket and were giving treatment. So, stricken runners are not unusual.

In the Ironman contests, crawling is so historically honored as to be singled out in the rules. On page 25 of the Ironman Florida booklet, for the marathon portion, I find this sentence: "1) NO FORM OF LOCOMOTION OTHER THAN RUNNING, WALKING OR CRAWLING IS ALLOWED" (capitalized in the booklet).

Julie Moss set the standard. It was 1982 and Ironman Hawaii was being broadcast on network television for the

Going Down Slow

first time ever, by ABC Wide World of Sports. As front-runner Moss approached the finish line, her strength bled out. Running, even standing, became impossible despite repeated attempts.

Her attempts grew feebler. Her limbs folded like linked bars. She fell in a heap. She entered a new realm. Crawling was the only choice left. She crawled.

She crawled, the crowd pressed in, it was pandemonium. TV viewers and spectators alike had never seen anything like it—an athlete determined enough to crawl, a woman athlete at that. In the confusion, the woman who had chased Moss all day now passed her without knowing it. She took the win but few remember her name.

What they remember is the searing courage of Julie Moss. No one dragged her across the finish line. Had that happened, the world would have been denied maybe the bravest performance ever seen in sports.

One person inspired by her performance was swimmer Mark Allen, classmate of Julie Moss at San Diego State. Allen, too, took up Ironman triathlon, eventually going on to win six Ironman world championships. *Outside* magazine called him the most (physically) fit man in America.

Julie Moss and Mark Allen married and had a son named Mats. His genetic potential for extraordinary endurance must be a good bet.

So, yes, sometimes racers crawl. You don't want to do that, to *have* to do that. At the least, it signifies you mismanaged your race, as apparently the man in Chicago had.

Going Down Slow

What of that Chicago runner who was crawling to the finish when he received help? What about his results? Was he disqualified?

Truth is, I don't know. I expect the director reviewed his case and relaxed the rule about receiving aid, letting his time stand. This resolution is a just one, especially if no age-group awards were involved. The director would recognize a decisive circumstance: The runner had not asked for help and was physically unable to resist it—kidnapped as he was.

Some 2,000 runners went to the limit of their endurance and stared into the abyss. They failed to finish the 26.2-mile distance. Each pushed the edge and felt its raw contour.

As I did. To each runner, the edge brings unique evil. In my case, leg cramps, springing from dehydration, nearly dragged me down. Had that happened, I might have been unable to get back up. Starting six miles from the finish and becoming deadly serious three miles later, my legs and feet alternated episodes of cramping, hard and hurting.

My stride jerked into a grotesque lurch, favoring whichever muscle was seized at the moment, hoping it would ease up. At times I ran wooden-legged, my foot twisted grossly to the outside. I gave up precious minutes, shuffling forward like a busted scarecrow.

I was competing for first place in the 65-69 age division, or hoping to. Once the cramping began, I doubled my fluid intake. By then it's usually too late, especially if

Going Down Slow

the day is hot. It was hot. The official high for the day was 84, which tied the high for that date set in 1960.

The official temperature is measured in shade four feet above grass. The street was paved with asphalt, not shade and grass. One runner said she saw 96 on a thermometer.

Heat was a factor in the outcome of the marathon. Some 45,000 had registered. Only 33,000 showed up to start. Of those, some 31,000 finished. For whatever reason—one guesses the hot-weather forecast—some 12,000 registered runners, many with bib number and timing chip already attached, decided: "Nope, I ain't going."

Indirectly or not, that particular circumstance led to a puzzler in my age division, sending me to scrutinize the rule book.

A man beat me by one minute and eight seconds.

I didn't know that until I'd left the race site, taken a shower and a nap. Since I didn't have a laptop with me, I called my wife back in Cookeville to get the bad news. Online results were unofficial at that time, the runners arranged in alphabetical order, not by order of finish. Jo Ann had to scroll through the list and, when she did, she found that a Dick Byrd of North Carolina had finished in 3:24:12, beating me by 1:08.

It was a buzz-kill. I sank into a morose hole. But I had to accept the hard numbers. I hadn't run well enough to win. Nutritionally, I'd prepared more carefully for this race than any I've done—only to blow it during the race itself, ignoring the heat and drinking too little.

I'd had a string going. I'd not lost first place in a marathon since June of 2004, on a hot day in Stockholm,

Going Down Slow

Sweden, thirteen marathons ago. Hard leg cramps hit that day, too, muscles like frozen snakes. After that race I lay on the ground for a long time, a long way from home, alone and unable to get up. My string stretched back to that blue Scandinavian sky where a white gull soared over, clouds drifted in from the south...

That string was snapped now.

A couple days after Chicago I was back home in Cookeville. I looked up Dick Byrd in the online race results. He was sixty-six. Results were still unofficial, but I made an interesting discovery — he was missing most of the split times, including the starting line itself. The rule book says a runner must have a starting time or he will be disqualified. Also, anyone missing multiple splits will be disqualified. Byrd faced double jeopardy.

The splits need explaining. At Chicago, a runner gets split times (accumulated time to that point) at eleven check points spaced out along the course. These include: the starting line, the half-marathon, the finish line and at each 5K — 5K, 10K, 15K, etc. A missing split may mean the runner took an illegal shortcut. Dick Byrd had split times for only 40K and 42K, the finish line, just two of the required eleven.

It appeared he had skipped the race and had jumped onto the course about two miles from the finish line. Was he a cheat? If so, he made a clumsy attempt, displaying gross ignorance of the marathon rules familiar to all runners. Maybe his timing chip had been defective, I thought, somehow fixing itself at 40K.

Never forget Google. I looked for previous marathon

Going Down Slow

times for Dick Byrd but found none. I did, however, find three recent half-marathon times. All were over two hours. One was 2:08. That answered the question: He didn't actually run the Chicago Marathon. A two-hour half-marathoner, inexperienced at the full distance, would push five hours in a hot Chicago Marathon. If he is able to finish at all.

He didn't run it.

But why did he fake it? It would take colossal arrogance to expect spoils from such an awkward trick. The race director would resolve all timing irregularities, I knew, before publishing the official results. At least I hoped he would.

On the third day after the race, the word "disqualified" appeared in the results after Dick Byrd's name. Correct outcome, but it didn't answer why he had pulled the stunt.

Then MarathonFotos put pictures online of all the racers. I looked up Dick Byrd's photos; there were a few. In each, he was running with a young woman. They crossed the finish line together and had a photo taken together.

I looked up the young woman, too. She was Pamela Byrd, thirty-six, from Georgia. She had exactly the same finishing time as Dick. I had my answer. Same last name, different states and thirty years younger—she was his daughter.

By race morning in Chicago, Dick had already pinned on his bib and attached his timing chip. Then when he saw the weather forecast he realized the marathon could not go well for him, a first-timer.

Prudence demanded he sit it out. Some 12,000 others

Going Down Slow

came to the same decision. But Dick, I figure, so wanted to share in his daughter's adventure that he came up with the perfect plan: Walk south on Michigan Avenue and wait for her at a point two miles from the finish. When he saw his child, he jumped in and ran beside her, a jubilant, smiling, proud papa.

I can't blame him. His daughter ran an excellent race. He was proud. He meant no harm. But his caper sank me in a multi-day funk. I walked around wondering what was going to happen.

On the fifth day after the race, the online results were finally revised, the runners listed in their order of finish. My name moved to the top of the 65-69 age division. The name Dick Byrd disappeared altogether.

The race director had enforced the rules. Dick Byrd was missing multiple splits, including the starting line. Hence he had been disqualified.

I had won. The marathon gods had known it all along; they just made me wait a while.

34

DISPATCHES FROM EL CAMINO

Thursday, June 25, 2009. The Grand Plan

Burgos, Spain—thirty-eight-year old Spanish runner Albino Jimenez and I are in our final week of preparation for an attempt to run across Spain on el Camino de Santiago—the Trail of Saint James. This trail, part dirt path, part city streets, stretches across northern Spain, from Spain's border with France in the east to Santiago in the west, and fifty-four miles beyond, to the ocean at Fisterra. Fisterra marks not only the end of land, as the name says, but was, in the old days, the very end of the World itself. Pilgrims have followed this ancient path for over a thousand years in order to visit the tomb of Saint James at Santiago.

We are planning an unsupported run, carrying what little we can on our backs. The total distance is some 519 miles, and we are allowing fourteen days for the crossing, thus facing daily runs of thirty to forty miles.

It may seem easy enough, but we are told that no one has yet run the total distance. That seems unlikely to me, but it makes little difference. Either way, we are going to run it—if we can.

Going Down Slow

Our start comes this Sunday, June 28, just over the border in Saint Jean Pied de Port, France. We face the Pyrenees on our first segment.

Albino has taken the lead, gathered information, and planned the stages, and he has chosen an unlikely partner: *un anciano americano.*

Our start comes just three days after my sixty-ninth birthday. We climb over 4,000 feet in the first fourteen miles. Thus, I blunder into my seventieth year.

As our run unfolds and when conditions permit, we will send updates. Odds are against us. We need all the luck we can get

Monday, June 29, 2009. Over the Pyrenees

"No bus goes to Roncesvalles," the girl behind the window said.

"But I read the bus schedule on the internet," Albino protested.

"You can't believe what you read on the internet."

"Well, the bus company ought to…"

Then he realized he might as well give it up. Getting ourselves to Saint Jean had turned into a hassle. We had driven a rental car to Pamplona, Spain. We'd planned to take a bus from there to Roncesvalles, the last town in Spain, and then take a taxi on to Saint Jean. But we were stuck in Pamplona, the very town we expected to run *to* on our first day of running. We pondered.

Idling taxis lined the curb by the bus station like buzzards on a limb. We decided to take one from Pamplona

Going Down Slow

to Roncesvalles and from there over the mountains to Saint Jean. Eventual price: 100 Euros.

The taxi wound out of Pamplona and headed up a long valley, gradually climbing the left side. I could see a clear fast stream below. I wondered if it was the one where Hemingway caught trout in *The Sun Also Rises*. On the radio Van Morrison was singing "Brown Eyed Girl." The driver took the Peugeot through numerous switchbacks, downshifting and upshifting. We finally slipped through the pass and headed downhill, losing radio reception. He tuned in another station. Bob Dylan was singing "Knocking on Heaven's Door."

Familiar music and thoughts of Hemingway, reminders of home filled the car. But over us towered the Pyrenees, foreign, forbidding and tall. Winding up and up, we had climbed so long and so high and still I had to lean close to the window and look up steeply to see their top. I was daunted by the prospect of running back across these mountains. Off to the south, where our trail was, I could see a bald peak. Tomorrow's path must go close to its top, I figured. The distance seemed so far, the mountains seemed so high, knocking on heaven's door seemed right. At that moment, I had a new view of what we were in for.

We had scheduled the start of our run for Sunday, June 28, at Saint Jean, France, but had discovered that, due to a local festival, no hotel rooms were available for Saturday night. Then we had located a farmhouse three miles up the trail, the way we wanted to go. We ran those three miles late Saturday and so got a head start. That

Going Down Slow

short distance gained 1,000 feet. The sun was fierce, and once we reached the house, I wanted to stand in the shade.

That evening we sat on the terrace, looking down on Saint Jean huddled astride the river in the valley below. In the pastures above, we could see sheep grazing, tiny tufts sprinkled on soft green. A model 6500 Ford farm tractor sat just below us, the manure fork on its front raised high, blocking part of my view. A farm boy, I would not have parked it with the lift raised; it could fall on someone.

During the night I had a nightmare and woke up screaming. Embarrassed, I hoped I had not disturbed Albino. But I had. A couple of weeks later I found out. When I had a second screaming nightmare he reminded me of the one here.

Next morning, Sunday, we continued our climb. We had 3,000 more feet to gain over the eleven-mile distance to the pass through the Pyrenees. El Camino follows the route over these mountains taken by Napoleon when he invaded Spain in 1808; it is a one-track blacktop now. The path occasionally makes off-road excursions and takes shortcuts. The trail is steep with hardly a respite. Interpolating from the profile in a book I have here — for a while I was a civil engineer — shows that one 2.5-mile pitch sustains an average slope of 9.8 percent. On the ground it is hardly so smooth. Short local pitches approach the steepness of stairs, the steps replaced by a wash filled with loose rocks.

It seems to go up forever, and you think you'll never make it. You know not to look up, but you do anyway. You see a road reaching to the sky. Your spirit sinks. Better

Going Down Slow

to keep your eyes down. Watch your steps. Push off left, then right, keep doing that. Don't think about the top.

That way, we reached the pass.

Shortly after the pass we entered Spain. The trail ran through wooded foothills on a rocky path. In the afternoon, maybe twenty-five miles into the day's run, I found myself in trouble. We were on a severely eroded and rocky stretch in dense woods. It was hot. Leg cramps hit, at first easy, then hard. A step up, a step down, a quick step, any kind of irregular motion, produced a painful cramp.

I was alone. Albino had gone ahead, long out of sight. If I fell and was knocked unconscious or disabled by cramps, he would not know. He was the one fluent in Spanish, and he had the cell phone. I had no such aids.

Following hard cramps I rarely recover running form. Our trek was going bust on the very first day. I made the only decision I could—slow down and double my drinking. My water bottle was running low, and running dry before the next fountain was my fear. Didn't matter. That seemed the only chance.

It worked, surprising me. When I caught up with Albino, he was waiting. He'd had no hint of the trouble I'd faced until I told him. He poured some water into my empty bottle.

We continued the trudge on to Pamplona, finishing some thirty-nine miles, and then had to go two more miles to find our hotel. They had already put up the wooden fences for the running of the bulls later in the week.

Looking back now, Sunday's run across the Pyrenees

Going Down Slow

seems glorious, a miracle I'm not sure I could repeat. I think I'll always remember it as one of my strongest runs. But it came at a terrible price. I'd done damage to my legs that I didn't know about at the time.

The portly old lady sitting behind the hotel desk at Pamplona was good natured and jovial. She laughed easily. When Albino told her we had run from Saint Jean to Pamplona that day, she knew it was a joke; we were teasing her. She laughed knowingly, enjoying the jest. And we laughed knowingly, too, enjoying her insight. She had seen right through us.

"She's a good old lady," Albino said as we walked to the restaurant.

While we were at supper, she must have wondered a little bit. When we returned she told us she'd called her husband. He had assured her it was quite impossible; nobody could run across those mountains in one day. She had us red-handed, our little joke caught in the spotlight.

We all laughed with gracious good-will. Of course we did. How silly! Nobody could run those mountains.

Wednesday, July 1, 2009, El Camino de Inferno

Albino continues on alone. This morning I watched him cross the bridge over the river at Nájera and then caught the autobus to Burgos, where he lives. He has a chance. He looked strong enough, in that minimized shuffling gait used by ultramarathoners. If it goes well for him I will see him here in Burgos tomorrow night. El Camino goes by his door. My run has ended in whimpering failure. It came at the

Going Down Slow

end of the third day, only 110 miles into the run, and five miles short of Nájera, yesterday's goal.

On Monday, as we were leaving Pamplona, the weather was hotter. My legs were so sore from crossing the Pyrenees the previous day that, at first, I could barely walk. Some forty-two miles stretched out to Los Arcos, our goal that day.

Mid-afternoon we ran out of strength. We had entered farm country. There was no shade. The sun beat down. You could feel the heat on your head under the hat. It lay there like a hot waffle. We walked together a while, trying to keep our run alive.

Walking in an ultramarathon is no shame, I told Albino.

"I'm feeling no shame," he replied.

Shortly we began running again, twelve miles from Los Arcos. Albino is stronger than I am. He moved ahead, finally disappearing over one of the rises in the dirt road ahead. The road was straight, golden wheat fields on each side, hills beyond. It could have been Nebraska.

Los Arcos hid itself so well you could get no encouragement from a distant view. You wonder if it is even there. The heat, the running, the crunch of dry gravel, the constant drinking, these were the realities. Los Arcos was a cruel joke. It did not exist.

Then I came around a curve in the dirt road. And there it was, no warning. And there stood Albino talking to an elderly gent with a cane just where the dirt road turned to pavement. As I trotted up, a passing farm truck threw up a cloud of hot dust. Albino had been waiting ten minutes,

Going Down Slow

he said. It was seven in the evening and we had started at eight that morning. I had run on legs so sore I could step on or off a curb only with grimacing pain.

After we had checked into a room, Albino's brother told him on the phone that Pamplona had reported the hottest temperature for all of Spain—40 degrees C, or 104 degrees F.

We ate supper in the hotel bar, the only choice. It was full of smoke and noise, loud drinkers and yelling kids. A sudden thunderstorm added to the din, and washed down the plaza outside. We hoped the rain meant cooler temperatures for days ahead, but that hope turned out to be vain. I managed to eat a fourth of my spaghetti. Forget the bread. A Tennessean would feed it to the hogs.

Food was a problem. We had to depend on the little stores and smoky bars. The food we found was unfamiliar to me, and the heat had taken my appetite. I wanted some salty peanuts, pretzels, a Snickers bar, but found none. I thought of the food my wife makes. I'd give a hundred dollars for a plate of Jo Ann's potato salad, I told Albino.

Salt shakers are not usually found on the restaurant table. I needed salt to fight off dehydration and had taken some in a plastic bag to eat occasionally. But it was inconvenient to dig out of my pack, and I didn't get enough. Despite having run forty-two miles that day I'd had very little to eat, and I knew I was getting weaker.

So, failure came on the third day. For breakfast I had orange juice, a doughnut, and a glass of warm milk. Milk is not popular in Spain. Good luck finding it cold. I applied some Icy Hot ointment to my sore legs. It did no good and

Going Down Slow

only added a disgusting stink.

We left Los Arcos running. Surprisingly, I led most of the morning. There were valleys and hills where the trail was rough and rocky, but I worked hard to set a good pace. Five miles an hour, I figured. But weakness distorted my view and made it seem I was accomplishing more than I was.

After nearly three hours, I stopped at a fountain in Viana and waited for Albino to catch up.

"There's no way we can do a half under three hours," he said. A half marathon, he meant.

It was true. According to his GPS we had not yet covered thirteen miles, and we were pushing three hours. It was shocking news. Until then I'd not known our distance, only the time. Given how hard I'd worked, I thought we'd come much further. My weakness was no longer a matter of guess work; it had been quantified.

Nine days earlier, Albino and I had run the Burgos half marathon. He ran a time of 1:31. Despite seven hours of jet lag and loss of sleep (the race came only twenty-one hours after I'd landed in Madrid) I ran it in 1:34. That time beat the Tennessee single-age state record I'd set in February.

Now we couldn't get under three hours. I could not deny that fact or escape the oppression of its startling truth. I felt finished.

We trotted on, both of us dragging and getting slower.

At Logroño, seventeen miles into the day's run, we had been reduced to walking. Cokes, one familiar drink but one I normally don't take, seemed to help Albino. He

Going Down Slow

would drink two or three at one sitting, while I would drink only one.

The heat made it hard to take food without getting sick. Even water, plain water, had become disgusting. We knew we had to drink a lot of it. We passed a street thermometer that read 42 degrees C, 108 degrees F.

We drifted out of Logroño like kiln-dried specters, hollow-eyed and gaunt, the juice sucked out of us. At fountains, we doused our heads and poured water on our shirts. That helped for a while, but it soon dried.

The fronts of my legs were so sore they felt hot to the touch, feverish, as if the quadriceps had been invaded by giant festering sores.

After twelve miles we came to Navarette. "That little town, whatever its name was," Albino scorned later. There was a bar with outside tables. A skinny Frenchman with an out-curving goatee and pony tail sat at a table near the door, smoking a joint.

We got Cokes. Albino quickly finished his, drinking three sodas altogether. I took one sip of mine and then rushed around the corner and bent forward, retching on ancient cobblestones. Nothing came up, just stringy slime and a dark stain from the Coke I'd just sipped.

Leaving Navarette, we were still walking. It was eleven miles through heat-blasted farmland to Nájera, to our hotel. The Cokes had given Albino some energy. He started talking about running. It was around five o'clock.

"We got to do some running if we don't want to get to our hotel tomorrow," he observed.

He was right, of course. At our pace we'd not hit the

Going Down Slow

hotel until nine that night. But I didn't think I could run enough to make much difference. I was weak as pond water. Ravaged legs, two days with scant food, the heat, the nausea, it all had taken a toll.

Since Logroño I'd felt like my run was over. I didn't know how to tell Albino. I didn't want to disappoint him; he had planned on this adventure so long. We both had. I kept playing out my string, hoping something would change.

It did. Albino started running. Two hundred meters out, I saw him turn once and look back to see if I was running. I was not. Nor would I. Albino vanished. I walked on, getting slower, slower. Farmers were combining their wheat. Chaff drifted over me, flies attacked.

Then the road turned lonely again, no one and no thing except wheat fields and hills rising in the distance. I walked straight at a humming sun.

A new thought hit: I might not make it. Goose bumps had run down my arm. Chill bumps are the last warning before heat stroke. My water, what about my water? If I am so slow that I run out before the next fountain — wherever that is — what then? There was no shade. I was in danger.

Melodrama invades such moments. I realized oblivion could find me on a dusty road in Spain, a prospect that struck me as fitting. The thought amused, but not for long. Recognition is not permission. My feet, by their prints in the dust, yet expressed denial. In action is truth; I was still going.

The road went straight, but the trail made a hard left. I might have missed it. It would have been a bad miss, I

Going Down Slow

now know. There were no fountains straight ahead.

A tractor approached from behind, carrying two men and towing a swirling plume of gritty dust. I had the sublimely stupid thought—hitch a ride on the tractor. I stepped into the weeds as it rumbled by. The men were sullen and met my wave with stony glares.

Around seven, I stumbled into Ventosa. It was there that I surrendered. I came to the albergue, a hostel for el Camino pilgrims. The smiling woman in charge said, "Hola!" She took my water bottle to the fountain outside and filled it. She didn't speak English. I don't speak much Spanish, but managed to remember all the words I needed.

I told her I needed help, that a friend and I were running el Camino, that we had come from Saint Jean to Pamplona, and from there to Los Arcos and were now heading to Nájera, that my friend had gone on but that I was unable to run. Could she call a taxi, and how much would it cost? I only had two twenties and two fives left. She said the amount but I misunderstood. She wrote the numbers on paper. It looked like 75. I was out of luck.

"Es setenta y cinco?" I asked.

"No. Uno," she replied and pointed at the seven. The number that looked like a seven was actually a one. The fare was 15 Euros. I could cover that.

"Es okay?"

"Si. Llama."

The taxi took me to hotel San Fernando in Nájera, where we had booked a room. I checked in, took a shower and waited for Albino. I hated to tell him the hard news—that I had quit.

Going Down Slow

Friday, July 3, 2009. "I'm Freaking Dying."

Albino is in Burgos. He made it in yesterday around three thirty. He is taking today off, and we are deciding what to do.

He called me in the afternoon of Wednesday, the day I left him at Nájera. His goal was Belorado, twenty-nine miles away, a short day as distance goes. But there was up and down to it and it was nearly all exposed to the sun. The heat was still humming.

He sounded discouraged, said he was again reduced to walking, that even that was hard. "I'm dragging my ass," is what he said. I told him sentimentally that my heart went out to him and that I'd be thinking about him.

Once in Burgos he told me what he'd thought in those dark moments out there alone, fighting the heat and barely able to walk: *I'm dying. I'm freakin' dying.*

So he'd thought, but he made it.

Next day, Thursday, he had made an earlier start, while it was cooler. He benefited from some cloud cover, and so he made the twenty-eight miles to Burgos — another short day — in good time, running all the way.

Now we have to decide what to do. Albino is with the doctor at this moment. He is fighting generalized soreness and had a massage last night. He has other problems. A fungus-like rash has enveloped his feet. The sweat-saturated environment is favorable to the growth of such things, I suppose. His intestinal problems started by diarrhea two days ago continue. He has dizzy spells.

As for me, my leg soreness is improved. But my

Going Down Slow

body weight is in the cellar. A normal weight for me is 142 pounds. Now I barely hit 134. That is awfully low for some one who stands 5-11. If I continue, my weight will go lower, and that worries me. Two or three pounds of the loss happened during the high-volume training in Tennessee, before I left for Spain.

Most of the weight loss came from the three days on el Camino, when I had too little to eat. My body was consuming itself, eating a pound or two of flesh each day. When I get back to Tennessee, I'll need some serious weight lifting to put some muscles back on my bony frame.

Weakness begets weakness. Last night I bent over to move a coffee table and strained a muscle in my lower back. It's the same injury I got a few years ago, on the Wednesday before the Saturday start of Ironman Florida. I recovered enough to finish that race. This time I don't have three days before Saturday, tomorrow.

Today we have to decide what to do. The heat wave that has gripped northern Spain seems ready to back off. We could decide to continue the run. Our goal is tarnished now. I've missed fifty-something miles, and Albino is enjoying a forbidden day of rest. We could still run across Spain. That is not a small thing. But it may be beyond our reach. You hate to give up. We have to think.

Given the quixotic turn of our run, it is easy to conclude that we are a couple of delusional fools unaware of the realities and demands of our adventure, Don Quixote and Sancho Panza rushing around Spain, tilting at windmills.

That is not true. We are both experienced long-distance runners. And we did our homework. Albino and

Going Down Slow

I studied el Camino separately, in different books. He made a number of trial stage schedules before we adopted the final one.

Further, last year Albino actually ran a 120-mile segment of el Camino on the Santiago end. And he had hiked the Pyrenees portion. We knew.

In his training, Albino ran twice a day, reaching weekly totals of eighty to ninety miles, mostly on trails. To compensate for my lack of youthful vigor I ran higher volumes, and logged several weeks over 100 miles. Eighteen miles became a standard morning run, and I ran several thirty-mile days. We were trained.

We were trained and we knew, and we brought it to the road. Our fitness, knowledge, information, experience—all that—comprised our meager pile of chips. It was all we had. It was a risk. We were willing to gamble. We pushed it all out on the table.

"Hah," said The Dealer, and sent a heat wave over northern Spain.

The unusual heat was the major factor in our run. In the weeks prior to our departure, I followed the weather in two cities, Santiago and Burgos. Daily highs fell in the 60s and 70s. Cold conditions at the higher elevations had concerned us more than heat—enough that we had included gloves, long sleeves and long pants in our packs, though we could ill-afford their weight. The heat wave came like a hard body blow.

We could not have prepared for the heat we encountered. It is possible to run in such temperatures, but only when supplied with copious quantities of fluids,

Going Down Slow

electrolytes, and balanced energy food. On an unsupported run those special things are not available. Once the heat hit, our run was doomed.

We knew what we were doing. And I knew all along it was a high-risk adventure. I said so. But I am willing to take risk. I don't regret it now. Even in failure, sitting here hurting, I don't regret it. Not one damned bit.

Sunday, July 5, 2009. We Decided.

A final word — we decided not to go on. Albino is still weak in the stomach and my back is still ailing. Although the temperature has retreated a bit, if we head into the plains it looks to come back, and el Camino there is almost fully exposed and fountains are less frequent.

It's the right decision. Although it's a disagreeable one, we have to abide it with whatever grace we can.

In writing my reports I've left out a lot — sometimes out of the need for brevity, at other times because I couldn't do any better.

Albino's run from Nájera to Belorado on Wednesday, the day I left him, deserved more comment than I gave it earlier. I believe that run was brave, dangerous, and maybe even foolhardy. Endurance athletes always go beyond the ordinary experiences of life. So who is qualified to say foolhardy — non runners who never venture beyond ordinary, or runners who always do?

Albino straddled a knife edge that day. By the time he reached Belorado, the sun had scorched his skin dark and his lips pale. He was nearly too weak to walk. He had

Going Down Slow

diarrhea and he was dizzy. Broiled in that oven, he was shaking with chills. Even after a hot shower and covering up in bed, he still couldn't stop shaking, he told me.

This was the day he remembered having the thought, "I'm freaking dying." From somewhere deep inside it, his primeval brain was trying to get its message out. I believe the thought was more accurate than he knows.

Earlier I made no mention of the beauty of the Pyrenees. Their features deserve appreciation separate and distinct from other mountains. But I can only describe them with reference to other ranges I've seen. At times their raw craggy fronts and deep valleys reminded me of the Colorado Rockies although their contours are generally more weathered. A grassy roundness suggested Wyoming. Sometimes sheep and horses grazed in the open range beside the trail. And passing through the heavy woods was like hiking the Appalachian Trail. There were many grand views. At most, we never stopped and only saw in passing.

Something else to note is the charm of the little towns we passed through each day. We drifted down Main Street, always called Calle Major, a narrow street of cobblestones, lined by medieval buildings. On the second story, flowers decorated wrought iron balconies. Sometimes a woman would appear there, cleaning her house. Sometimes nothing was moving at all and the whole town seemed deserted. "It's like everybody has gone to church," I told Albino. Then you'd come to a bar with outside tables, and a few pilgrims were sitting there with their backpacks. An old man with a cane would shuffle down the street or sit

Going Down Slow

quietly on a bench.

You'd find a fountain, a masonry or brass stand with one or two faucets. Cool sweet water gushed at the push of a button. At some, water ran perpetually. The fountains gave life.

Late April or early May might be a better time for attempting el Camino. But cold weather could bring hypothermia then. One can visualize rain and wind on a cold day in the mountains, and books had warned about it. Our experience was of course the opposite of cold. We enjoyed the sublime irony of carrying the extra weight of warm clothes while suffering heat exhaustion. A degree of luck with the weather is essential to complex trips. Better luck might have made a big difference in ours.

In the end we failed. That's our fault, not anybody else's, and not the weather's. We didn't get it done. We'll learn what it teaches, and travel on.

Saturday, July 4, 2009. The Beautiful Art of Rejoneo

The bull needed to die but could not. He stood looking dully ahead, his shoulders slicked with blood oozing from the eight darts sticking in them. A sword stuck out of his back. Cuadrilleros, the bullfighter's helpers, swarmed around. The matador who had made the weak stab walked up, studying the bull's face. The spell was bad. The crowd was uneasy. We watched. Cuadrilleros prepared to chop the spinal cord. The matador stopped them. He raised his hand, palm outward as if appealing for peace.

The bull was already at peace. He didn't want to fight

Going Down Slow

any more. He needed to die but could not. We waited. The bull stood. It was taking too long. The people murmured. The matador had performed poorly.

Then the bull fell, toppled more than collapsed. He laid still, his legs sticking stiffly out. The blade had finally done its job. Relieved, the crowd gave scattered applause. A team of three mules trotted in, pulling a long singletree, and dragged the dead bull out. His broad flank made a smooth curving path in the dirt.

The matador was from a wealthy family, Albino told me. Perhaps he didn't need to fight bulls for money and only did it for women and glory. He walked away dejected. He would not gain the bull's ears or tail, the prizes awarded to a matador for a good kill.

Albino and I were celebrating July 4th in Burgos, Spain, not where we meant to be on that day. Our run had failed. We had found a restaurant called Richi's that Albino had heard served American-style food. We ordered the classic—hamburgers and fries. In my pocket was a small piece of cardboard cut from a Band-Aid box. It was folded over and taped at the edges. Sandwiched inside were two toothpicks topped by tiny American flags, the kind you find sticking in the muffins at a backyard cookout in Tennessee, which is exactly where I had found them a few weeks earlier, at my sister's cookout in Mount Juliet, Tennessee.

We stuck the flagged toothpicks in the hamburgers and sang the Star Spangled Banner. Then honoring the American tradition of violence, we decided to go to a bullfight.

Going Down Slow

It was Saturday afternoon, the last day of an eight-day bullfighting festival bearing the ponderous name Feria Taurina San Pedro y San Pablo, a festival so grand that one saint was not enough. It took Saint Peter and Saint Paul both.

This last evening was reserved for a historic kind of bullfighting known as corrida de rejones, developed hundreds of years ago for training the cavalry. In rejones, the matador works from horseback. He serves as his own picador, sticking the eight barbed darts known as banderillas into the bull's shoulders, and he kills the bull from horseback, too.

We'd just seen the first matador of three, Fermín Bohórquez, who was thirty-nine years old. Although his record was respectable, luck had not been with him on today's bull. In 2007, his best recent year, he had appeared in sixty events, gaining 107 ears and five tails. He would fight one more bull here today. Perhaps he dreaded it.

The matadors appeared in order of increasing skill. Hermoso de Mendoza, forty-three, was next. He had appeared in 120 bullfight festivals in 2007, gaining 278 ears and thirty-three tails. In 2008 his production dropped to less than half that. The festival program described him as "...without doubt the best rejoneador of all time." Still plenty formidable at forty-three, he was maybe no longer as quick or as strong as he had been. His age favored a decline.

The third matador, Diego Ventura, was from Lisbon, Portugal. At twenty-seven years of age, the youngest, he had gained the position of headliner. He appeared in

Going Down Slow

sixty-three festivals in 2008, gaining 167 ears and sixteen tails. He turned out to be a cheerful crowd pleaser, carrying out his deadly work with the exuberant glee of a kid having a water fight, smiling broadly and gesturing with raised arms after each good move, seeking approval and getting it.

It is the bravery, intelligence, and athletic skill of the horse that amazes the most. The horse wears no armor, yet works inches from the bull's horns. One lucky upthrust can rip his belly open, letting his entrails slip heavy-sliding into the dirt. For the horse, stakes are grave.

The bull's charges are quick. The horse must avoid the horns with better quickness, yet bring his rider in close enough to plant banderillas and thrust the sword.

Altogether, the matador sticks eight banderillas into the bull's shoulders, four on each side. Their colorful handles dangle downward, rolling and pulling the flesh where the barb entered. This helps infuriate the bull. On the last set, the matador inserts both barbs at once, one in each shoulder. It must be done powerfully and quickly.

Horse and rider communicate by unknown magic. As the bull charges, the rider leans far out, holding no reins, tilting his body nearly horizontal in order to reach the bull's shoulders, a banderilla in each hand. The horse knows what his rider needs in this vulnerable position. He must be precise in permitting the charging bull to come close, while yet avoiding the horns. If he makes an unexpected step he could dump the rider on the horns.

The horse of Ventura knew where the limit was. Once, the bull got just close enough to rake a four-inch gash up his ham. The cut turned bright red in the afternoon sun.

Going Down Slow

A rejoneador uses three horses to kill each bull, substituting when his horse grows tired. The work is strenuous, and the horse needs rest. Toro competes against a relay, getting no such rest.

A horse can outrun a bull. That is not his normal job, but Ventura's had a special trick he sometimes showed a charging bull. The horse ran, staying just inches in front of the horns, his tail practically in the bull's face. Then he did a full-circle pirouette, maintaining his forward motion and distance from the bull all the while. This required that he run sideways to the right, backwards, sideways to the left, and finally forward again, outpacing the bull throughout the rotation. This move delighted the people. The crowd roared its approval.

He had another trick. Bull and horse stood facing each other, taking measure. The horse then raked the ground a few times with his hoof, like a bull does. Then he straightened his leg and pointed it at the bull. A horse can't talk. But this one spoke clearly. Everyone understood what he was saying:

"You, Toro! I'm talking to you! Bring your best."

Toro could not know that no bull ever left the arena, not until the mules dragged him out. All he could do was fight hard. And die bravely.

Ventura delighted the crowd and killed his bull. In the last moment, after he'd already thrust the sword, he jumped off the horse and ran up to Toro, shaking his finger in his face, scolding Toro in words we could not hear.

Bohórquez, the first matador, who'd had hard luck, must have watched this dominating performance. Now it

Going Down Slow

came time for his second bull.

And his luck had not improved. Unlike Ventura's smiling countenance, Bohórquez's face wore a sweaty red scowl. It seemed hard for him. He even failed to plant one of the banderillas. It fell out and laid there. He couldn't erase that failure or cover it up. The garish proof, red and white, lay in the dirt mocking him.

Finally he rode to the wall and called for the sword. The trumpet played the lonely tune it plays before a bull dies. Toro charged, but the sword of Bohórquez did not strike. A matador must hit a small spot and shove the blade completely in, a demanding athletic challenge. Bohórquez brought the bull in close, charge after charge. But he could not make himself strike. We wondered what he was waiting for. Something like target panic had gripped him. He couldn't pull the trigger. It was like a baseball pitcher losing his stuff.

"He's lost his confidence," I said.

"Yeah." Albino could see it too. All the people could. The humiliation was very public.

When the sword finally did plunge, it was tentative and puny. Toro stood, half the blade sticking out of his back. He had won. The matador could not kill him.

But he had to die anyway. A cuadrillero rushed up and chopped his spinal cord. Toro fell in a heap. Bohórquez walked away frustrated and took up a position behind the wall near us, the scowl solid on his face. No one spoke to him.

The second bull of Ventura was the finale. As before, the cocky Portuguese dazzled the crowd with his playful

Going Down Slow

confidence and nonchalant flair, gleefully working the bull. Bohórquez watched it all.

When the sword of Ventura fell, no part of it was left showing except the handle, sticking out of the back of the bull. Toro stood perfectly still. Ventura jumped out of the saddle and ran up to him, nearly touching his face. The triumphant matador dropped to one knee, spread his arms back wide and thrust his chest into the face of Toro, mocking the stricken bull. The people cheered wildly.

Toro didn't move. He didn't care. He looked at Ventura with dead eyes. Bulbous strings of crimson slobber drooled from his mouth, and red foam gathered at his nostrils.

Toro collapsed. The crowd roared. Ventura strutted, arms high. The people waved scarves, handkerchiefs, hats, anything they had. The stands turned to a stirring white flurry. Raucous applause continued. The judge, who was positioned behind and above us, flopped a tassel onto the front of his desk—it looked like a bull's tail. It meant one ear.

They go by the crowd's reaction; they have a computer to help them, Albino told me. A cuadrillero cut off one of the bull's ears and handed it to the matador. He held the ear high, walking in front of the cheering people, and then threw it to some waving hands. Cheering continued. The judge flopped out another tassel. And again, Ventura strutted, holding the ear up for all to see before throwing it in the stands.

Cheering persisted but tapered off a bit before the judge could award the tail. It depends on the place, Albino

Going Down Slow

said. Some towns are harder than others. Ventura had to settle for two ears, a triumph nonetheless.

I glanced at Bohórquez, the hard-luck matador. He had watched it all. He stood alone behind the wall. The scowl was hard on his face.

35

THE TITAN

Following our aborted attempt to run across Spain, I was still visiting with Albino Jimenez in Burgos when startling news reached us from the U.S.A.—the shooting death of former NFL quarterback and Tennessee Titans football player Steve McNair. We learned that he'd been shot on July 4th, a day Albino and I had celebrated by going to a bullfight. He'd been shot by a distraught young woman in his Nashville apartment as he napped on the sofa, after which she'd turned the gun on herself.

McNair had completed a distinguished career and was loved and respected by players and fans alike, including me. He had seemed basically a respectful and decent man, striking me as a country boy at heart. But his reputation as an individual clashed jarringly with the tawdry reports of his death—shot in an apartment a long way from his wife and family, involvement with a woman much younger than himself, heavy drinking, partying, and so on.

In 2006 it happened that I had written a brief story about a chance encounter I'd had with him in 1998. The story was written as a composition assignment in a Spanish class I was taking. I re-wrote the remembrance in a fuller version, and in English, for the newsletter of my running

Going Down Slow

club, the Nashville Striders, a club containing Titans fans.

And that was it until the news came to Albino's Burgos apartment. Hearing that, I called my wife back in Tennessee and asked her to search my desktop computer for the story file. I didn't even remember the title. She found the file and e-mailed it to me. His death had suddenly made the story timely. I read the piece and, without a single change, submitted it to the *Herald-Citizen*, the Cookeville newspaper. It ran in the following Sunday edition under a note from the editor (which I'd also drafted) that established the context of the piece.

While fans were mourning his death, the story served as a gentle reminder of his life. The story did something else. It offered a glimpse of the quarterback at the peak of his power, and, while it was only a snapshot, the view was a different and surprising one. Subsequent events in his life made the ending of the story poignantly prescient.

From Albino's apartment in Burgos, the piece flew to the *Herald-Citizen*, and from there to the doorsteps of the readers. Here it is, as they read it that Sunday, still unchanged.

At the Houston airport in May of 1998, my mother and I were boarding a Southwest flight bound for Nashville. Prior to that trip Momma had never ridden on a jet, and she wanted to sit where she could look out. She took a window seat at the front, and I sat down next to her.

Soon a tall black man took the seat next to me and nodded. I thought I recognized him, a football player. I asked him if I was right. He smiled kindly and extended

Going Down Slow

his hand—it was thick and tough like a farmer's hand. A gentle manner reflected his Mississippi rearing.

It had only been a year since the Houston Oilers had moved to Nashville, eventually changing their name to the Tennessee Titans. I asked him if he still owned a house in Houston.

"No, I live in Nashville now," he said, expressing with that answer what I took to be a commitment extending beyond his personal residence to his team's new home as well. He'd been to Mexico on a vacation, he told me.

During their first year in Nashville the Titans' stadium had been under construction. Without a place to play their home games, team management had considered a number of local college stadiums, but finally decided on playing at the Liberty Bowl in Memphis.

That choice proved to be a disaster. Political tension, if not outright enmity, had long existed between Memphis and Nashville. Fans from the Bluff City were not anxious to embrace a team that belonged to Music City.

The Titans had found few friends by the riverside. At one game, against Pittsburgh, the visiting team had actually enjoyed more fans than the home team, a humiliating rejection for the Nashvillians.

I told him I hated that they'd had to play in Memphis and that it would be much better once they started playing in Nashville.

"Yeah, it was pretty tough playing in Memphis," he said.

"You'd been better off playing at a high school than

Going Down Slow

playing in Memphis."

He laughed at the irony in that comment, absurd yet true.

After that, I dropped the conversation, realizing he probably endures boring talks with fawning fans all the time. Three young women occupying the seats facing ours carried on a raucous conservation, hoping for his attention—and getting none. Instead, the man leaned back and took a nap.

I'd felt a bit uneasy talking with such a celebrity. We had little in common: He was half my age, twice my weight and a hundred times as rich. And, by comparison, I owned scant athletic credits.

In college, I'd lettered on the rifle team, breaching the national top twenty, and winning my team's most valuable player award. While I treasure that, it seemed to pale beyond mention. And shooting glory had been a long time ago.

Perhaps a better athletic link was carried by the message on my T-shirt, a bold ad for the Golden Eagle 10K in Cookeville, an event of only the previous month which had been my first ever road race. In that first race, I had won two trophies—first in my age group and first master (over fifty there)—and discovered at the age of fifty-seven a talent I didn't know I had, one that has since led to numerous age-group titles and over two dozen state records.

Looking back now, I think my timidity was unfounded, and that I deserved to talk to the man as an athlete, one to another. Our difference was one of degree,

Going Down Slow

not principle: He plays football, I run. We both compete.

In any case, he was courteous to me that day. And I fondly recall shaking his hand—the hand of a man who earns his living throwing a football. He does it well enough to be called by the name "Air." Two years later he would lead his team to the Super Bowl. Three years after that, he would earn the League's co-Most Valuable Player Award.

When we reached Nashville, it was late that night; not many people were around the airport. I glimpsed the quarterback as he headed down the concourse. He was framed by the harsh light and receding walls.

Steve McNair walked alone, shoulders slumped, eyes down. It seemed the image of a lonely man.

36

FOUR WHO RAN KOMEN

My buddy Angela Ivory was one of the two runners I was delighted to see come to Cookeville for the first local Komen 5K. That first race fell in October, 2009. The Komen races are well-known among runners across the country. They benefit the fight against breast cancer. Angela came for just one main reason: I asked her. My running buddy Josh Hite, who lives in Cookeville, also scheduled the race. I've sometimes referred to Angela as an "extreme runner." I don't know another term that better describes what she does. The term "elite marathoner" is how I describe Josh. He has earned that term. Although both are friends, there was a connection between them I had not realized until this first Komen U.C. race. It came out in talks I had with Josh when we occasionally met up on our runs around town.

So here is a story about two runners who came together in my town to fight cancer. Two runners who had a history I didn't know about, two runners who the world would think are very different from each other. Angela, who was forty-one, is an African-American from Memphis in West Tennessee, and Josh, who was thirty-one, is a white boy hailing originally from politically-conservative

Going Down Slow

East Tennessee. Very different, the world thinks. But the world is often mistaken.

One thing they had in common was that both ordinarily favor races much longer than three miles. Angela had not run such a short race in five years. Friends kidded her that maybe she couldn't.

Some six years earlier Angela Had discovered cancer in her breast. It changed her life, but not in the way you'd imagine. She endured the usual weary horror—lost a breast, lost twenty-two lymph nodes, and endured months of chemotherapy and radiation.

None of that bothered her much; she was already skilled at endurance. It only altered her arc. A year or so later when the medical aggravation was over, she started a new phase—running a marathon every weekend. She ran forty-seven in one year. In barely more than a year, she ran a marathon in each of the fifty states. This coming close on the heels of hard cancer.

She was just starting.

She told me about making two new goals: run *two* marathons in each state, and run an ultramarathon in each state. Technically, of course, an ultramarathon is any race longer than 26.2 miles; typical distances are thirty-one miles, fifty miles, sixty-two miles, and 100 miles.

As the Komen 5K rolled around, she only lacked five marathons for the first goal and eighteen ultras for the second goal.

Each weekend required a trip for Angela, usually a long trip. To make time for her weekend travel, she'd usually take leave on Monday or Friday from her job with the

Going Down Slow

State of Tennessee, where she works as an environmental engineer. The weekend before the Cookeville race she was at a trail marathon in Lincoln City, Indiana. The weekend before that she was at a twenty-four-hour race in her hometown of Memphis. Before that, Bellingham, Washington, and so on. That's how it goes for her.

All this, she does while fighting cancer. Because after four years, it returned. For two years before the Komen race she had lived with its return. The return started with a sneaky back pain that she thought was caused by all the running. She went to a chiropractor, and she tried physical therapy. Neither helped.

She then had MRIs and a bone scan. The images showed that breast cancer had metastasized as an inoperable tumor on her lower spine. It had eaten holes in her pelvic bone as well. She was taking a medicine to rebuild her bones and another medicine to inhibit the production of estrogen, which the tumor fed on.

She lived in continual pain. Her iron count sometimes got so low that just walking made her out of breath, and she occasionally had to take iron infusions. She has a bone scan every four months to look for signs of new cancer. Except for her spine and pelvic bone no new sites had appeared.

In her online blog, "See Tiger Run," Angela discusses her ongoing treatments candidly and with humor, absent of any self pity. And through it all, she runs. Still. Could anybody in the whole round world deserve more to be honored at a Komen race?

Local marathon ace Josh Hite was a runner hitting the

Going Down Slow

top of his game. He had penciled in the October 5K, too. Within the year, Josh had won three marathons, and he had finished among the top three seven times.

He was striving to run about two marathons per month and so far had run thirteen for the year. He was on track to complete twenty to twenty-two marathons in the calendar year, he told me.

Conventional wisdom holds that an elite marathoner should not run more than two or three marathons per year. Josh scorns that practice. Additionally, he runs high mileage during his training, and would finish out the year at over 4,000 miles. His success had led him to a sponsorship with Marathon Guide, an online race service.

For its part, this 5K was the first such race for Komen Upper Cumberland. The Affiliate had only been approved by the national organization for three years. In that brief time it had raised and granted nearly a quarter-million dollars to non-profit organizations working to improve education, screening and treatment for breast cancer throughout the fourteen-county region of the Upper Cumberland.

How the affiliate was formed is a story that President Eileen Stuber told me. "The impetus was being a breast cancer patient," she said. "And when I was through with that I felt like there were lots of things that patients needed that weren't available to them."

She had discovered her breast cancer five years earlier. Surgery, radiation and chemotherapy followed. As it had for Angela, cancer changed the life of Eileen: She was inspired.

Going Down Slow

"I started looking at what was out there," she said. She discovered Komen, the national organization. She and her physician husband Harry made a trek to the Mission Conference in Washington, D.C. They were impressed enough with Komen's work that they decided to form a local affiliate.

"They said, 'Here's the application,'" Eileen told me. "It was two inches thick." She chuckled and then added quickly, "I'm not kidding." I didn't think she was.

One element of the application was called a "Community Profile." That required demographics of cancer in the fourteen-county area. A huge undertaking of data-gathering followed. Eileen enlisted several colleagues in that sweeping effort. A lack of needed data and consistent record keeping emerged as one of their discoveries. That fact made their job harder than it should have been.

"We learned about poverty and illiteracy," she added.

It turned out that only thirty-nine percent of women who needed screening were being screened, and there was an excess of late-stage cancers among those who were screened, diminishing the odds of a stricken woman's survival. So Komen U.C. set two goals: raise the screening rate to fifty percent and reduce the incident of late-stage cancers.

The application itself took a year and a half to finish. And it all culminated, finally, in what Eileen called the signature event, the Race for the Cure 5K. So on that Saturday, Eileen and all the other Komen volunteers were joined by Angela and Josh and hundreds of other

Going Down Slow

runners—some of whom were cancer survivors—in a collective celebration of life and a united resolve to fight breast cancer to a sulking standstill. It's a good fight.

It was fitting that Angela and Josh Hite met again, and here. Their first meeting had come just in the previous June, at the Moonlight Boogie in Ellerbe, N.C. That meeting cemented them in running folklore. Josh had heard about Angela but had never met her before then.

That Ellerbe race had started at six in the afternoon, and so proceeded into moonlight. Both a marathon and a fifty-mile race were being contested, the two distances laid out on courses that partially overlapped. The temperature at the start was 102 degrees, Josh told me. He was running the marathon while Angela was running the longer distance.

After the race Angela told me how it had ended up. "There were only two from Tennessee. He was first and I was last. We were perfect bookends." She enjoyed that metaphor and wasn't ashamed of being last.

Around twenty-one miles into the race, Josh had lapped Angela on a common portion of the two courses, coming up behind her. He was leading the marathon, but the heat had stolen his strength, and he was barely able to go on.

"I was just trying not to crawl," he said.

He had to keep going if he were to hold off the man he'd passed a mile back. Josh pulled even with Angela. He recalled what happened next:

"Angela, help me. I'm about to fall. Just run with me," he said.

Going Down Slow

"No, honey, I can't keep up with you," she told him. But she smiled and encouraged him. "You're doing great! Just keep going. Just keep going."

"But I'm only running nine-and-a-half minutes per mile," he protested.

"That's all-out for me," said Angela.

Josh grabbed her hand and pulled her along a short ways, drawing energy from her exuberance and praise. She told him he was looking great, that he had it all wrapped up, that he was making her proud.

Josh went on to win that race. The energy that pulled him through the last few miles, he credited to Angela.

"Her positive energy was beyond encouragement. She had a positive energy about her…better than anyone I've ever seen. Period."

So it was that the one who was last helped the one who was first.

On that searing night in North Carolina Josh had not known about Angela's cancer. She joined his fight to win the race there; four months later he joined her fight against cancer in Cookeville.

The second Komen U.C. race sent me in search of women again. Not just any women. I wanted women who were smart, strong and photogenic, women who had something to say. Women with interesting backgrounds made for an interesting newspaper story. I needed two of them, and I went looking. It didn't take long before I knew which two I wanted; they were friends already. Oh! There was one other requirement: They had to have had breast

Going Down Slow

cancer.

So I turned up two friends, women of different generations, different backgrounds. Either one alone might have filled the bill, but I liked the idea of two women of widely different backgrounds joining in a common cause. Jill White and Margie Stoll accepted my invitations.

Local runner Jill White was half the age of Nashville's Margie Stoll. Jill was reared in rural Smith County and had always lived in Tennessee, while Margie lists the urban locations of St. Louis, Chicago, Philadelphia and Washington, D.C. as her past homes. Both women boast athletic credentials. They had never met but their paths would soon converge. So here is a story about two women, with two stories—but one goal.

I'd run races with Jill. A few years earlier I had accompanied her to the Country Music Marathon, where she ran the half marathon distance despite not having trained for it. Then for two or three years I didn't see her. There was a good reason, I soon learned.

Jill, who was thirty-three, had attended the first Komen 5K. Her blond hair was just then growing back out, and she wore a baseball cap for cover. The big C, it had held her back for a while. Despite her recent bout, she may have won her category at the race. She thought she was the first cancer veteran across the finish line. Then she realized she'd failed to put the timing chip on her shoe. "No chip, no time," is the warning all racers know. "I was so mad!" she told me.

She wouldn't make that mistake the second year.

She learned competition early, when she was growing

Going Down Slow

up on the family farm near Gordonsville, Tennessee. Her father put up a basketball goal. He showed her how to shoot a hook shot. The hook shot didn't take, but other shots did.

Jill, who stands five feet eight inches, played forward four years for the Gordonsville Tigerettes. She was co-captain during her senior year.

She recalled some games for me. In one, against Trousdale County, she scored twenty-eight points. "I was a three-point shooter," she said simply.

And so she was. What was your favorite moment? I wondered. That question brought a twinkle.

"The real highlight was my senior year and playing Celina, a big rival, and we were down by two points." Although not the intended shooter, as the last naked seconds ticked off the clock, she found the ball in her hands and could not help but do what instinct and her dad's teaching and four years of basketball playing demanded: she put up the shot. It went in.

"I shot a three-pointer, and we won!" The gym erupted in celebration. "And it was crazy!"

Then life after high school settled in. A stint at Volunteer State, interrupted by work in a factory and in a nursing home, eventually led her to Tennessee Tech, where she earned a B.S. in Business Administration.

She also won the Golden Eagle 10K just before her spring graduation. She'd taken up running in college and had finished several road races and even several sprint triathlons. She had transferred her competitive spirit from basketball to racing.

Going Down Slow

"I took up walking and then walking got boring. I started running." She had been running ever since. Except for one rude intermission:

Just six months after marrying insurance agent John White, she discovered breast cancer. And her course changed.

Margie Stoll's story began some thirty-six years before Jill White's. Margie, who was sixty-nine years old, had re-defined running in the state of Tennessee, at least for the older set. Age group state records are maintained for each year of runner age. Margie held fifty of those records, ranging from the one-mile distance through the half marathon. *Running Times* magazine had ranked her as the third best runner in the U.S.A. in her age group. At the 2009 National Senior Games Margie won two gold medals and two sliver medals.

Born in 1941, Margie grew up in Lombard, Illinois. She described it to me as, "a pretty small town in those days. There was a cornfield at the end of my street." The house she grew up in had been in the family since 1936. "So I never had to change friends. I had the same friends from kindergarten through high school."

Her bucolic beginning was bound to end. She went off to Washington University in St. Louis, where she earned a degree in French. After working briefly for a brokerage firm, she resumed studies, at the University of Chicago and gained a teaching certificate.

But she gained much more; it was there that she met husband-to-be Hans, who was working on a Ph.D. in finance. They married in 1967. By then Dr. Stoll's work

Going Down Slow

had taken him to the University of Pennsylvania.

There then came a two-year stint when they lived in Washington, D.C. while Dr. Stoll worked for, among others, the Securities and Exchange Commission and the Federal Reserve.

It was there, in 1969, that Margie took up running — and in a very unusual place. "We lived near Arlington National Cemetery, and I used to run through the Cemetery. They probably wouldn't allow that now," she said wryly.

But why? That was before the running craze. She ran for exercise and because she liked the feel of running she told me.

Meanwhile, her husband had developed into a distinguished scholar of finance. The family eventually settled in Nashville in 1980, when Dr. Stoll accepted a position at Vanderbilt University.

They had been settled in the new town for a year. Then cancer called. That brought a brand new challenge, one unlike running or finance, either.

Cancer comes around at unhandy times. Margie would tell you that; her discovery came in 1982 when she was new in Nashville and without nearby friends. Jill would tell you that, too; she was just beginning a marriage. Although the cancers of the two women fell thirty years apart, there seems a weary sameness to the treatments they described: a round or two of surgery followed by six months of chemotherapy.

Those treatments are dreadful and make a patient feel awful. Jill described the solemn mood in the car when

Going Down Slow

husband John would drive her to Nashville. "It was quiet. We didn't talk very much. I had to mentally prepare myself." Get on her game face, like playing basketball.

All her hair came out: "Eye brows, eye lashes, everything." For her, losing her eyebrows was the worse. Their loss most made her appear enfeebled, she thought. "The good thing was I didn't have to shave my legs," she said laughing.

Margie had gone through a similar routine in 1982, but with a special cruel twist: she couldn't talk about it. Breast cancer was somehow considered embarrassing and shameful back then, hushed up. Stricken women suffered in silence.

Margie can talk easily and candidly about her experiences now. But she told me, "I wouldn't have said all this until about five years ago." The Komen races in Nashville, which she'd attended, changed that, released her. Remembering that race, she said, "It seemed like a festival, a total different atmosphere than the hospital."

Margie can look back on breast cancer with the gathered wisdom of thirty years. She prefers the word "veteran" over "survivor." Her thoughts on why are compelling:

"I think of a survivor as someone who has gone through a lot of pain and hardship — I like to think of myself as a veteran. The ones who are the real heroes are the ones who went through the pain and had a harder time — and somehow it was stacked against them. Because they died, that's why there is an organization like Komen."

Margie Stoll and Jill White know how to suffer hard

Going Down Slow

and they know how to run hard. Race Sunday came. They toed the line in common cause. Both women walked away, victorious. Margie was recognized as the first cancer veteran, and as the first overall women over forty.

The nature of Jill's victory was different. It was one she'd already told me about. She'd told me before I even wrote the promotion story, and had asked me to keep it secret, to omit it from the story. She'd not been ready to reveal the news. She was apologetic and hated to ask me the favor. But I agreed with her.

After all her illness, the debilitating treatment, the dreadful trips to Nashville, the chemotherapy—after all that, the life-affirming news she'd told me was: she was pregnant. "I hope that doesn't spoil your story," she said.

37

WRETCHED UNDEAD HOUND THE HAUNTED HALF

"The horde of hollow-eyed ghouls making a death march along Cookeville city streets next Saturday will turn out to be a pack of sleepy-eyed runners competing in the 2nd Annual Haunted Half Marathon. For some, the worst nightmare ever; for others, a glory-dream."

The Haunted Half sports a ghostly theme that appealed to me. I decided to have some fun with the whole goofy thing. The race's website promised racers a "Spooktacular time…a wonderful weekend of health, wellness, fun and activity…"

Well, maybe.

Glory-dream? One dream weaver was Angie Clark. No scar-faced guy with blades for fingers could catch her. The Celina native, follows a rigorous training program, regularly running farther than the race's unlucky 13.1-mile distance.

I'd met her at a local 5K a few weeks earlier, and she agreed to be the subject of a promotion article. As the Haunted Half approached, I had a long talk with her.

"I follow a combination of two or three training plans, and I run forty to fifty miles per week and do two days of speed work and one long run," she said.

Going Down Slow

If the Tennessee Titans football team trained so thoroughly, they might avoid a turnover nightmare.

For Angie, who is thirty-one, the training pays off. She had won the women's division of the recent Fall Fun Fest 5K, posting a time of 21 minutes, 8 seconds. On the Saturday two weeks later, she was the second woman at still another 5K.

That hardly tells the story of the last race. Saturday is the day she does her long runs. To complete both the 5K race and her long run, she compromised:

"I ended up doing that same course five times that day. I did it two times before the race and two more times after the race." I reckon the two prior trips around the course might have taken some edge off her 5K speed. It would mine. Her total distance for the day came to 15.5 miles.

Angie works as an academic advisor and instructor in the general curriculum program at Tennessee Tech. She earned an M.B.A. there in 2004.

She neither ran cross country in high school nor college. Rather, she took up running on her own while in college. That curious fact—lack of varsity experience—seems almost normal in my experience, especially among some of the good women runners I know.

"I've always been into exercise, but I never enjoyed it until I took up running. I like the way runners look and so that's why I tried it. I like the sense of accomplishment I get from it," she said. Well, there's her reason, but it didn't occur to her in time for running on a varsity team.

As Angie was preparing for the Haunted Half, the

Going Down Slow

race director was preparing for 300 expected runners. I wrote: The race draws runners from other states—other realms. Look for Neytiri, the Na'vi from Pandora; for Leatherface from Texas; for a lurching hockey mask; Lady Gaga; Darth Vader; the Wicked Witch of the West; and bats out of hell.

I noted how the course turns just two blocks shy of running down Elm St., thus avoiding any chance of a slasher nightmare on that evil street. And further, how the course ends on the quadrangle in front of Memorial Gym, where suffering runners can collapse on the grass.

Metaphors flutter like bats; it's easy to crack wise. Elm Street aside, the real suspense and misery in any race comes from the running itself. A runner fights to exorcise the seductive little voice whispering oh so sweetly: *You can stop. It will feel so good. Why don't you stop?*

The race goes to the fit, the trained. Others fall behind, some way behind. Bad luck for those poor wretches. Laggards will be arrested and thrown into the pit where porta potties are pumped, I warned with over-wrought irony.

Angie Clark, I knew, could quickly and readily travel the distance. She'll blow past the leather-faced cannibal before he can get his chainsaw cranked, I predicted.

No stranger to long distance, she has run four marathons, including Country Music, Louisville and Rocket City. At Rocket City she finished the 26.2-miles in 3 hours, 28 minutes, winning third place in her age group and—more importantly—qualifying for the Boston Marathon, a dream she had held hard to.

Going Down Slow

She has a more outrageous adventure planned before that big dinger in Boston. Her relay team of twelve members will run from Chattanooga to Nashville, 168 miles, in the so-called Ragnar Race. The thirteen-mile Haunted Half is only a warm up for her.

Truth is there *is* hellish effort in running a competitive race. Athletes call it pain. It feels like a nightmare. The only escape from the running is to keep running…until the finish line. Or quit and face the shame of failure. Between the pain of running and the shame of failure, most runners choose pain.

38

A SPECIAL GUEST AT A SPECIAL RACE

This I didn't know when I went: Each year this race has a "special guest," and this time it was little four-year-old Emma Smith, who was born with spina bifida and who is my great niece.

I'd never been to the Race for Jordan, had never run any race in Carthage, Tennessee. Driving down that morning I could not have known I was heading for an intersection of racing and family.

It was not the normal date for the race. The seventh running had originally been scheduled for the first Saturday in May. That was a day of storms, and a 1000-year flood in nearby Nashville. Dangerous lightning forced cancellation, and the race was re-scheduled for June 12th.

But I had not known any of this prior to the Sunday before the race, and the way I discovered it then was unlikely: I went to a family reunion.

Hadn't planned to go. My only reunion connection was my paternal grandmother, who died when I was only five. I barely remember her. So, I expected to see a lot of people that I barely know or don't know at all. In the end, I decided to go in order to take my eighty-seven-year-old aunt. She always loves it. While I was there, a tan young woman came up to me.

Going Down Slow

"Can you run a 5K?" she asked.

"Uh...yes, I think so." I said, surprised.

"I thought so, since you're wearing a marathon tee shirt."

She was right. I was wearing the tee of the Country Music Marathon, which I'd finished just six weeks earlier. The young woman was Karen Hackett. She was the Director of the Race for Jordan 5K.

Jordan was her son. He'd been born with a heart defect. He only lived four months. His short life was filled with medical procedures. After his death, Karen and her husband Steve had started the race to raise money for other afflicted children and their families.

"We raised $30,000," she said.

She was talking about last year alone. A thousand people had registered for the race, "donated," she called it. Around 500 people actually showed up to run.

"It's good that you can make something good from..." I stammered.

"Try to..."

Still, I probably would not have run the race except for a final unlikely event. A few weeks earlier, running friend Bill Baker had asked me to find a race near Cookeville for June 12. He and his son were coming to town for a wedding, and they wanted to run a race that day. I didn't know of any. After Karen told me about the Race for Jordan, I sent Bill a message. He replied that they would probably run the race.

That meant I had to run it, too. To not make an effort to see them during their visit would be rude I thought. Out

Going Down Slow

of courtesy, I had to go run. The final irony: they failed to show up.

A race re-scheduled, a reunion visit not intended, a tee shirt worn, visitors who wanted a race—all these unlikely events colluded in a crazy defiance of mathematical probability, so that as dawn spread its light across the mid-state that morning, I found myself barreling down I-40 toward Carthage, Tennessee. From a universe of infinite opportunity an infinitesimal probability explodes to outrageous reality. It happens all the time.

Upon arriving, the first person I saw was Karen. She was walking across the parking lot waving. That's when she told me about the "special guest," and that this year it was my nephew's daughter Emma. I was astonished. I see Emma's family only occasionally.

She told me another thing: "This year we got it certified." That meant that the course had been certified by USATF to be the correct length for a 5K (3.107 miles). A record finish time could thus count as an official state record.

Until then I'd not even considered that particular issue. Suddenly it grabbed me. The course starts at a playground and runs out-and-back along the road to Cordell Hull Dam, nearly flat most of the way.

Age-group state records are kept for each year of age. I had set the 5K record for a sixty-nine-year-old male in March. That course was not favorable to a fast time. So a week later I went to another 5K and broke the record I'd just set. That second course was hilly and not fast either. I was frustrated that the record didn't reflect my true capability.

Going Down Slow

Given a chance before my seventieth birthday, I knew I could improve the record for a third time. Suddenly a certified flat course had dropped in my lap two weeks before my birthday, a last chance. I don't know if a runner has ever set three records for the same distance in one year. I doubt it.

About 500 runners showed up. The race started under a blistering sun at 8:00 a.m. The first half-mile I ran in eighth position. Then I began picking off runners, eventually moving up to fourth. That's where I finished, unable to catch number three, a thirty-two-year-old man, just yards ahead. My time of 21:05 went seven seconds over my state record.

It was failure. The flat, and certified, course had been a gift. The day's heat took it away.

Suddenly I spotted little Emma, across the parking lot with her dad, Chris. When I walked up in sweaty racing clothes, Chris was flabbergasted. The last thing he expected was to see his uncle. Not a runner, he had dutifully brought Emma so she could be part of the festivities.

After a bit of amazed talk, Chris left Emma in my care temporarily while he went to his truck. Emma, who walks well without braces, was wearing a ponytail, blue sunglasses and a tiny maroon race tee. She looked like a doll ought to.

We walked to the finish line to welcome runners home. Emma stood smiling, clapping her hands the way I showed her. Her mom Ashley was still out on the course.

Emma's dad returned and shot a syringe full of pink fluid into her mouth. She drank it without a whine. The

Going Down Slow

medicine she takes prevents sweating, Chris explained. They have to be careful in hot weather. The doctors think she can get off the medicine soon.

A little later, at the awards presentation, they lifted Emma into the bed of a pickup and introduced her. She looked out over the crowd, still smiling. A lady with a bullhorn stood beside her and read her story. It detailed the family's desperate trips from Gordonsville to Vanderbilt Children's Hospital, how that hospital had helped them, had saved Emma, had saved them.

Hearing that, it suddenly hit me like a brick: Children's Hospital is an organization I usually contribute to. I've written those checks without once realizing the hospital might be helping an actual member of my family. But it is so.

The lyric to a pop song goes something like, "All you give is all you get, so give it all you've got." Proving the songwriter's truth, little Emma smiled at the gathered people.

The photographer made pictures of me holding the special guest in my arms. Emma smiled for the camera. On cue, she leaned over and kissed her grizzled great uncle on the cheek.

The crowd drifted away, the parking cleared out. I stood on the pavement alone. I wanted to think about what had happened. The best way to think is to run. I started running and lapped the course again.

Life plays out at a race. Life intensified, life distilled and pressed into a small space. Surprises are part of it. A race is never just a race.

39

FOURTEEN ELITE FOOLS

Looking up from his cell phone, Josh Hite interrupted the caller to confirm what he had just told him:

"Wouldn't you say that the sucky part of the course was Cane Creek School parking lot?"

"Yeah, that's about right," I agreed.

We were sitting around Josh's dining room table, several runners eating, drinking and recovering from having just finished the first-ever marathon in our hometown of Cookeville, Tennessee. And Josh was talking to his friend about the course, specifically the sun-blasted part that meandered around the perimeter of Cane Creek Elementary School.

Here's what you can do: Start at the Recreation Center in Cookeville's Cane Creek Park. Run down CC Camp Road to the Park entrance; circle Cane Creek Lake, returning to the center. Continue on the park path the other way, past the softball fields to the Tommy Thomas Bike Path on Jackson Street. Follow that path past the school a short ways and make a turnaround. On your way back to the Recreation Center, just for good measure, detour around the perimeter of the school parking lot.

You will find that you've just run 5.24 miles. If you

Going Down Slow

repeat that four more times you will run precisely 26.2 miles, the length of a marathon.

At 7:00 a.m. on a Sunday morning in August, that is what fourteen "elite fools" attempted to do: Run a marathon. In the South. In August. On a course largely exposed to the Sun.

Your doctor wouldn't recommend it.

How did such a thing happen? Credit Josh. A couple of months back he decided to host a marathon in Cookeville. On our runs we talked it over. I was noncommittal. But he soon listed the "Event" on Facebook, sending messages to various running friends, inviting them to run it. At the time, he was calling it something like "Not Yet Named Marathon." He advertised it as "NO FRILLS marathon... No certification. No shirt. No fee." Along with the narrative, he also posted two inviting photos of Cane Creek Lake.

Enter Trent Rosenbloom, friend of Josh and the director of Nashville's Flying Monkey Marathon, a joke of a marathon that has become the Rocky Horror Picture Show of all marathons, so popular that after online registration started for the 2010 edition, the race filled up in only thirty-two minutes. Trent knows how to promote a sadistic joke.

Trent hung the handle "Blister in the Sun Marathon" on Josh's race and listed it on the website of the Marathon Maniacs. The name "Marathon Maniacs" explains itself.

Thus, the race was born, or at least a virtual storm of electrons about it was.

Replies rolled in: Maniac Jeff Matlock allowed "I'm

Going Down Slow

in for the...No Name Run In The Sun Running is Stupid Hot Hilly Humid Marathon." Later he tried to back out, calling it "crazy...insane." But Josh eventually shamed him into coming. Photographer Elly Foster demurred, claiming, "As much as I would like to be in the company of such elite fools, I regretfully decline." Local Ironman Susan Ford declined with the dubious endorsement, "This is crazy. I just love it."

A smattering accepted. Josh switched to e-mail for those doomed runners, twice sending out race updates and bad news about hills and heat — six days before, and forty-eight hours before. Those messages were addressed to "Masochists," and ended with the signature "Sadist." The last one announced, "You have only forty-eight hours until the soul in your shoes start to melt." It's not clear that the word "soul" in the place of "sole" was really a spelling error.

In any event, Sunday came, as it always does. Trees stretched their early morning shadows across the fourteen runners standing on the pavement before the Recreation Center, where Queen City Timing had set up an electronic start/finish line.

We shoved off.

Josh was hoping to win his own marathon, but he was afraid of Gary Krugger, a compact, angular runner from Edinboro, Pennsylvania, who wears a plaited ponytail hanging to his waist and who had won the 2010 University of Okoboji Marathon. They took off together. The rest of us strung along behind, trotting along at various speeds.

The race dragged on. For me, it would be a special

Going Down Slow

challenge to just finish. The night before, just ten hours earlier, I'd run the Race After Dark 8K (5 miles), which had started at 8:58 p.m. By the time I'd finished, taken a shower and had a snack, I got in bed around midnight. And I had to get up at 5 a.m. for the Blister Marathon. I got precious little sleep. But there was maybe a bigger factor than sleep deprivation: rest.

In lieu of competing in that 8K — a race he could have won, along with its prize money — Josh elected to pace me through the distance. His high-tech runner's watch reads out instantaneous pace, distance, and elapsed time.

The state record for a seventy-year old male was 37:00, and I was hoping to break it. Josh's pacing helped me do that. I finished in 33:58, running an average pace of 6:48 per mile. I thus ran a state record, I was the first finisher over fifty-five, and I won $100 prize money for that last fact.

I had gone all out and saved nothing for the next morning's marathon. In the last half-mile stretch my speed had steadily increased to 6:15. But at a terrible cost.

Now knee-deep in the marathon, I had to pay. I could only go slowly, a reality the heat would help assure.

On my first outbound pass toward the school I met extreme runner Angela Ivory. She is fighting cancer and cannot run as fast as she once could. After a bout some seven years ago, the cancer recently metastasized to her spine and has since spread to her liver, lung, and skull. Josh gave her an early start so that she would not finish so late in the day. She has completed some 170 marathons and 100-plus ultramarathons. A wounded

Going Down Slow

warrior, she soldiers on.

Despite the heat and threat of cramps, my race ironically passed pleasantly. Ha! Thanks to going slow. It's the racing that makes it hard, not the distance, a sage noticed.

Drama started on my fourth lap. As I approached the boat ramp someone was yelling. I turned to see Josh 100 yards behind. He was in his fifth and final lap, a lap ahead of me. He was alone and in the lead, but he had blown up.

"Dallas, wait!"

I stood waiting. He was reduced to walking. He wanted company to help him keep going.

"Go with me," he said.

He had done as much for me the night before. We went into the woods together.

"Dallas, this sucks."

"Yeah."

He was irrational, afraid Gary Krugger was going to catch him. Although Krugger was nowhere to be seen, Josh kept mumbling pace numbers:

"…if I can just run ten-minute miles…" Then a few seconds later: "…if I can run twelve-minute miles…" Then he'd go over it again.

But it made no sense figuring pace without even knowing where Krugger was. Josh had dropped him on the second lap and then gone hard on his third lap to put him out of sight. In his fourth lap then he had gone deep into his energy reserves. Finally, now, he had hit bottom. He could only run brief distances, and then he had to walk again. He was obsessed with Krugger suddenly catching him.

We reached the high trail on the north shore. It offers

Going Down Slow

a commanding view of the trail behind us, including the long levee we'd just crossed. Krugger was nowhere to be seen. I looked at the woods across the lake.

"If he's out there, he must be in the trees," I said, referring to the woods on the lake's south side.

"He'd be over there," Josh said, pointing farther back, along CC Camp Road.

I didn't know why he was worried. To finish, Josh had only a half-mile to reach the Recreation Center. After that all that was left was the two-and-half miles out-and-back to the school.

"He couldn't catch you if he had a motorcycle," I said.

Then I remembered where I'd last seen Krugger. Martha, Josh's wife, had set up a table loaded with food and drinks in the shade at the center. When I left there on my fourth lap — which was slightly before Josh left on his fifth lap — Krugger wasn't going to catch anybody.

He wasn't running. He was standing in the shade having a hushed talk with his girl friend, a pretty blond woman named Morgan Cummings. She was on crutches from a stress fracture in her hip. She is a marathoner, too, and she's been known to even run on her crutches.

We returned to Martha's table, Josh yelling, "Ice water! Ice water!"

Krugger wasn't there. We headed toward the school, Josh's last segment, and suddenly met Chris Estes, a big man with the physique of a body builder. He was maybe three miles behind Josh.

"Did you get Krugger?" Josh asked.

"What?"

Going Down Slow

"Did you pass Krugger?"

"Yeah."

"Way to go, dude."

Josh had it. Krugger wasn't even second; Chris was. And either one was farther behind Josh than Josh was from the finish line. Josh had only to go to the school, pass through the parking lot inferno, and return to the Center. He could walk all the way.

Which he mostly did, winning with 3:32:07, a time far off his capability. Chris held onto second, and Gary Krugger ended up third.

Meanwhile, Angela Ivory had joined with a friend, Diane Taylor. When Angela completed her last lap, Diane still had a whole lap to go. Angela decided to stay with Diane for another lap, thus covering a distance of 31.4 miles, 50K. Hence Angela finished Cookeville's first marathon, *and* created, *and* finished ad hoc Cookeville's first 50K ultramarathon.

Most runners talk about their PR, by which they mean "personal record," or their best finish time. After this hot, hilly race, I heard a new term—PW: *personal worst.* I set one myself.

Twelve of the fourteen elite fools actually finished. Once they returned home, Facebook began to crackle with irony and absurdity. The post of Trent Rosenbloom, who'd help Josh plan the race, summed it up best: "That was silly."

40

AFTER THE FLOOD

Josh wanted sixteen, and I had fourteen. That is, he wanted to go for a sixteen-mile run, and I had a fourteen mile loop. My fourteen-mile loop went into Jackson County, a rural place where the dogs run free; and past Cummins Falls where the water runs wild.

The water of Blackburn Fork jumps off the falls and meanders down a narrow valley for ten miles before it joins Roaring River. You might call the valley a gorge; it is pretty narrow at the bottom and bounded by steep wooded slopes with some bluff outcroppings. A road surfaced with creek gravel, paved in places, follows the stream on its journey.

But I didn't even mean to go there, down the gorge, I mean. The fourteen-mile loop stayed above the valley. It merely went *past* the falls, staying on top. But, see, Josh wanted sixteen miles that morning.

The weather was hot, August hot. One bottle in a waist pack is not enough for such heat. The well-equipped ultra runner made preparations. I dug out the backpack I use for journey runs and such. It's a tiny thing probably designed for the shorter torso of a woman. But it is just right. It is short enough to leave room for my regular waist

Going Down Slow

pack below it. So I can go with both the waist pack for my bottle and still have a bit of cargo room in the little backpack.

The backpack is large enough to hold a pair of long pants, a wind jacket, a pair of gloves and emergency medical kit. The pack was a bladder pack before I took the bladder out. Now it's just a pack. It's what I use for ultramarathons; so I don't need drop bags, or for a crew to meet me two hours before or two hours after I need an item. I travel light and carry everything I need. That way, I have it when I want it.

What Josh needed was sixteen miles. In August that distance crosses the line for a one-bottle run. So I duly filled two extra bottles and put them in the little pack. Just in case. Those two bottles may be responsible for what happened, because without them, I doubt we would've made the decision we made that day. Or, more accurately, failed to make the decision we should have made.

Because he did say sixteen, and once I'm pretty sure I further heard "or more," and I only had fourteen. I figured we'd just run down a side road for a mile—"or more"—and add that excursion to the fourteen miles of the loop. Which side road exactly I didn't know. We could take our pick.

So we shoved off at my house into the building heat, heading toward Jackson County, each runner with a bottle strapped to his waist and with two extra bottles in the pack I was wearing.

Six miles into the run we were approaching Blackburn Fork, when we made the decision on which side road

Going Down Slow

we'd pick for our extra-distance excursion. The signpost said Blackburn Fork Rd. I was very familiar with the road from having ridden my bike all over Jackson County. The road stays up on the rim for a mile and a half before it drops suddenly into the gorge, making sharp turns and switchbacks.

We headed down it. Soon a pickup approached from behind, pulling a farm implement. We edged over.

"Dallas, you going all the way? the driver asked, stopping.

"Nah, we're just going part way."

I'd never seen the man before. I shook his hand and redundantly told him my name. He said he recognized me from having read my newspaper stories. He had a reason for asking his question, because the road was closed. On back roads in that country, what road closure signifies is not so much a legal condition as a physical one—it's impossible to travel it.

We knew a little of what had happened on upper Blackburn Fork, at least its two branches near Cookeville. Ten days earlier, a strong flood had covered roads, disrupted travel and work and school schedules. The two main branches of Blackburn Fork pass into Jackson and converge maybe a mile above the falls. The concentrated energy of the two branches had combined in a catastrophic way. The flood had gathered strength downstream to a degree that Josh and I didn't yet imagine.

I'd actually seen some of the damage on the end of the gorge near where Blackburn Fork joins Roaring River. But most of the gorge was closed off. Only a few people

Going Down Slow

live in it, and generally speaking the gorge lies beyond the experience of most of the local population. People didn't know what had happened there.

So I thought maybe Josh and I could penetrate just a little ways and then cut and climb back out. I was carrying two extra bottles of water, after all. The road I had in mind crossed the stream on a single-lane bridge and climbed up to a ridge called Seven Knobs in Jackson County. So I asked,

"What about the bridge…"

"It ain't there," the man cut me off — his way of telling me I had a poor idea of what was down there. That bridge had been there since 1937, I believe he said. He mentioned how deep the mud was, and he talked about how he'd once enjoyed canoeing on the stream. Then he drove on, turning in to his house just up the road. Josh and I resumed our run.

Another three-quarters-mile brought us to the edge of the rim, where the road dipped sharply down. There in the road stood the obligatory Road Closed sign that people in this part of the country simply ignore and drive around.

Half way down the hill we came to a view of the valley floor, although screened and obscured by dense tree foliage. Through the leaves, we saw tan. Where the fields and pastures below should have been green, we saw expansive desert tan, desert in Tennessee. The flood had stripped away green living plants and replaced then with acres of deposited gravel bars, or gouged out the bottom land to bedrock, in either case replacing the green background with an alien tan overlay, at least from our

Going Down Slow

distant view. Although no stranger to floods, it was the first time I'd realized that a flood can change the very color of environs.

We rounded a switchback, the hill's last sharp curve, and leveled out on the valley floor. Approaching the place where the creek swings in close to the road, the creek on our left and steep hillside on our right. (And here, I've used the work "creek" for the first time. Some will argue with that, because the state legislature has designated the stream a Scenic River. So they claim it's a "River." But in my experience, locals refer to the stream as a creek, the legislature notwithstanding. I'll continue favoring the local and historical "creek" over the legislative term.)

The road disappeared into a dark chaos of tangled trees uprooted by the flood and swept into random piles. The road surface vanished under a deep layer of mud, now rutted by truck tracks, but the tracks didn't go much farther.

There sat a car. Josh and I picked our way through, to find a young man and his girlfriend. The young man appeared quite drunk. They were just standing around looking in amazement, as we approached. We were at a one-lane bridge where a branch known as Dry Creek flows underneath just before its confluence with Blackburn Fork. The bridge was partially covered by uprooted and broken trees. The branch had washed out the approach on the other side. End of road.

After talking a bit with the man and woman, Josh climbed down the other end of the bridge. It was a three or four foot drop. As I followed, the over-solicitous young

Going Down Slow

man insisted on helping ease the old gent down and grabbed hold of my upper arm, which had the unhelpful effect of depriving me of the use of one hand. Nonetheless, I made it down without breaking an ankle. Josh and I picked our way though some more downed trees and broke out on the road again.

"He's been drinking Mimosa juice," said Josh, the former bartender.

"He wanted to help me. I didn't need it, but he wanted to. That's okay."

The road curved left, hard against vertical bluffs. The flood had gone high up on those rocks far above our heads. The creek, calm and pastoral now burbled across the gravel shoals below us innocent of all the violence it had brought. I looked for the right place because I wanted to show Josh something about the bluff.

"These are the bluffs I'm running in front of on the cover of my book, *Falling Forward*," I told Josh." This is where we made the picture, these bluffs." I showed Josh the place where my friend Charles Denning had gotten the low angle by stepping part way down the creek bank, to a level below the road.

"He photographed me running up and down the road in front of these bluffs." In one frame, the shadow of a tree on the bluff had loomed menacingly over the motion-blurred runner. The runner's shadow ran across the rocks. Although the runner was blurred, his shadow on the rocks was jarringly sharp; it was reduced in size and preceded the runner as if the runner rushed toward his diminished future. These fleeting shadows, the ephemeral quickness

Going Down Slow

of life caught in images cast against timeless rocks and threatened by the looming darkness filled the photo with metaphor. The picture inspires me yet. Its feeling of menace had come true — this location had drowned under fifteen feet of rushing water.

Farther down the road, the roadbed simply disappeared, gouged away by the flood's force, the road bed itself replaced by gullies and ridges. Josh and I picked our way through. In the distance I could see where a small rustic bridge had spanned the creek. It was gone. One steel girder remained, its end cast in the near abutment and held tight. The flood had bent the three-foot-deep girder like a noodle and aligned it with the flow direction. Charles and I had made running pictures on that bridge, too. He had laid down the floor and made a photo showing the splintered wooden floor as I ran by. Now Josh and I had no way to even record the bridge's absence, or any of the other devastation around us. We had no camera; Josh wasn't carrying his cell phone as he usually does.

A white frame house sits on higher ground on the right. Two dogs came tearing out barking invectives. I don't worry about dogs when I run with Josh, although Jackson County is full of unleashed menacing dogs. He has a black belt in Karate. I trot happily on, leaving him to deal with any malevolence. I figure he'll just kick the shit out of one if he needs to. There is a danger in that, too. The owner may come after you with a deer rifle in his hand and vengeance in his heart. He places the welfare of his dog a couple of rungs above that of two strangers on foot. But these two dogs I just sweet-talked, and they turned into

Going Down Slow

tail-wagging pussycats. Their owner was more guarded,

"Who are you guys?" she wanted to know. So we stopped and talked, and convinced her we were harmless. They'd gone without power for seven days after the flood, she told us. During those days her husband had stayed up guarding the darkened house. They'd had suspicious-looking men come around late at night, would-be looters they'd figured. She had a reason to be cautious with strangers.

We went on, running through devastation like we'd not seen before. Whole groves of mature trees swept down and flattened like so many corn stalks. Stretches of the creek bank had been denuded, the trees uprooted or broken off and carried downstream and left in house-sized piles. Just past the woman's house a creek bottom cultivated in soybeans had been simply erased, gouged to bedrock in places, buried by gravel and television-sized rocks a few feet deep in other places. It was as if the Colorado River had coursed through this narrow canyon and scoured it out.

River bottoms and creek bottoms have existed ever since humans first occupied this land, thousands of years ago. I believe this because you can find stone points thousands of years old on the surface or in the top few inches of the soil. The soybean field experienced a flood it had not seen in a similar span of time. By coincidence, only two months had passed since Nashville had endured what the U.S. Army Corps of Engineers called a 1,000-year flood. Josh and I had run the Strolling Jim forty-one-mile ultramarathon at Wartrace, fifty miles south of Nashville,

Going Down Slow

that very day. And now this place, hit by a similar flood. But Josh and I were not talking about that—until suddenly we were. We were trotting along in amazed and morose silence, when out of the blue he spoke,

"Global warming's not happening, right?"

"Right!"

We were being ironic. Climate scientists have told us for decades that global warming will bring storms of enhanced intensity and frequency. Within two months, Blackburn Fork and Nashville had both obeyed that prediction. Severe weather is here. We'll have to get used to it. We've done nothing to stop it. And it's too late now. It will only get worse. The polluters and their lobbyists together with their stupid and dishonest politicians have won.

We passed where the seventy-year-old bridge leading to Seven Knobs used to stand. No sign of it was left, no abutments, nothing.

Josh had become the mule now, carrying my little pack. It contained two empty water bottles. We each were running low on our last bottle. The creek water wasn't safe to drink, we knew.

About half way through the gorge, Zion Road comes in from the east rim and joins the main road, which crosses the creek there. But not anymore; the bridge was gone, the main road cut in two at that point. To the left of the bridge approach is a grassy lawn where a brick house had stood. It had been cleanly swept away, its pieces, bricks and all, scattered downstream. The concrete walks remained like the house's silent signature.

Going Down Slow

The bridge at Zion was the most emblematic scene of the flood's power. It had been the only modern structure spanning the creek. Its entire three-span deck, still attached to the beams underneath, had been swept downstream sixty yards and spun into a skewed alignment with the creek, the near end left resting on the bank, the far end out in the water. Even the two piers, hammer-head-shaped monoliths, had been toppled and carried downstream sixty yards or so and left lying in the water like giant overturned mushrooms.

The bridge had been of routine construction like dozens of such structures I'd designed myself working for the then-Tennessee Department of Highways. This one was worth maybe half a million dollars. Its near abutment was the only part of the entire three spans left in place. That abutment was now covered by a house-sized pile of trees.

Josh and I worked our way through downed trees to a point upstream where the creek flowed shallow over a gravel shoals. We waded across the creek and climbed up to the road on the far side and ran on.

For a long time now Josh and I had been past turning back and rejoining our loop home, even though we were running low on water. We'd gone too far. We were committed to wherever we ended up now. And we'd not even discussed that decision. We simply kept going forward, too fascinated at the destruction to turn back. It's a safe bet no one had ever before run the length of this remote road. It's an equal bet we were seeing the destruction in its entirety like no one yet had. We could

Going Down Slow

only run on now, the town of Gainesboro our likely target—for the reason that it was the only one possible, however far it was. It was a hot day, and our lack of water was becoming worrisome

You are never prepared. I'm not. We were running on gravels, dirt and washed-out gullies, and wading the creek. And what was I wearing? Why the lightest pair of lightweight trainers I'd been able to buy, not trail shoes. That is a good way to break an ankle. Both of mine have been broken, but I think they recovered stronger than before. Sometimes I get away with negligence.

There's a memory on this road I told Josh about. Many years ago I made a special ride on my mountain bike through here. It was one of the most alluring valleys in Tennessee and a favorite place of mine. I guess that changes now. Jim Smith and I rode our mountain bikes through here, as we later did many times. What made that particular trip memorable was that my youngest son Joel, maybe nine, rode with us, as did Jim's son Andy, a few months older than Joel. Andy had muscular dystrophy which affected his legs, and he couldn't ride a bike. He came along on his all-terrain-vehicle, a three wheeler.

There was a place in the road then where a flowing branch came into the road, turned and ran with the road. Branch and road were one for a few feet. You rode down into the water, followed it a bit and then it turned from the road and went on while you climbed back onto the roadbed. At the start of the trip Jim and I told Joel and Andy about that place, about how they'd have to go through the water. They got excited. You'd think we'd told them

Going Down Slow

they'd see Santa Claus. While we rode alongside the creek that day, they kept asking about when we were going to ride through the water. And, of course, they did love it once we got there, splashing the water and whooping.

The three-wheeler was a blessing for Andy, allowing him to participate in trips like the ride we took that day. A year later he was killed on it, when a school bus hit him on the subdivision road near his house. Jim lived in a rural development called Dry Creek then and I still owned a house there myself, having recently moved. Our houses were on the head of the same Dry Creek that flows into Blackburn Fork where Josh and I entered the gorge on our run today.

At that place where Andy and Joel had enjoyed the water there stood a faded old house close beside the road, one surrounded by outbuilding, and fruit trees, the home place of an old-time family. Josh and I were running by that place as I told him the story. The house was now gone, swept away by the flood and scattered in pieces. An old woman had lived there alone, I've heard. She was lucky enough to take refuge in a barn on higher ground. A young man on an ATV, successor of Andy's, rode down, apparently on a trail through the woods, and rescued her from the barn.

Down the road a hundred yards from the house site, Josh and I discovered a giant pile of trees thrown up against still-standing trees beside the road. Mixed into the pile and scattered beyond it were items from the house: a microwave oven, floor fan and so on, and articles of clothing hanging like prayer flags from the brush. We

Going Down Slow

found home-canned jars of green beans and pears, muddy but looking perfectly good to eat once wiped off.

"Something's dead," Josh said. I noticed the scent about the same time. We began looking, wondering if it was the body of a human, a pet, or a farm animal. Josh and I spread out. We poked around in the piles of brush. The scent came and went. I began back tracking the wind. Concentrating, I was aware a car passed. (The one bridge left standing was the last one near Roaring River Road and crews had repaired the road on that end enough that cars could come in from there.) I followed the scent to a depression against the road bank, and found a collection of minnows that had been trapped and died there when the flood receded. I called Josh over and we stood looking down at little fish that stunk out of proportion to their actual size. Mystery solved without drama.

"Was that two women in a red convertible?" I asked.

"They were not attractive."

"Uh."

When you hold an ace in the hole, you need to be certain it actually is an ace. Charles Denning and I once went hiking in the mountains in the dead of winter where it can get dangerously cold. Our route was long and the sun got low and we began to wonder if we'd make it to the truck before dark. Spending a night in the wilderness began to seem a possibility. There were many overhanging bluffs and caves where we could take shelter. If need be we'd just build a fire for warmth and light. For Charles' benefit I dramatically produced the butane cigarette lighter I carry for such emergencies, held it up and gave it a flick. Results

Going Down Slow

were notable for their absolute absence: no flame. Flick, flick, flick, flick, and still no flame. In fact, no flame ever came from that traitor of a lighter. I should have checked it beforehand. It had been stored with my hiking stuff for a long time and had lost its pressure, I reckon.

By the time Josh and I crossed the only bridge left standing on Blackburn Fork—out of four—our water was nearly gone. We'd been stretching it out. But, of course, that only allows one to get more dehydrated and does little to conserve the total combined fluids contained in bottle and body.

My ace in the hole was just one half mile farther. A spring seeps out of the bluffs beside the road. An ancient plumber of springs had stuck an iron pipe in the bluff crevice decades ago, capturing and running the pattering little stream right out to the thirsty traveler. Just stick your bottle under it. And you don't even have to turn off the faucet that the plumber didn't provide to the everlasting spring that never stops.

When we got there, the everlasting spring that forever brings cold, life-giving water, that non-ending stream of the thirsty runner's dream, that very spring had, in point of fact, gone bone dry. We'd get no water there. I've filled my bike bottle there. I'd never seen it dry before. My ace had turned into a joker.

It was a half mile further to the Roaring River Road, and from there, an uncertain distance on to Gainesboro—maybe in the range of six to seven miles, I vaguely figured from my memory of riding the road. My guess would prove to be not bad wrong, and would end up pushing

Going Down Slow

our total distance to twenty-one miles by the time we reached Gainesboro.

We headed down the two-lane blacktop, fully catching the sun's heat now, running beside Roaring River. Our lack of water began to tell. Josh is half my age, hence, more able than I to shuck off the heat and dehydration. Nonetheless, we ran together down that road carrying empty bottles in our waist packs and Josh carrying two empties in the backpack, little more now than relics of a water-blessed past.

Occasionally we walked, getting gradually tired and slow. Josh ran on. I began to trail behind. Cramps had set in on my legs. I could only go so fast before the cramps seized hard. I did what I could.

"Josh, go on. Don't wait for me." But he did wait.

"The first thing you'll come to is a liquor store," I said.

It was true. On the lower end of Roaring River—preceding the town itself—sits a campground belonging to the Corps of Engineers. The liquor store, as well as a companion grocery store, sat across the road from it. Because of the campers, that had once been a good location. Then the campground closed, followed by the grocery store. Now, only the liquor store remained.

"At least I hope it's still there."

But I didn't know for sure. I hoped we could fill our bottle there. But I feared it might have dried up like the spring.

Ultrarunners know you can log a long distance if you simply keep going forward. We were getting closer, but also getting thirstier. So thirsty, that Josh took a chance. We

Going Down Slow

came to a house on a slope above the road. We could see a frost-free faucet standing in the yard beside the house. Josh carried the empty bottles across the yard. I stood in the road watching to see if he was going to be shot. He lifted the faucet handle. Not one drop of water came out. Apparently it had been disconnected.

He looked around and found a coiled water hose connected to a faucet on the house's foundation. Now he was really pushing his luck. If anybody was home, they'd likely hear the water flowing in the pipes under the floor. Josh turned on the faucet and filled all four bottles. He came walking back smiling. Nobody showed up waving a shotgun.

"You were taking a chance."

"I figured it was die of thirst or be shot."

I took a long swig. And at once spit it out on the hot pavement. The water out of that hot hose tasted like water out of a tractor tire, full of chemicals, the taste thereof anyway.

"That stuff'll kill you!"

We trudged morosely on, still thirsty, carrying the weight we didn't need of the water we didn't dare drink. But we were getting close. Soon we came to the closed campground, the gated roads and weeds between camp sites. And I knew we were there.

The liquor store was, too, and still open, even though there were no customers until we walked in. Yes, we were customers. Josh had revealed his ace in the hole—an emergency twenty-dollar bill. A lone woman sat behind the counter.

Going Down Slow

"You got any Cokes or Dr. Pepper?" I asked.

"We don't sell anything but liquor." That's all their license permits, she told us.

"Well can we fill up our bottles? You got a bathroom or something?"

She took me to bathroom in an unfinished utility room at the back, and turned on a light. While I was pouring out bad water and filling bottles with good water, Josh was prowling around in the cooler. He found a drink called Jim Beam Cola in an aluminum can, and a margarita by Jose Cuervo in a plastic bottle. I saw him purchase two of the colas. Then he called his wife Martha on the store's land line to see if she could drive to Gainesboro and pick us up. Arrangements were made: we'd meet her at the Marathon station, which, with a name like that, was the appropriate place.

We walked out of there smiling, and drinking the colas, in violation of open container laws, I am sure. It was afternoon now and we'd had nothing to eat, but the cold colas compensated for that. We had about a mile to go, and we walked down the shoulder sipping on the cans. Josh and I happened to actually be talking about how we were surely violating the law when the sheriff's car passed.

"There goes the sheriff, Josh said. And then, "Well, he's not stopping."

"I don't give a damn if he does." My patience with all things contrary was worn out.

Suddenly Josh crushed his can.

"Man, you finished that in a hurry. I'm sipping on mine to make it last longer."

Going Down Slow

"I got a couple of those margaritas in the pack."

"Oh."

So we opened the margaritas, kept walking, and finished them too. When we hit the Marathon station we saw Martha pulling in at the lot. She'd been prompt. Josh and I had just had two quick drinks on empty stomachs. We went in the station's store.

"Want to get some beer, Dallas?" Josh said. He had a ten spot left from the emergency twenty. We went to the cooler.

"Budweiser is what you want," I said. I pulled out a quart can. Josh grabbed a quart of Corona Extra. We sat them on the counter and got in line to pay behind a couple of other customers. A uniformed officer, a woman with a badge and a gun got in line behind me. I turned.

"Catch any crooks today?"

Nope, she didn't. I was telling her we'd run from Cookeville, that we'd come through the flood damage on Blackburn Fork, and had she been up there to see it yet, and she hadn't, and then I became aware of a querulous discussion going on behind my back. I turned to see what in the world was going on now.

Josh was holding the ten out, but the clerk wouldn't take it. He was demanding an ID, and Josh was trying to tell him we'd been running and didn't have any and…

My patience really was exhausted. I didn't want to hear it. I snatched the ten out of Josh's hand and thrust in at the clerk.

"Here, I'm buying this stuff. Do I look old enough?"

The clerk made a slow grin, took the ten and gave

Going Down Slow

me the change. I turned and dropped it into Josh's hand. We scooped up our beers and dashed out. Martha was waiting.

Josh and I drank the quarts while Martha drove us back to Cookeville. She dropped us off at my house, turned around and left us standing in the driveway. It was mid-afternoon. We'd now each had the equivalent of four drinks on an empty stomach. I unfolded a couple of yard chairs in the shade in front of Josh's car, where he'd parked it that morning.

"Josh, you want another beer?" I had a refrigerator stocked in the garage.

So that's how we finished the day, sitting in the shade and nursing a beer each, talking about the day's astonishing scenes. We'd seen a remote rustic valley, one of my favorite places, devastated by flood damage unprecedented in our experience. We'd run twenty-one miles on a hot August day with not enough to drink, and with nothing to eat — on a run we'd never intended to make in the first place. We'd spent extra time exploring damage, and, thus, had gotten more dehydrated than twenty-one miles would usually indicate.

Around three-thirty we finally got something to eat. Jo Ann brought out sandwiches, ham on croissant.

PHOTOS

Songwriter Stan Lawrence
(photo by Betsy Srichai)

Shuffling across an endless Kansas prairie
on the Heartland 100 course.

Mildred Garret points to the painting
she made in memory of her father, Isaac Garret.

Isaac Garret
(photo courtesy of Mildred Garret)

Bill Curzie plays second base
in the age-group World Series

Anthropologist
Glen Freimuth

Assistant expedition leader
Fran Mauer served 21 years as
a biologist in the Arctic Refuge

Emergency Room doctor
Ethel Chiang

Expedition leader Don Ross, former
assistant director of the Arctic Refuge

Indomitable Angela Ivory enjoys
a non running moment.

Susan Ford closes the last mile of
her first Ironman.

Rock climber Meredith Ollier
ponders the long view down.

Albino Jimenez at the Burgos Half Marathon
one week before our El Camino attempt.

Jill White prepares
for her second Komen 5K

Margie Stoll, the third best runner in the
U.S.A. in her age group (photo by Hans Stoll)

"Special guest" four-year-old
Emma Smith.
(photo by Kathy Piper)

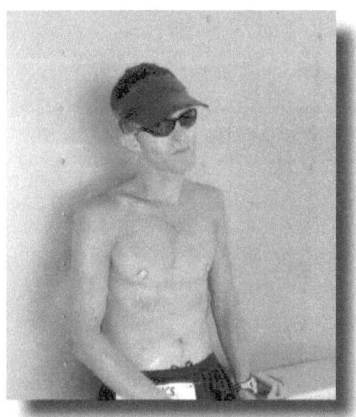

Josh Hite sits dehydrated and
exhausted just after winning
the Blister Marathon.
(photo by Trent Rosenbloom)

Two days after Josh and I first ran through
the flood damage I returned, shown here
running where a road used to be toward
where a bridge used to be.

Appendix

MY WINNING YEAR

With this appendix, I broach a topic it has been my policy to avoid in writing this book: me.

It's true, I write first person stories which have me in them, but those are adventure stories in which I've been directly involved. (Sometimes they were told to me by someone involved.) In any case, there is a big difference in writing first-person stories and, on the other hand, writing stories about...you know, "Me," Me with a capital M, facts and data about me. The first focuses on the adventure, events that actually happened. So this chapter is a small exception.

What brought it on? Why did I think anyone in the whole round world would want to read about what you will find below?

I had a pretty good year.

As a racer, that is. My annual racing report summarizes it. I could put up similar reports from other years, but this is the most recent one I have. I decided I'd put it up for whatever informational, instructional or inspirational value it may hold, and maybe it holds none. But if you are a racer also you may find it interesting. Or maybe not. Anyway, here it is. At the least, maybe it establishes my

Going Down Slow

running bona fides and confirms my qualifications for writing a book about running adventure.

Annual Racing Report, 2010
Dallas Smith, Age 70; DOB June 25, 1940

SUMMARY

Miles run: **2612**

Total no. races: **26** (two ultramarathons; seven marathons; one half marathon; two 10-milers; two 15Ks; two 10Ks; one 8K; one 4-miler; eight 5Ks)

State records: **11** (six at age 69, five at age 70)

Age-group competition: **undefeated**

Times in top 10 overall: **11**

RACE LIST

(age-graded time in parentheses; **Record.** = single-age state record; o.a. = overall)

01. Callaway Gardens Marathon, Jan. 31, 3:26:26 (2:32:30), **9th** o.a

02. Mercedes Marathon, Birmingham, Feb. 28, 3:28:13 (2:33:39)

03. Fall Creek Thaw 15K, Fall Creek State Park Mar. 6, 1:05:22 (48:03), **Record.**

04. Tom King Half Marathon, Nashville, Mar. 13, 1:33:07 (1:08:30), **Record.**

05. Running to Beat the Blues, Nashville, Mar. 27, 21:07 (15:30), **Record.**

06. Mule Kick 5K, Columbia, TN, Apr. 3, 20:57 (15:23), **Record.**

07. Purity Moosic City 10K, Nashville, Apr. 10, 42:08, (30:55), **Record.**

08. Country Music Marathon, Nashville, Apr. 24, 3:21:11 (2:28:15), **Record.**

09. Strolling Jim 41.2 ultramarathon, Wartrace, TN., May 1, 6:59:38.2, (5:09:04)

10. Scenic City Trail Marathon, Chattanooga, May 22, 4:38:11 (3:24:46)

Going Down Slow

11. Cane Creek 5K, Cookeville, June 5, 20:58 (15:22), **3rd** o.a.
12. Race for Jordan 5K, Carthage, TN, June 12, 21:05, (15:26), **4th** o.a.
13. RC Cola-Moon Pie 10-miler, Bell Buckle, TN, June 19, 1:14:51 (54:52)
14. Goodlettsville 4-miler, July 31, 27:28 (20:05), **Record.**
15. After Dark 8K, Cookeville, Aug. 8, 33:58 (24:49), **Record.**
16. Blister in the Sun Marathon, Cookeville, 4:32:11 (3:19:52), **7th** o.a.
17. Baxter Street Fair 5K, Baxter, TN, Sept. 4, 20:09 (14:43), **3rd** o.a.
18. Fall Fun Fest 10K, Cookeville, Sept. 11, 44:21 (32:23), **5th** o.a., **Record.**
19. Run4Don 5K, Gainesboro, TN, Sept. 18, 21:11 (15:28), **2nd** o.a.
20. Heavenly Host Lutheran School 5K, Cookeville, Sept. 25, 22:07 (16:08), **2nd** o.a.
21. Komen 5K, Cookeville, Sept. 26, 20:39.62 (15:05), **5th** o.a.
22. Shelby Bottoms Boogie 15K, Nashville, Oct. 2, 1:05:07 (47:34), **Record.**
23. Nashville Ultra 50K, Oct. 16, 4:37:49 (3:23:35)
24. Team Nashville 10-miler, Goodlettsville, Nov 13, 1:11:39 (52:17), **9th** o.a., **Record.**
25. Flying Monkey Marathon, Nashville, TN, Nov. 21, 3:35:36 (2:37:48)
26. Miss Gulf Coast Marathon, Waveland, MS, Nov. 27, 3:25:02 (2:30:04), **10th** o.a.

Acknowledgments

Albino Jimenez and Josh Hite didn't write one word of this book. But their fingerprints are all over it. If you are going to write a first-person adventure book, then you need to go out and actually find some adventure. Thanks to them, it found me. Each of these two guys has managed to drag me along repeatedly on his respective young-man adventures. I don't know why they do. I think it's because I'm easy. I can be talked into it. I don't always exhibit the prudence you'd expect and demand from the bridge designer I used to be or hesitate at the possibility of discomfort like you'd think an old man would.

And so it was that when Albino suggested I join his outrageous plan to run across Spain on el Camino de Santiago, I reflected for maybe one millisecond, and then allowed how that sounded like a good idea. That invitation led to my most outstanding endurance failure—and to a very great adventure. ¡Muchas gracias, amigo! The run was a failure, but the stories are not. I don't regret it, and I still thank you for it.

And then one day there was Josh planting the idea of running down a local gorge just recently reamed out by a flood likely exceeding any seen since pre-Columbia times. Sometimes a planted idea grows quietly. I reckon that happened to us. We found ourselves running through miles of devastation wrought by an innocent-looking creek that had decided to roar like the Colorado, sweeping down whole groves of mature trees like dead cornstalks, uprooting many and stacking them in house-sized piles, and splintering houses like dead sticks. After twenty-one miles of running that hot day, dehydrated and hungry, we finally stumbled into a liquor store in another town that was allowed to sell liquor but not sodas. That law was not our fault.

Without Albino and Josh, this book would be thin, vanishingly thin. Thanks, men!

Angela Ivory left a searing imprint on these pages. Her courage and grace in the face of cancer makes me question my own strength. Cancer aside, her intelligence and humanity can teach anyone how to live.

I remember talking with her a decade ago. She was yearning to run an ultramarathon, just tossing the idea around. Thrown off by her humility, I failed to glimpse the quest ahead of her, that she would become an extreme runner. A few years later, after I discovered her running saga, she was reluctant to let me write the story—obeying her dislike of self-promotion. Only after I pointed out how her story could help others did she finally agree. I wrote frankly and vividly about how cancer attacked her, avoiding euphemisms. Rather than taking offense, she appreciated that angle, glad I'd kicked cancer in the mouth.

I was proud to break Angela's story. Many of her running friends had been as ignorant as I had. It is my happy privilege to dedicate this book to her. I hope she is pleased.

Comes now Valerie Connelly, reared in Chicago, but currently living in rural Tennessee, which strikes me as a big change. After traveling a good bit of the world and making a living as a teacher of French language and literature, and by any number of artistic skills, including music and painting, today, among other things, she publishes books. She agreed to publish mine. That she carried out the editing in such good humor says something about her patience. She laughs easily, flatters me shamelessly, and we got along fabulously. More to the point, she made the book better than it would otherwise have been. I thank her for her wisdom and skill, and for doing all the things I don't know how to do. We may do it again.

My long-suffering wife Jo Ann looks forward to me writing a book like a root canal. That's my fault. She knows I'm going to drift around abstracted, obsessing about the book, walking into furniture and losing my car keys. But endure it she does — twice now. More than that, she serves as my front-line editor, spotting my unproductive tangents and awkward sentences. One of the best proofreaders I know, she's saved me more than once from submitting a story filled with embarrassing errors. Thanks, Jo Ann. Maybe this is the last one. I don't know.

Photo of the author by Elly Foster

ABOUT THE AUTHOR

Dallas Smith has won his age group at the New York City Marathon and the Chicago Marathon, among many others, and finished second in the 2011 Boston Marathon. He has finished Ironman triathlons and 100-mile ultramarathons. He holds several dozen single-age state records in the state of Tennessee for distances ranging from 5K to marathon. He is the author of *Falling Forward: Tales from an Endurance Saga*. Professor Emeritus at Tennessee Tech University, he lives with his wife Jo Ann in Cookeville, Tennessee.